The
Model Posing Guide
for
Fashion and Glamour
Photography

Table of Contents

Introduction

The model is standing in front of the photographer and he says "All right, let's get started!" and puts his camera up to his eye. The photographer expects the model to start posing for his camera. The model starts "Okay, what do you want me to do?" expecting the photographer to tell her how to pose. Awkwardness ensues...

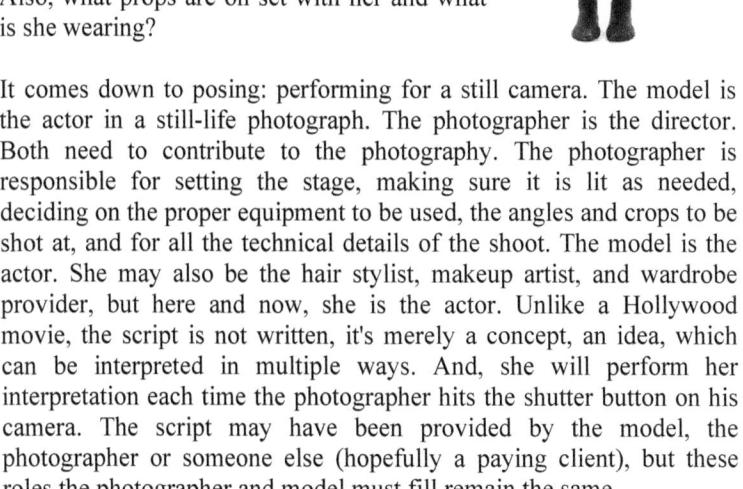

Sound familiar? What's wrong with this scenario? Is the photographer or the model to be blamed? The answer is probably both. The photographer should have prepared the model with information on the nature of the shoot. He should be giving direction on what he's expecting the model to do and what emotions or expressions he wants her to show. On the other side of the lens, the model should have some idea of what she is doing. What was she told the shoot was about? Why is the photographer shooting her? She should have requested and been given some of this information when the session was booked. Also, what props are on set with her and what is she wearing?

It comes down to posing: performing for a still camera. The model is the actor in a still-life photograph. The photographer is the director. Both need to contribute to the photography. The photographer is responsible for setting the stage, making sure it is lit as needed, deciding on the proper equipment to be used, the angles and crops to be shot at, and for all the technical details of the shoot. The model is the actor. She may also be the hair stylist, makeup artist, and wardrobe provider, but here and now, she is the actor. Unlike a Hollywood movie, the script is not written, it's merely a concept, an idea, which can be interpreted in multiple ways. And, she will perform her interpretation each time the photographer hits the shutter button on his camera. The script may have been provided by the model, the photographer or someone else (hopefully a paying client), but these roles the photographer and model must fill remain the same.

ABOUT THIS GUIDE

This book is aimed at helping models (and photographers) learn the rules of modeling and use them as a base for creativity when it comes to Fashion and Glamour Photography. The rules are based on observations of the human body and how it looks when reduced to the two dimensional world of a photograph. Certain sections of the guide will apply to photographers or models and again may relate to only Fashion or Glamour, but the concepts apply to any type of modeling photography. The first section deals with the rules of posing and other concepts, while the second section is a compendium of poses in various categories to give you a hand when you are planning a shoot or even during a shoot.

Fashion and Glamour Photography are included together in this guide because they are very similar. The main difference between the two types of photography is that Fashion Photography focuses on a product (clothing, shoes, jewelry, etc.) while Glamour focuses on the model. Photography done for a model's portfolio or a model photographer's portfolio will more often than not, fall into these two categories.

Fashion Photography is what you will see in catalogs and magazines that are selling apparel. Once practiced in rigid terms and only in the studio settings, it is now practiced in a variety of ways including not only beautiful surroundings and natural poses, but also the mundane to the bizarre. Over time, Fashion Photography has itself become fashionable artwork, and you will sometimes see fashion images hanging in frames anywhere from the corner coffee house to the finest museums. The main purpose, however, remains the same, to showcase a product to the viewer.

Glamour Photography refers to the work done for men's magazines or boudoir photography where the emphasis is on sensual/sexy poses coupled with a fantasy environment. While the term has broader meaning today and includes nude photography, like that in Playboy™, sexy photos like in Maxim™ or FHM™, boudoir photography done for a woman's significant other or the current "glamour portrait" studios, it still means the same thing – focusing on the subject and making her look her best. These same styles and poses are also used in models' and photographers' portfolio work.

HOW TO USE THIS GUIDE

The best way to use this guide is to read through it and then keep a copy handy when you're on a shoot. Take it out and look through it for ideas when you get stuck or just want to refresh your memory on certain things.

COMMUNICATION

It is important to be upfront with your photographer (or client) about your limits. Will you do sheer or topless shots? Is a thong ok? Be very clear with your photographer about what you are and are not comfortable with BEFORE you begin shooting. Communicating what you won't do is just as important as what you will do. Don't be afraid to talk to your photographer DURING your shoot either. If you're not feeling well, need a break or just have to go to the bathroom, say so!

Don't forget, as a model, you are not yourself in front of the camera; you are an actor playing a part. You are portraying the look and type of person that the photographer, client, or art director feels is necessary for the job. Don't get offended or take it personally if the client wants to use you in a manner that you feel is not the real you.

PRACTICE

The best way to begin learning to pose is to practice posing in front of the mirror and the camera as much as possible. You should get an idea of what looks good and what doesn't by doing this. A professional model should be able to easily move between many different poses. Practice your balance and condition your legs. Many times you'll need to hold a difficult pose or maintain a pose that feels like you might lose your balance. Studying your photos will help you find out what types of poses make you look the best, to identify what your strengths and weaknesses are and how to emphasize or hide them.

WHY POSE?

In general, posing is about two things: making the model and/or the outfit (or other product) being modeled look the best it possibly can. This means posing in ways that emphasize the model's or the outfit's positive attributes and de-emphasize the negatives. Posing also provides a variety of images that will later allow the model, the photographer or the client to choose the photo that best accomplishes that goal.

In Fashion Photography, it is important to make sure that the product will be clearly visible in the resulting photography. A number of poses should be used that show the front and back of the outfit, as well as any special features. Minimal accessories should be used to place focus on the outfit or item being modeled, but this will vary by client, as some may wish to include accessories that are also theirs. As the photographer or model, it is important to keep in mind where these images are supposed to be going. While creativity is a plus for any type of shoot, artistic may not be what the client is looking for. Time should be spent evaluating the client's needs and what is sought for the finished images. While shooting, the model and the photographer need to be watchful for details that might ruin an otherwise perfect shot: Are there any tags or loose strings showing? Does the clothing lie flat on the body? If there are any ties or knots on an outfit, are they done right? Do the strings lay flat or are they twisted? It is also essential that the person modeling the product look their best too. Attention should be made to the model's hair and makeup, as well as their overall appearance.

Glamour Photography is about the model being photographed and usually means making her appear beautiful, desirable and sexually appealing which is why you'll often see it in model portfolios. While Glamour Photography is often suggestive or provocative, it is not sexually explicit in nature. The fine line that distinguishes Fashion, Glamour, Erotic or even Pornographic Photography is the intent of the photography. It is up to you as a model to know what you are comfortable with.

The Rules

There are some rules to posing that should be followed. You may need to break some depending on the situation or for creative reasons. If we remained always rigid to these rules, there wouldn't be a tremendous amount of variety to work with and photography would be very boring. However, they are good to follow in most circumstances, especially when you are just getting started.

PROPS

All poses are built on the props available, which is everything in the set, including the floor, walls, your outfit and you. (How long is your hair? What can you sit on? Lay on? Lean against? Play with?) Interaction with your environment is the primary key to posing. This is why posing nude can be so difficult. If you're having trouble posing, ask your photographer for a prop! Just about anything you get can help generate new pose ideas.

START WITH A BASE

Consider your body from the waist down as a base for your poses. By varying your upper torso, arms, hands, head and facial expressions, you can generate a number of poses while expending very little energy. To create a pleasant standing base, place your weight on one leg and let the other one relax. This gets your hips tilted and will naturally put a bend in your other knee. Try to make that bend visible to the camera by pointing the toes away from the camera. In general, you want the camera to see two separate legs, so even if your legs aren't visibly separated, try not to run them right next to each other. This applies to sitting poses too.

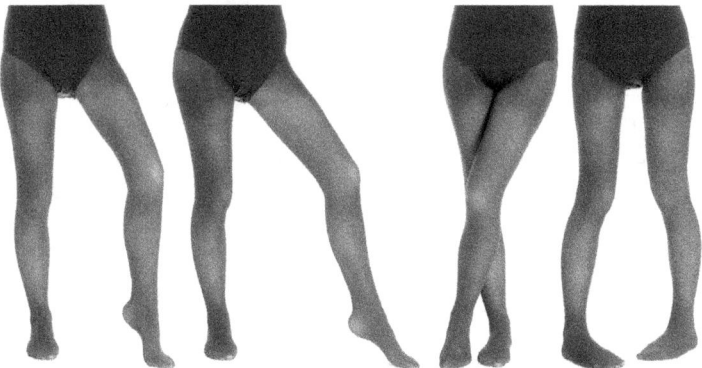

IF IT BENDS, BEND IT!

You frequently hear models and photographers use that expression and it's true; if it bends, bend it! Overall, the body should follow a gentle curve or wave, starting at the head. Make the most of your own curves by rolling your hips back, arching the back and lifting your chest. A slight twist at the waist will make you look more alive and creates a slimming effect at the waist.

ARMS

Keep the arms off the body, as that can give a heavier appearance. Ideally, your elbows should be bent and off your sides. The exception to that is to bring the arms in to cover the side of the body giving a thinner appearance. When done from the front, this has the extra advantage of creating additional cleavage. (The arms need to be brought in from the sides as opposed to down, which can flatten the bosom.)

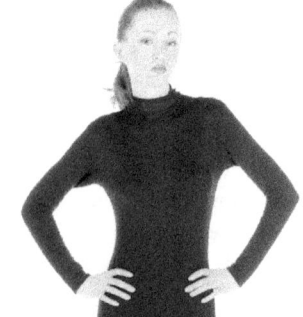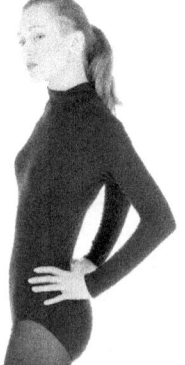

Whatever you do, make sure you don't totally hide an arm behind you as you will look like an amputee in the photo. Usually, all it takes is a small move to bring your elbow or fingers into view to correct this.

HANDS

Unfortunately, the hands show a person's age more quickly than any other part of the body and we don't usually use any cover up there. The backs of your hands may show wrinkles or veins, even if you're still very young. Also, showing the flats of your hands will make them look wide and manly. So, try to minimize the hands while keeping them in the shot, by turning them to the side. Hands typically look thinner and longer if seen from the side. Bending the wrists also helps make the hands look more feminine, especially when on the hips (bend the wrist and kick the elbow out.) And remember to curl the fingers slightly so that they look relaxed, especially when your hands are simply dangling or you've got your thumbs in your belt loops.

Hands can be placed just about anywhere; in or behind your hair; grabbing the straps of a bikini, the edge of a shirt, tucked into your clothes, on your hips, hanging loosely down, across your body, or interacting with any props you've got on the set with you.

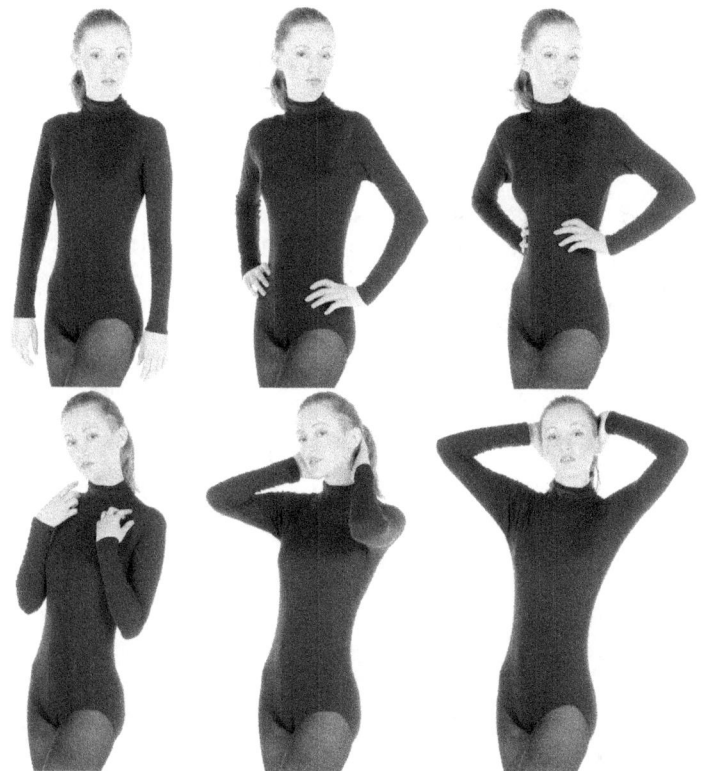

When grabbing bikini strings or the lapels of a blouse, turn the hands under to avoid showing the backs. With a blouse, use the hands to push in for cleavage.

When putting your hands to your chin, two things to avoid are the 'fist' and actually resting your chin on your hands. Instead, use only one hand, and extend the index finger (with a light curl) for a more seductive look. If your hand is under your chin, support your head with your neck, not your hand!

HIPS AND WAIST

When the hips and waist are perpendicular to the camera, they will appear the widest they can in the final image; when parallel to the camera, any roundness to the tummy will be pronounced, so turning partially to the side will help minimize both. Some other things you can do: crawl toward the camera, with your hips slightly above your shoulders; lie down on a fluffy blanket or mattress; use a wall or vertical prop to partially hide behind.

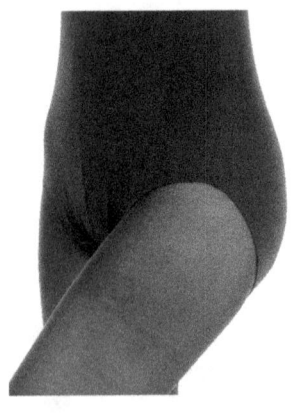

A twist in the body at the waist makes you look more life like by conveying a sense of movement. It also helps pull in some of your stomach, smoothing out the abdomen.

When standing at an angle to the camera, roll your hips back (pop your butt out) to create more curve. In addition, bringing the leg near the camera up creates a rounder rear.

When sitting or reclining, roll one hip slightly up from the resting surface to give your hips a pleasingly rounder and more three dimensional look. If you are sitting and the photographer is

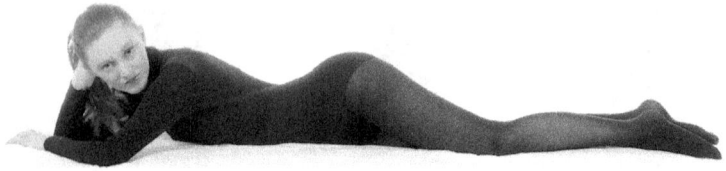

shooting at any down angle, try to keep your weight off your thighs altogether, as that will help keep them from flattening and looking wider than normal.

SHOULDERS AND CHEST

The same problem exists for the shoulders and can be solved the same way. Also, using a quarter turn, of the shoulders, the curve of the breasts and back is more visible. Try to keep your shoulders from becoming a straight horizontal line in front of the camera. Tilting the shoulders helps create a pleasant curve through the length of the body.

Lifting your chest as if you were holding a deep breath will result in a bigger bosom, a tighter stomach and an improved posture. Learn to do this through muscle control, instead of by breathing deeply, which can be tiring during a shoot. Just be careful not to tense up while doing this. Turning the body to put your bust in profile is also more appealing.

To emphasize or increase your cleavage, lean forward and use your arms to push your breasts together. Most of the time, this should be done as subtly as possible by bringing the arms together at waist or crossing your arms in a natural fashion. Good posture will help too.

To de-emphasize your cleavage, you would do the exact opposite. Lean back and keep your arms apart and off your sides. Stretching the body out with your arms beyond your head and shoulders will have a slight reducing effect too.

FEET, LEGS AND BUTT

Depending on your photographer, you may be asked to wear shoes or go barefoot. Unless told otherwise, plan on wearing shoes. Wearing high heels extends the visual length of the legs and makes them look sexy. If you're not wearing shoes (and maybe even if you are), pointing the toes helps tighten the calf muscle and extend the legs. It doesn't matter whether you're standing, sitting or lying down.

Make sure that when you're kneeling, your legs and feet don't run straight behind your knees, hidden from the camera. Instead, turn your calves to one side, both in or out.

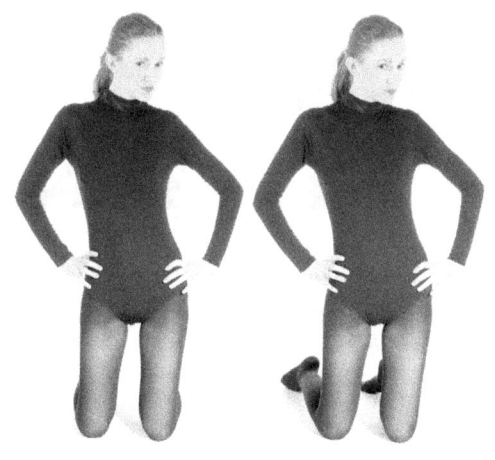

Don't feel that you must face the camera for every single shot. Try to turn around for at least a quarter of your shots. When you do, don't forget to roll your hips back or pop your butt out for that extra bit of curve.

HEAD

Imagine there is a string attached to the top of your head that is pulling upwards. This has the benefit of keeping your neck elongated, your posture straight and might help keep you on your tip-toes as well. Keeping your chin up can help to avoid neck wrinkles and double chins, but don't overdo it either. When turning your head, you may have some creases that form in your neck. Try to minimize these by keeping your head up and tilted away from the camera or hide them by leaning in and tilting your head down to hide them. Sometimes your outfit or strategically placed hair will help cover this too. For variation, tilt your head and twist your neck slightly in conjunction with your facial expressions.

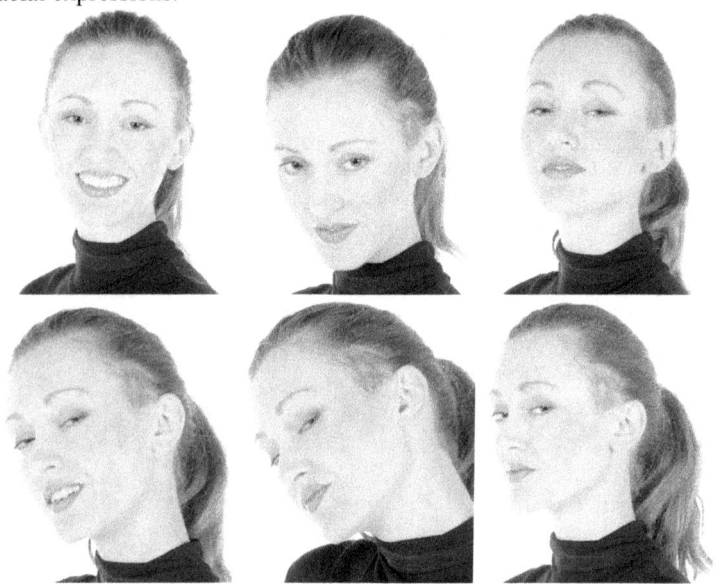

FACIAL EXPRESSIONS

A model uses posing to portray a mood. The mood can be reflection or a contrast of the environment she is being photographed in. While physical interaction with your environment will create an interesting photo, it's the expressions that will really sell the mood of an image. This is where imagination, the art of pretending, is really important. It's why an intelligent, educated and well-read model is so desirable; she has imagination.

A good model will have several expressions to use during a shoot. Don't use the same face (big smile!) for every pose. Try a small smile with your lips slightly parted, a pout, a laugh, a scowl, a smirk, or even a frown. Your facial expression is part of the overall pose and should have some variety.

Here is a list of moods that will help you generate different expressions: aggressive, agonized, anxious, apologetic, approving, arrogant, blissful, bored, covetous, cold, concentrating, confident, curious, demure, determined, devious, disappointed, disapproving, disgusted, distasteful, eavesdropping, ecstatic, enraged, envious, exasperated, exhausted, frightened, frustrated, grieving, guilty, happy, horrified, hot, hung-over, hurt, hysterical, indifferent, innocent, interested, jealous, joyful, loaded, lonely, love struck, meditative, miserable, naughty, negative, obstinate, optimistic, pained, paranoid, perplexed, prudish, puzzled, regretful, relieved, sad, satisfied, seductive, sensual, sexy, shocked, sheepish, smug, surly, surprised, suspicious, sympathetic, thoughtful, undecided, wholesome, withdrawn.

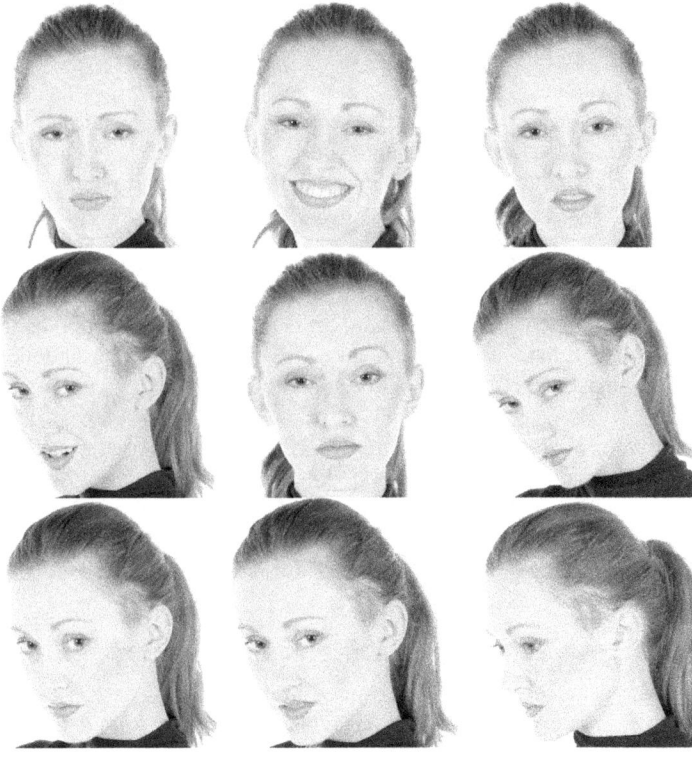

If you get stuck, use the five vowels (AEIOU) to generate some others, A and E are both open mouth smiles, I and O are two different surprised looks, and U looks like you're blowing a kiss.

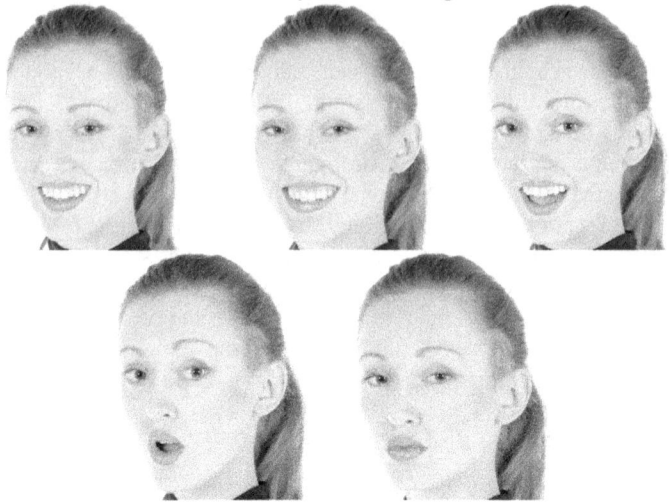

Remember to make sure that your body is saying the same thing that your face is and don't feel that you must always look straight into the camera. It is not only acceptable, but expected that you will be looking off to the side or even completely away for some of your poses.

OTHER CONSIDERATIONS

Posing should come easily. Remember that the reason the photographer is using a model instead of a manikin is that he wants his photos to be of a living thing, showing and evoking emotions. While modeling is work, the actual activity should be something like play.

Keep your location/setting in mind as that will somewhat dictate your poses. When shooting outdoors, don't let the elements affect your posing. It may be cold or extra sunny out, but you don't want to let that show in the photo! Likewise when looking into bright studio lights. If it's too bright, try closing your eyes for a few shots as if you were relaxing.

Beware of shadows! In particular, when putting your hands in your hair (a classic modeling pose), make sure that your elbows are not casting a shadow across your face. This can happen anywhere and hopefully your photographer will notice it, but try to watch for this yourself too.

Depending on your photographer (who may like to give directions or none at all) it will help keep your shoot moving along if you keep moving. Don't always wait for directions, but keep in mind that does not mean dancing around either. Remember, this is photography not video. Move gracefully from pose to pose, but stop and hold each pose for a half second so the photo will be sharp. You may be able to keep time with your photographer if you can hear the shutter of the camera. Occasionally, you will run into a photographer that manages every aspect of the shoot including your posing. In this case, listen to the photographer and pay attention to what he or she is trying to accomplish.

Poses should be comfortable, but some will not be. Be careful not to let it show that you are uncomfortable. If the pose is painful, let the photographer know! Also, pay attention to your photographer. He or she should be giving you feedback on how you're doing. Ask questions if you need to.

Posing can be a tiring exercise, but you need to keep your energy level up both physically and mentally. If you are feeling down, it is ok to ask for a break. Take some deep breaths, refresh yourself and resume working when you are ready. Take some energy bars and water with you to your shoot to help keep your physical energy level up. (Don't forget to eat!) Try to group your poses to avoid repeatedly standing and sitting as that can be tiring on you and your photographer.

One last note about your outfits: Whether they are the subject of the shoot or just clothes you brought to shoot in, make sure that they look like they're supposed to. Make sure straps are flat and all visible tags are removed. If you have clothing that requires tied ends (like a bikini) make sure the strings are cut to the proper length, finished off and tied at an even length. Clothes should be clean, pressed and lint free. Shoes should be scuff free and clean looking.

Posing for a Fashion Shoot

Many of the poses found in the Pose Photo Guide can be used for Fashion Photography. Some of the poses may need to be varied to make sure that the item being modeled is as visible as possible. You will find the most used poses in Fashion Photography are standing poses. It's easier to show off the apparel being shot.

There are some specific types of apparel that may need to be shot in certain ways, such as shoes or jewelry. While posing, keep in mind that you are trying to sell the item you are wearing. Cropping is done as tight as possible for the outfit or clothing to be shown without wasting valuable space in the catalog or web page. Exceptions to that may be when the work is editorial in nature, where a whole scene may be presented or even a group of models showcasing a number of outfits or something creative as specified by the client.

PANTS, DRESSES AND SKIRTS

Pants, Dresses and Long Skirts are usually full length shots from head to toe. Shorter skirts and dresses may be ¾ length shots if the hem falls above the knee, eliminating the need for shoes or the floor to be taken into consideration.

BLOUSES, SHIRTS AND JACKETS

Tops are usually shot as ¾ length shots.

BIKINIS AND LINGERIE

Bikinis and typical lingerie are usually done as ¾ length shots or full length. Care should be taken to follow the client's format (sexy, casual, relaxed, etc.) When shooting lingerie for a catalog, it is particularly important to know what should be hidden, what should be shown and how.

SHOES

Shoes are usually shot as part of an entire outfit, just above the ankle or to the top of the thigh for boots.

JEWELRY

Jewelry is usually not shot on a model, but when it is, the focus and framing is all about the jewelry.

HATS AND SCARVES

Hats and scarves are done as head, head and shoulder or bust shots to show the item in its entirety.

POSING FOR A GLAMOUR SHOOT

Glamour poses are more focused on the subject and tend to be more sensual and/or suggestive in nature. They are done for a number of reasons: the photographer's or the model's portfolio; a publication; a website; or even artwork. Some of these poses would not be used in Fashion Photography because they are too provocative or simply aren't useful for showcasing apparel. There are, of course, exceptions, such as lingerie work or advertising designed to shock the consumer.

Some discussion between the photographer and the model should take place to determine what will and what will NOT be shown in the photos.

WORKING WITH YOUR PHOTOGRAPHER

In any type of shoot, it is important that you and your photographer have a level of rapport and trust. That is even truer when it comes to doing any type of glamour shoot (or modeling lingerie). Even if you are not doing nudes, there is a chance that your photographer may see you exposed. If this is not acceptable to you, then you should avoid doing these types of shoots.

Expect that some shots will be taken with the photographer closer to you for a close-up or cropped effect. Depending on the photographer, the equipment being used or the effect that is trying to be achieved, close-ups may be taken by using a longer lens (or 'zooming in') or the photographer may simply move in closer for the shot.

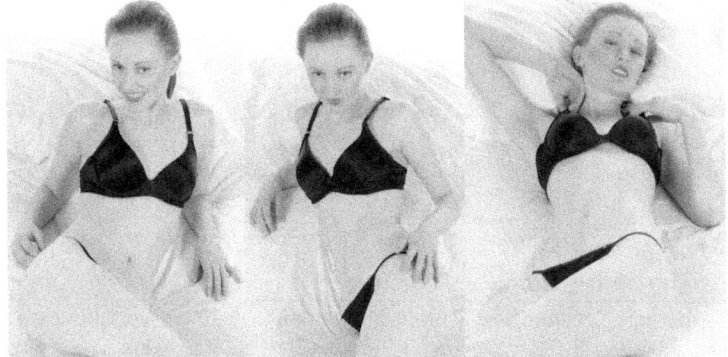

The above were taken from about 6 feet away on a ladder.

The photographer may come in even closer for detail shots. Usually the photographer will let you know what he or she is doing, but don't be startled if your photographer is suddenly shooting two feet away from you! (Hopefully your photographer will be kind enough to talk to you during the shoot!)

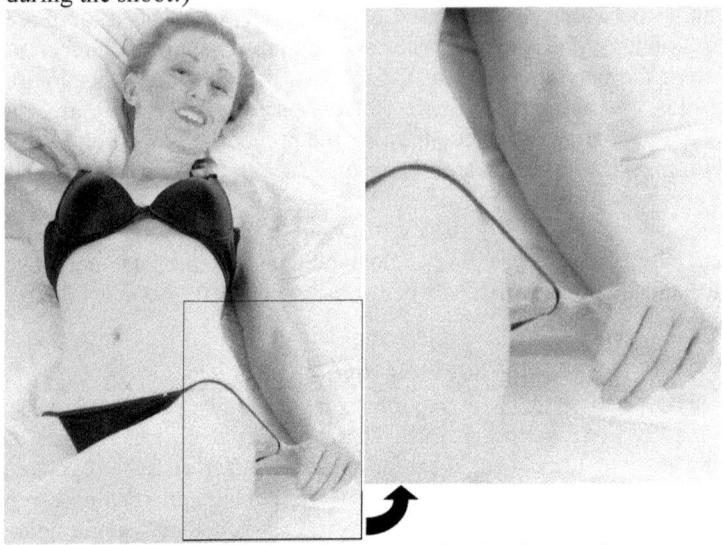

The above is an example of a CROP made after the shoot on the computer. The final print will be able to be, at most, only 11 by 14 inches.

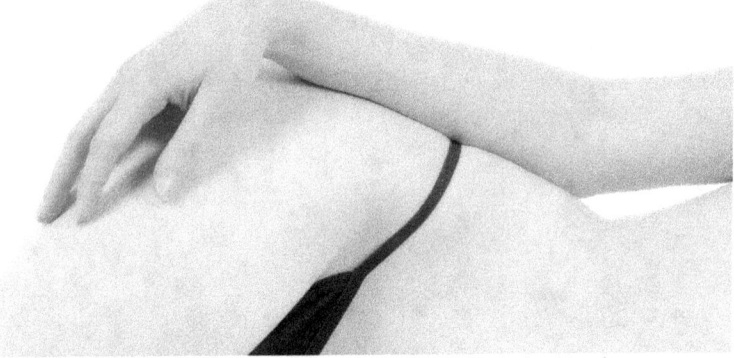

This image, taken much closer, will allow for a 36 inch wide print.

POSING FOR THE RUNWAY OR STAGE

Despite being related to Fashion Photography, Posing on a runway or stage is much different than posing for the camera, even if you are getting shot while you're up there. Usually, the event and your activities will be choreographed. In general, you will strike a number of poses at certain points and may be expected to walk off-stage OR wait while other models join you. If there is no formal choreography, find out BEFORE hand what you are expected to do.

Being Prepared

While this section is not about POSING, it will help you prepare so you will be ready and relaxed before and during your shoot, which will let you concentrate on your posing.

PREPARING FOR A SHOOT

Your body is your "product" and you need to keep it in top shape. As a model you are judged on your performance and your looks. You need to maintain a healthy weight level and exercise on a regular basis to keep muscles toned. You should not look anorexic. Note that models of any size are expected to maintain a stable weight, even if that weight is plus-size. Good, healthy eating habits include lots of fruits and vegetables. Also avoid caffeine, smoking, alcohol, and other substances that will deplete your energy and health. Make water your drink of choice.

Don't make any changes to your appearance before a job. No perms, colorings, or haircuts unless you are requested to do so. Longer hair is usually preferred on models. Try to limit make-up except for actual jobs and interviews. Make-up blocks pores and can cause acne and pimples. Bathe a couple times a day and use appropriate skin care products to keep your skin as healthy as possible. Avoid tanning as being sunburned will not help and a pale model can be made to look tanned easier than getting a tan model to look pale. If you do tan, tan in a tanning booth in the nude to avoid tan lines.

Manicures and pedicures are a must for any model to keep their nails in great shape. Never, ever, bite your nails! Next to your face, your hands get a great deal of attention in modeling, so take care of them!

Unwanted body hair should be shaved **at least** 8-16 hours before the shoot. Waxing should be done **at least** 24 hours before the shoot. This will give enough time to allow any red marks to fade.

For most clothing shots, the model should expect to pose without underwear on. Underwear colors and patterns show through lighter clothing or may create lines or bumps in the fashions being worn. Typically the model will wear only the clothes provided. If you are posing in revealing clothing, such as lingerie, swim wear, or nude, come to the photo session wearing loose fitting clothing and if possible, no socks or underwear. Anything that presses on the body creates reddish pressure marks that may take an hour or more to go away. If you have a shoot like this, do not wear any tight clothing or clothing with elastic in it for at least a few hours before the shoot. If possible show up early for your shoot, undress and put on a robe, this will help your skin lose any pressure marks it may have.

If you are doing a test shoot, portfolio work or work that requires pieces from your own wardrobe, pick out clothing ahead of time which will give you a variety of looks and which flatter your figure. Avoid distracting patterns that lead the viewer's eye away from you. Bring a wider selection of clothes than what you will need. That way you will have backup outfits and choices to pick from.

SHOOT BAG

It's a good idea to have a shoot bag that you can simply grab and bring to every photo session. That way you will be ready to go on any job at any time. Below is a list of suggested items to include in your shoot bag. These items should only be used for photo shoots, so that the bag is always stocked and items of clothing will be in "like new" condition for the photos.

Makeup Items

o Blush Brush
o Blushes
o Concealer
o Cosmetic Sponges
o Cotton Balls
o Cotton Swabs
o Cover Sticks
o Eye Drops
o Eye Liners
o Eye Shadow
o Eyebrow Brush
o Eyebrow Pencil
o Eyelash Curler
o Facial Cleanser

o Facial Tissues
o Facial Toner
o Foundation
o Lip Balm
o Lip Brushes
o Lip Gloss
o Lip Pencils
o Lipsticks
o Mascara Remover
o Moisturizing Cream
o Nail Clippers
o Nail File
o Nail Polish
o Nail Polish Remover

o Pencil Sharpener
o Powder Brush
o Powder Puffs
o Scissors
o Skin Conditioner
o Sun Screen/Lotion
o Tooth Brush/Paste
o Towel
o Translucent Powder
o Tweezers
o Wash Cloth
o Water Proof Mascara

Hair Care Items

- Bobby Pins
- Brush
- Clips
- Comb

- Curlers
- Curling Iron
- Elastic hair bands
- Hair Dryer

- Hair Spray
- Hair Straightner
- Styling Gel
- Styling Mousse

Clothing Items

- Assorted Inexpensive Jewelry (earrings, bracelets, necklaces)
- Bath Robe

- Bras (Black, White and Nude)
- Several pairs of panty hose (Black, Nude and other colors)

- Shoe Polish
- Shoes
- Sneakers or slippers
- Thong underwear toned to match skin

Miscellaneous

- Appointment Book
- Band-Aids
- Book (to read)
- Business cards

- Clothes Pins for loose clothing
- Comp-cards
- Masking Tape

- Notebook and Pens
- Portfolio
- Safety Pins
- Small Mirror

Pose Photo Guide

Most poses are independent of the clothing being worn. When using this reference, it's important to see past the clothing shown and look at the pose. Feel free to experiment and vary the poses to suit your style and the mood that you are going after. The General Poses can be used for Fashion and Glamour photography with few exceptions. The Prop and Clothing Specific Poses are meant more for Glamour Photography. *Note: Not every pose can be done by every model, so if a pose is causing you pain, stop and try something else!*

GENERAL POSES

STANDING

The most common poses used for Fashion Photography.

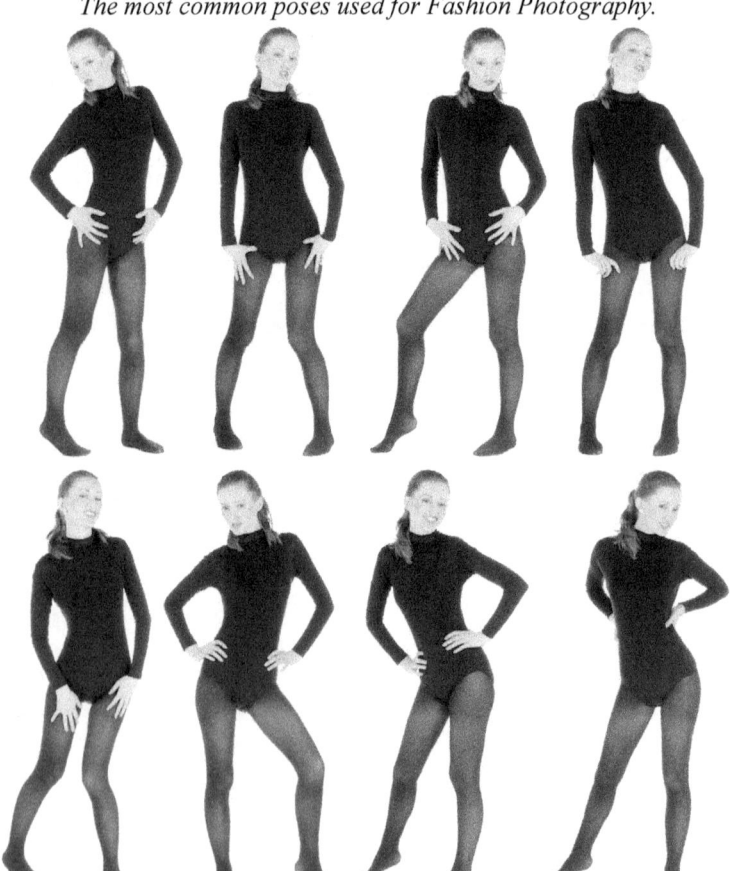

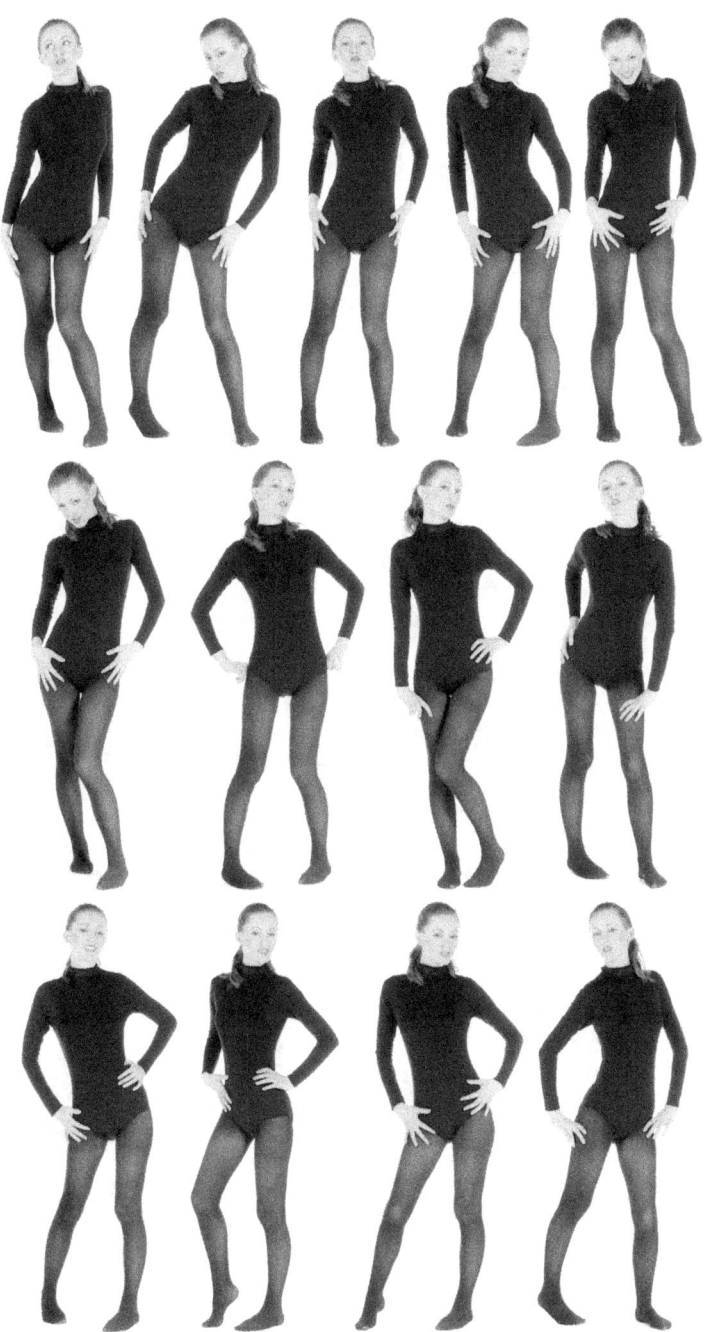

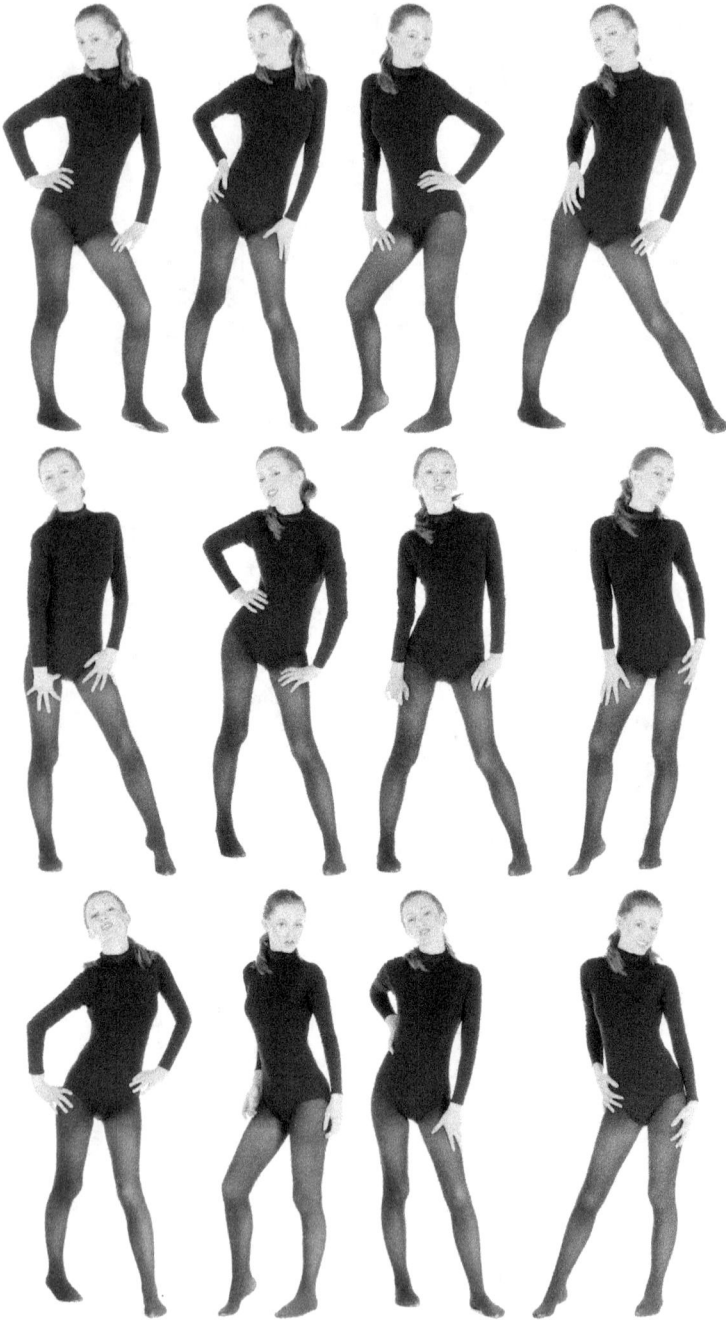

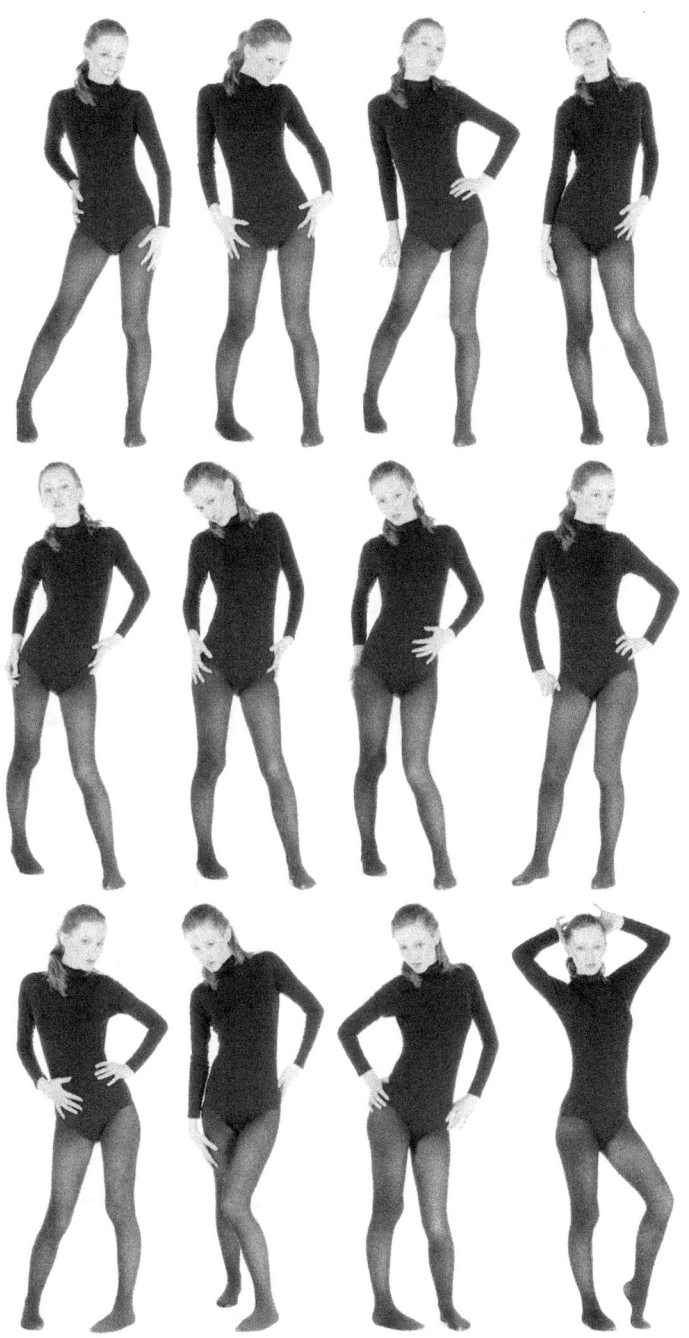

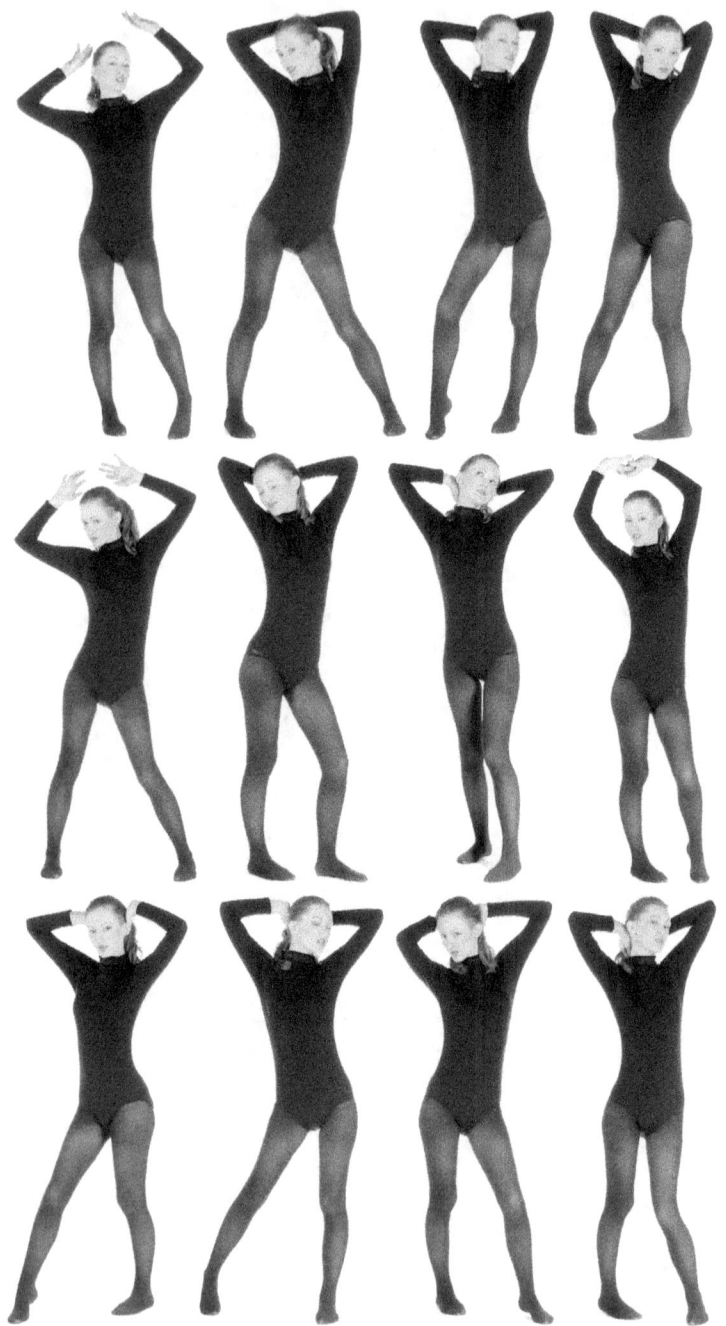

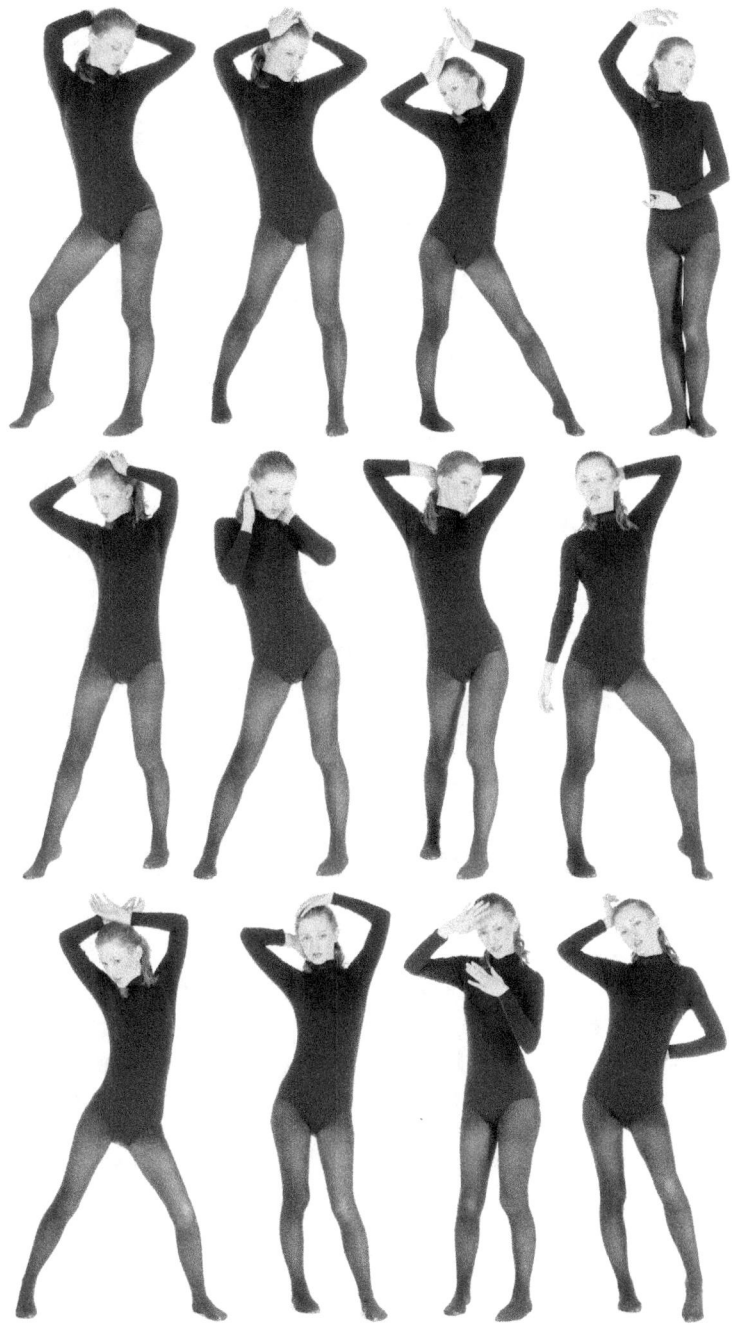

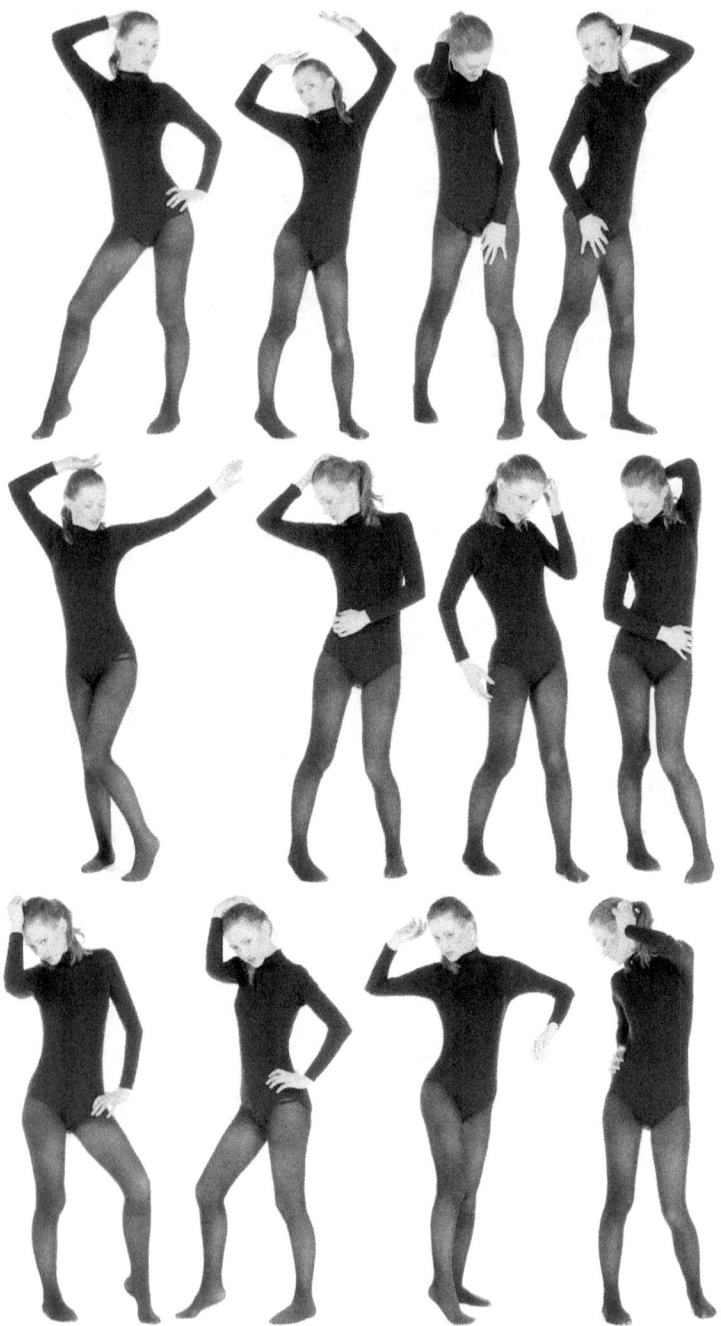

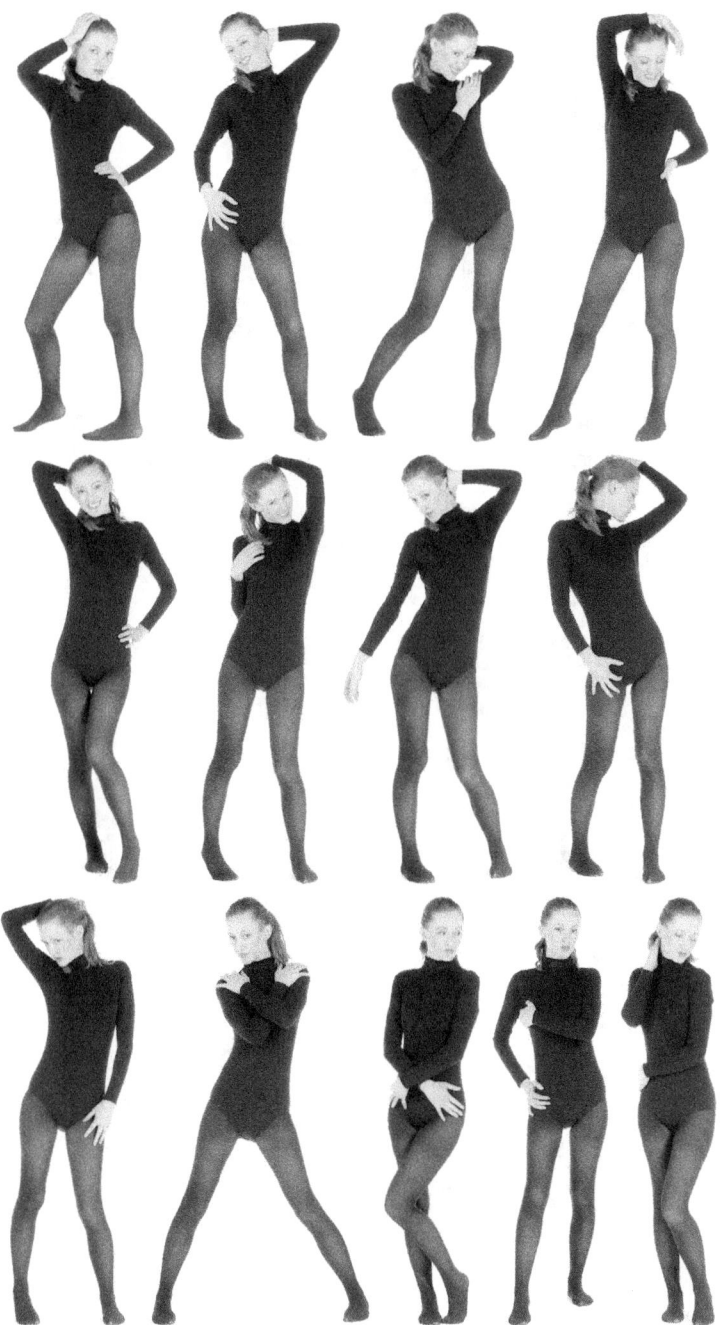

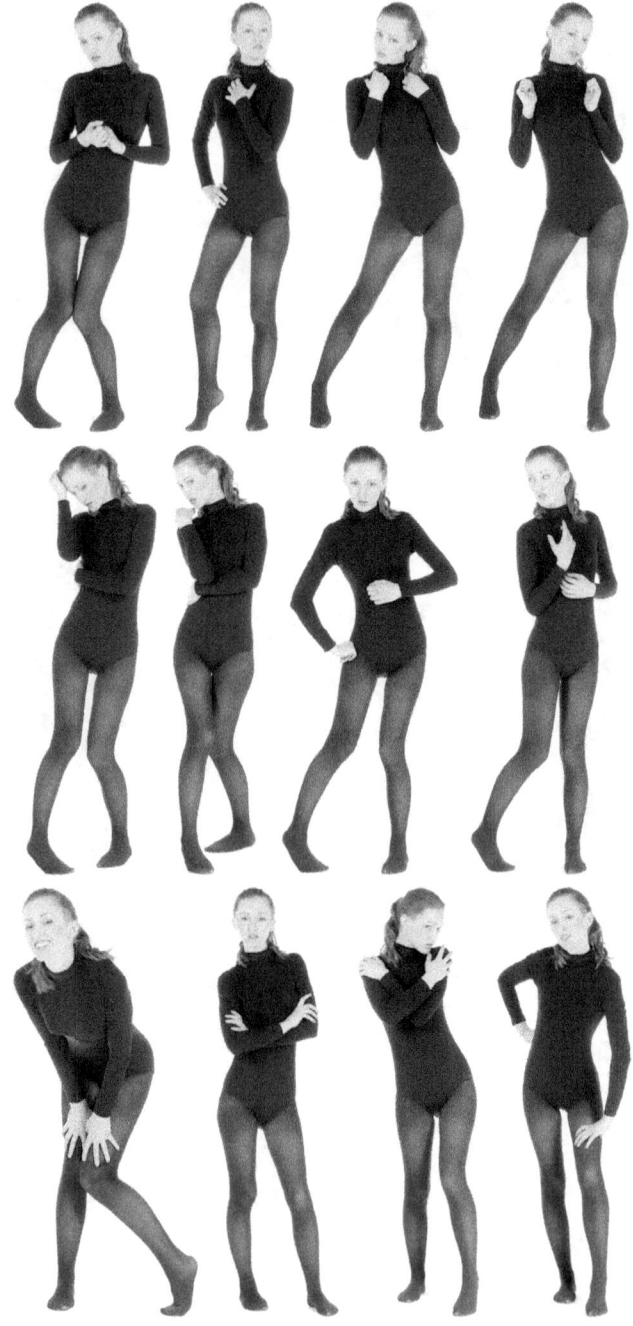

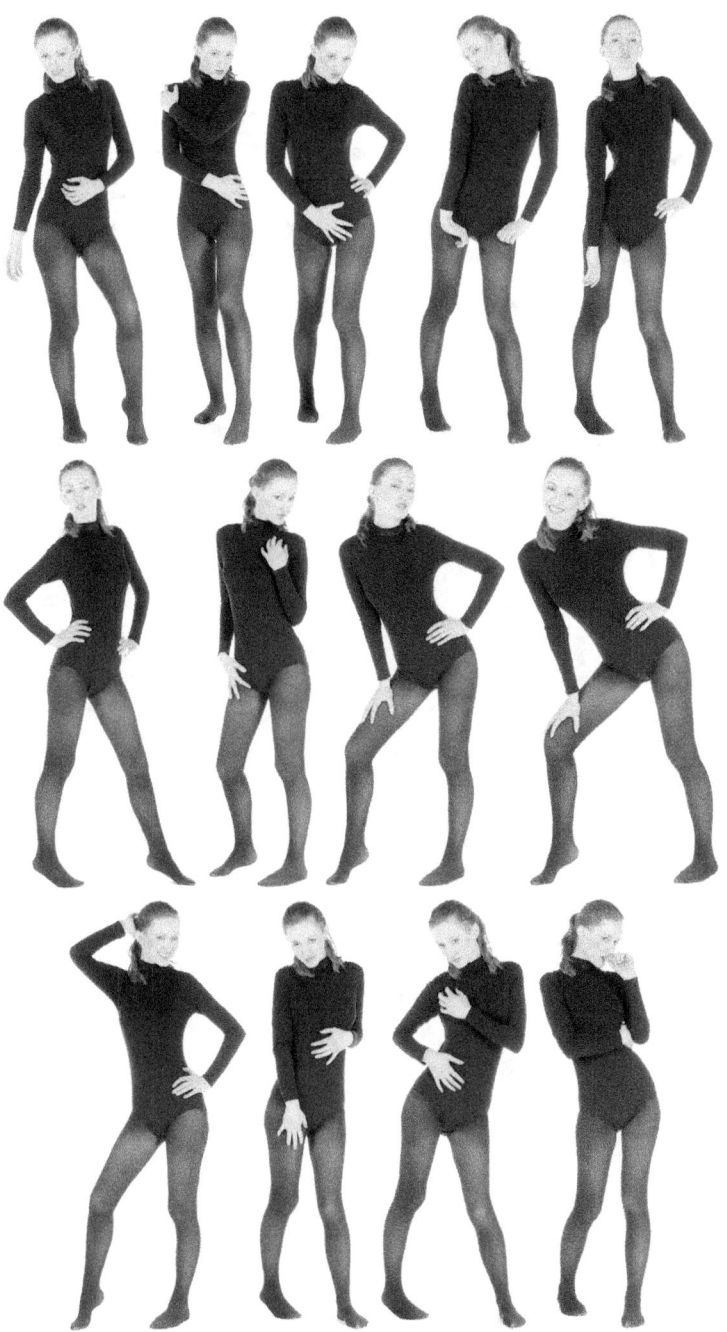

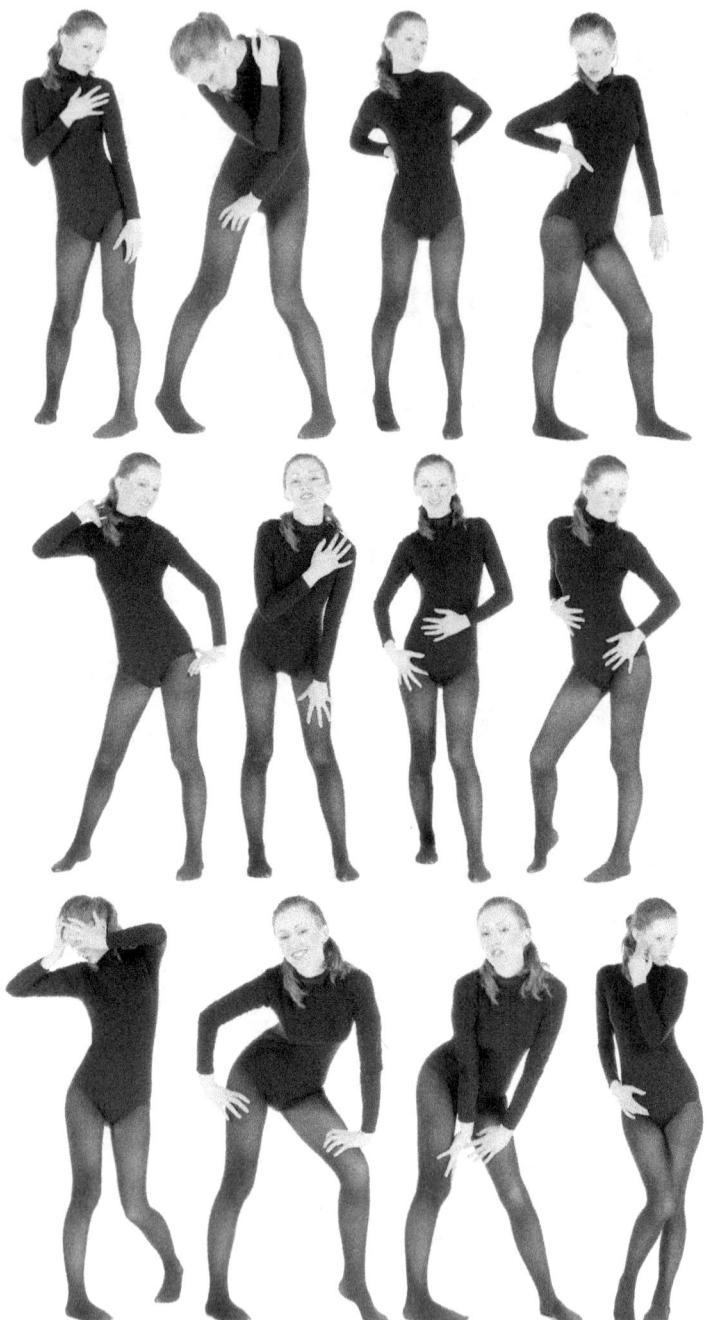

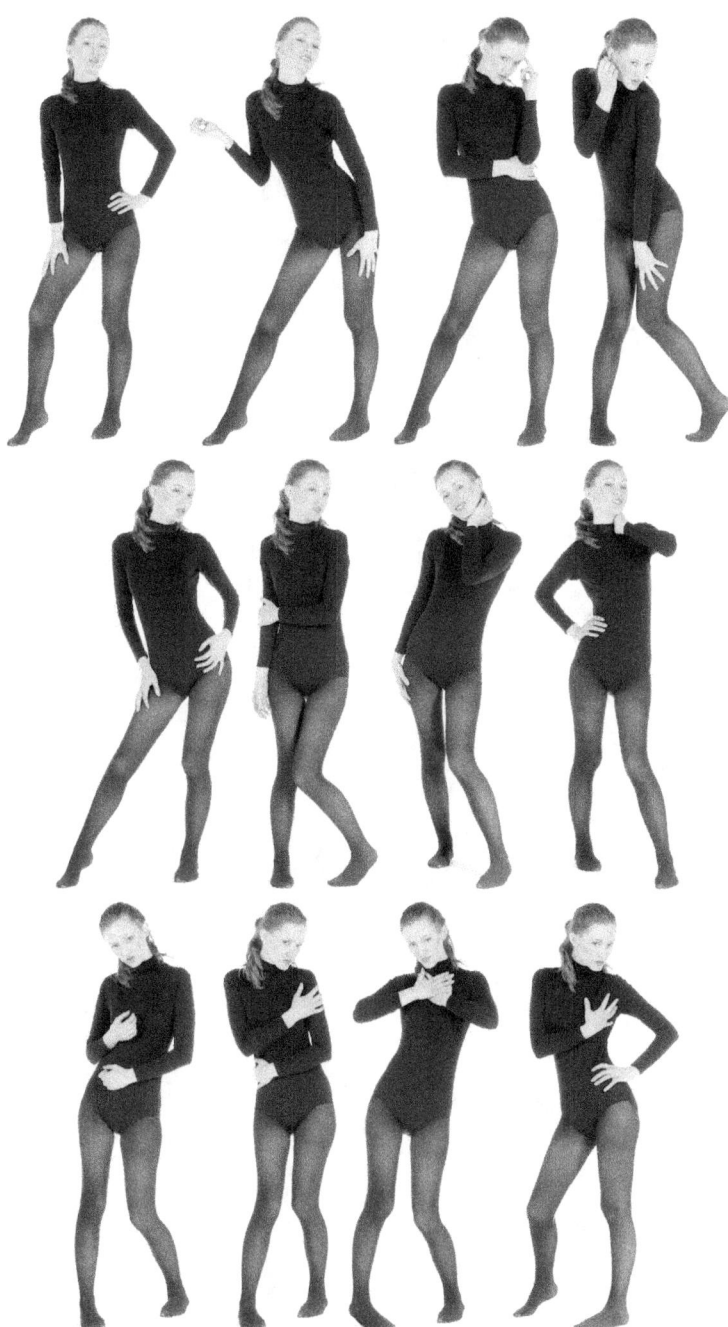

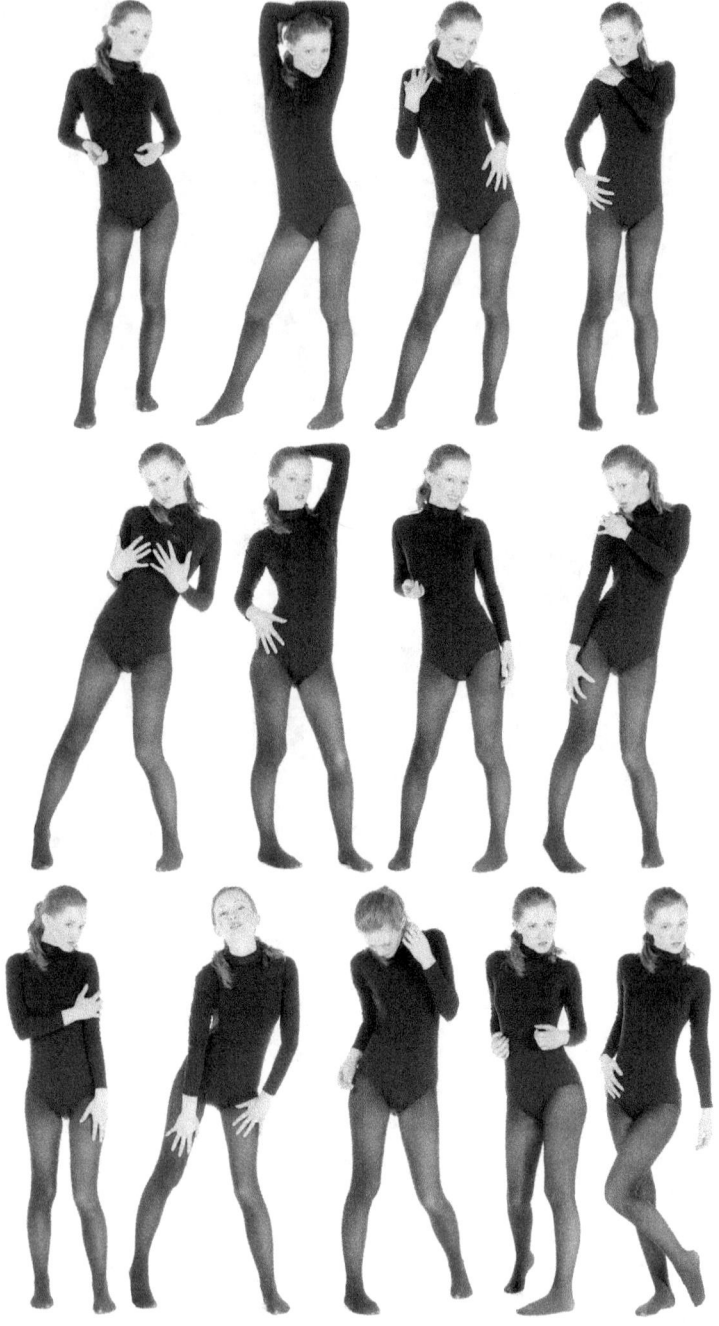

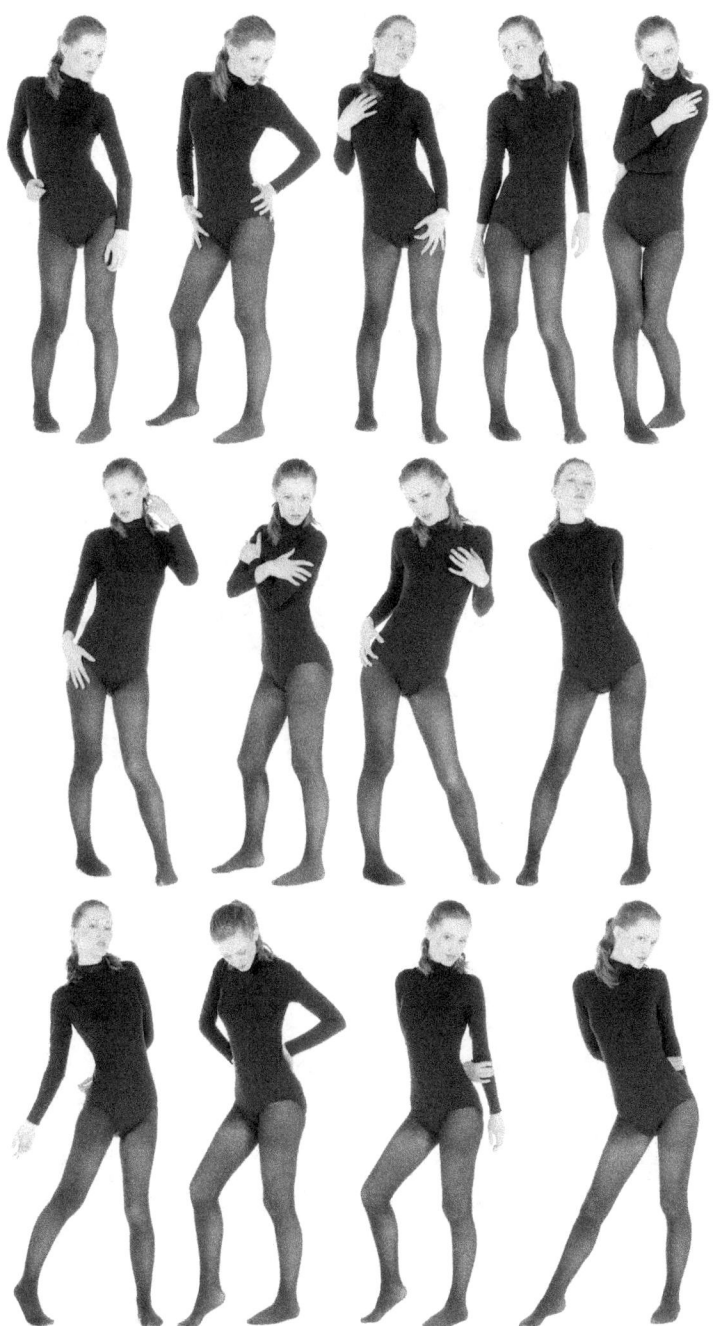

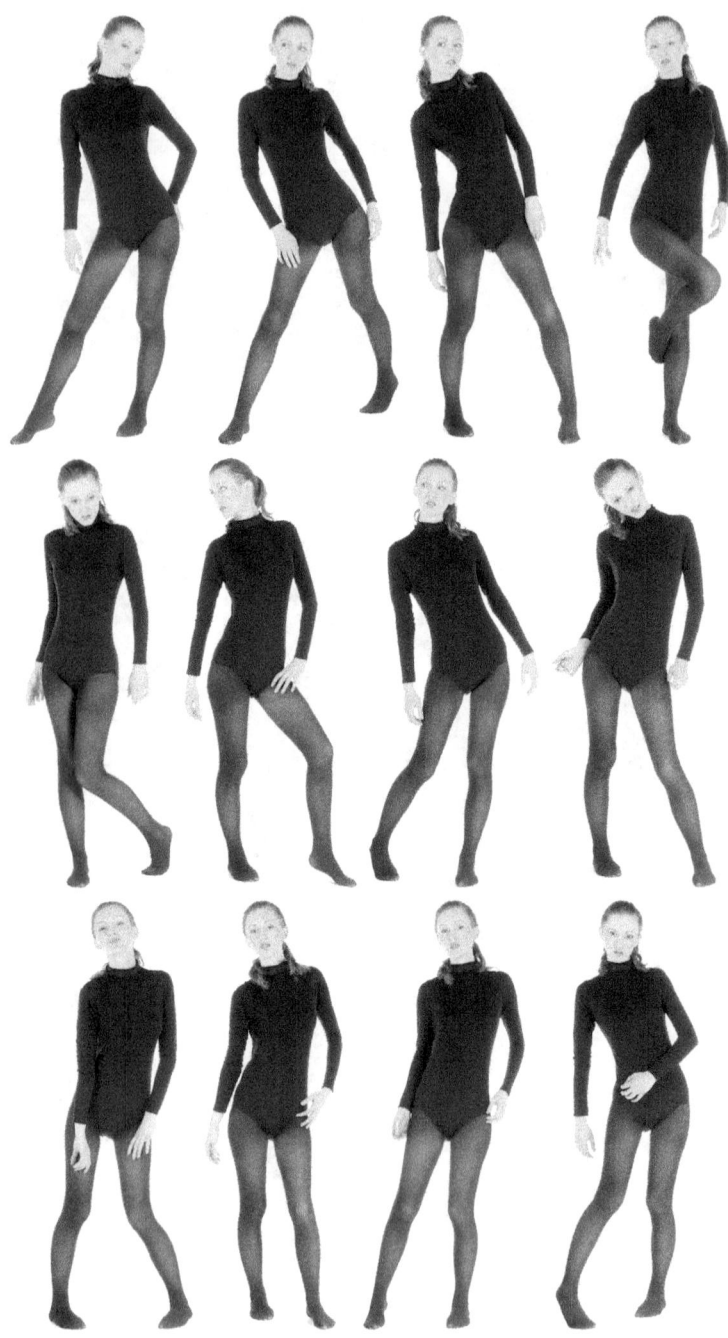

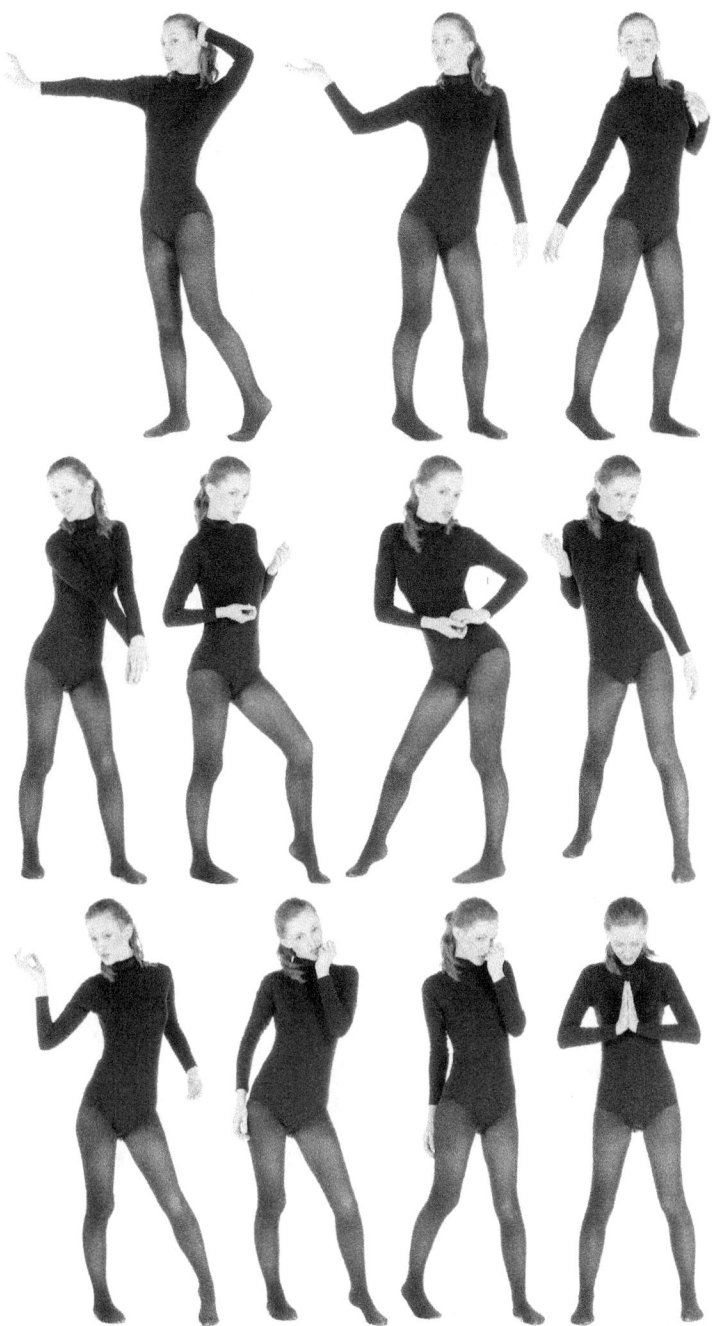

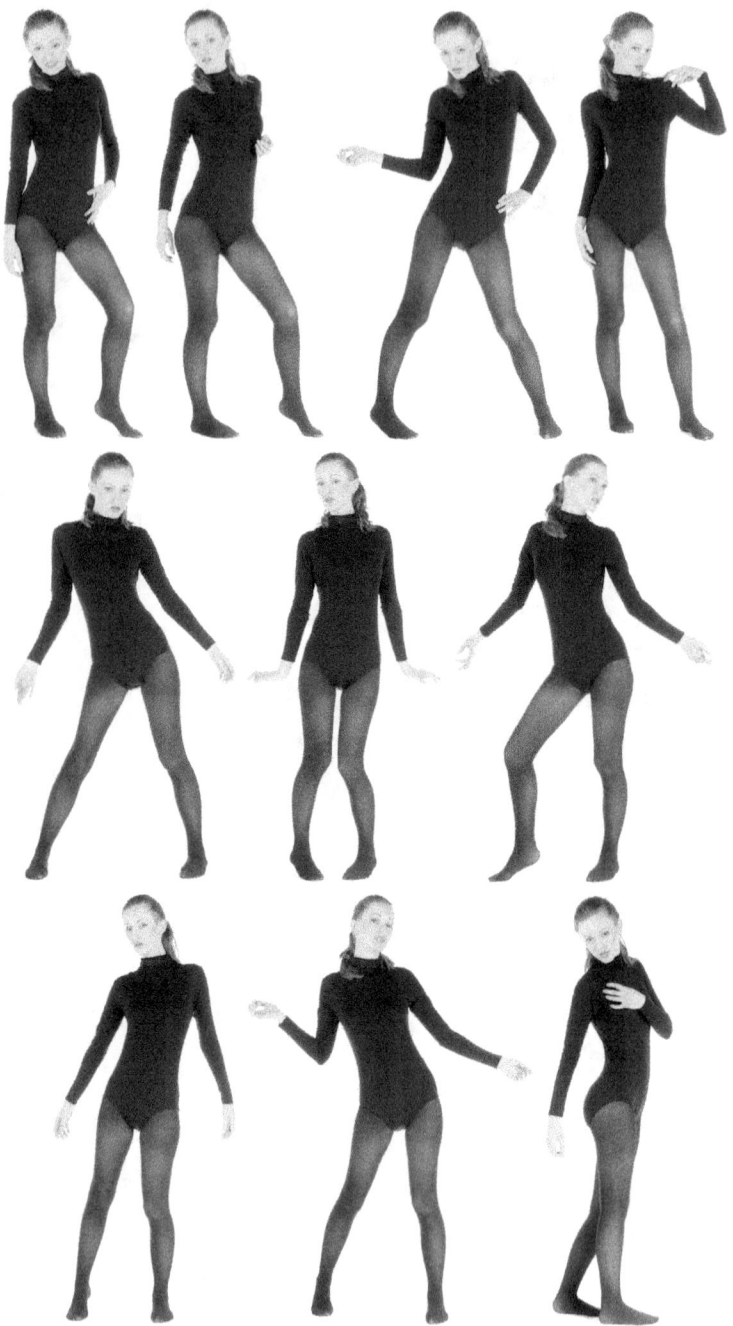

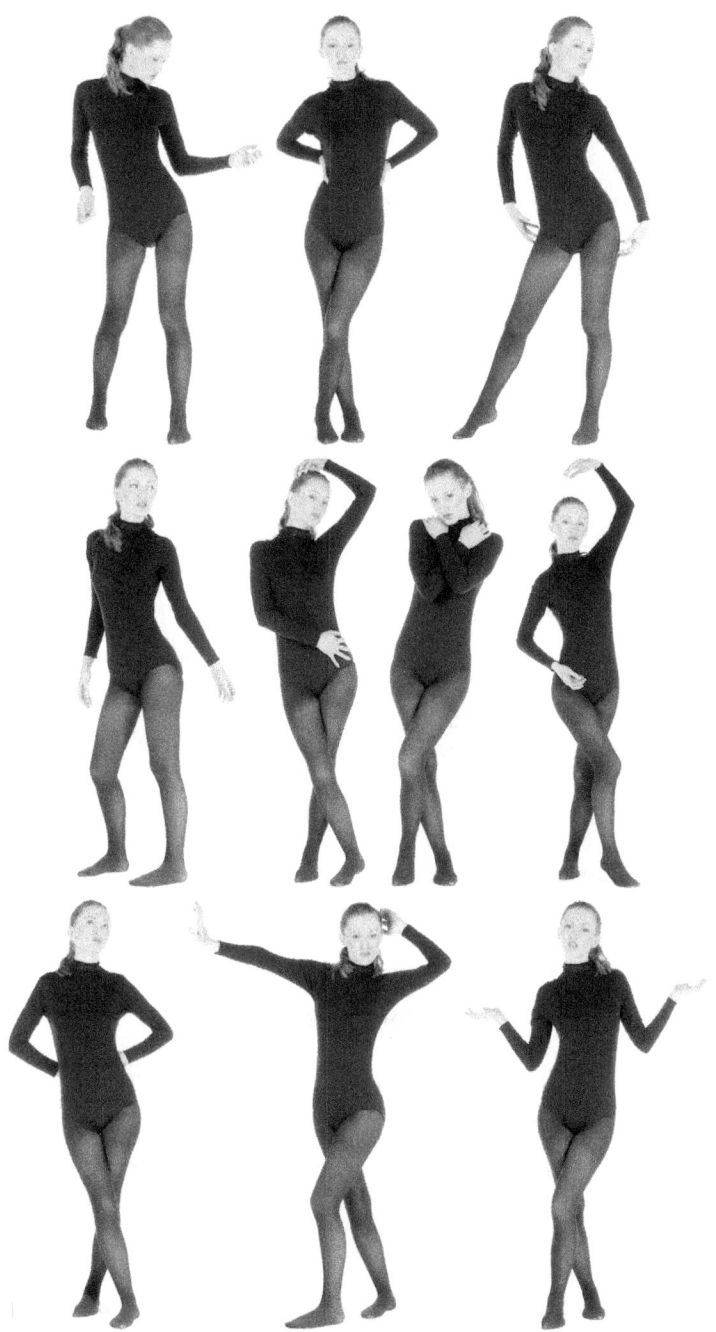

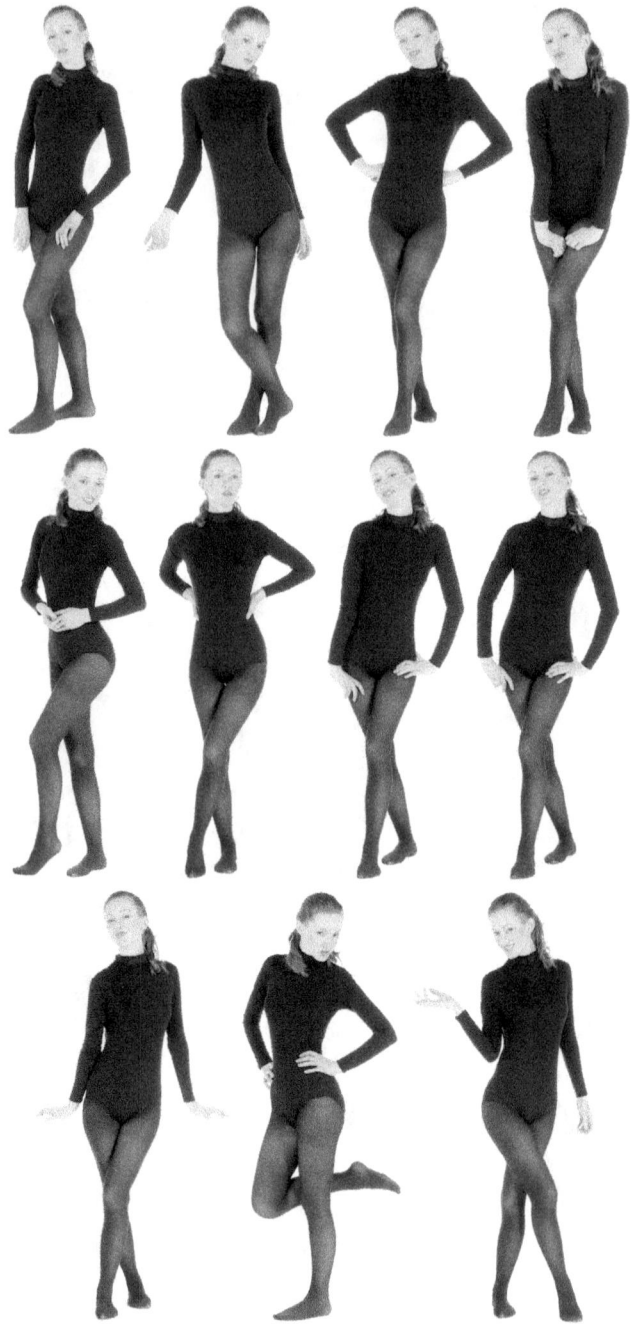

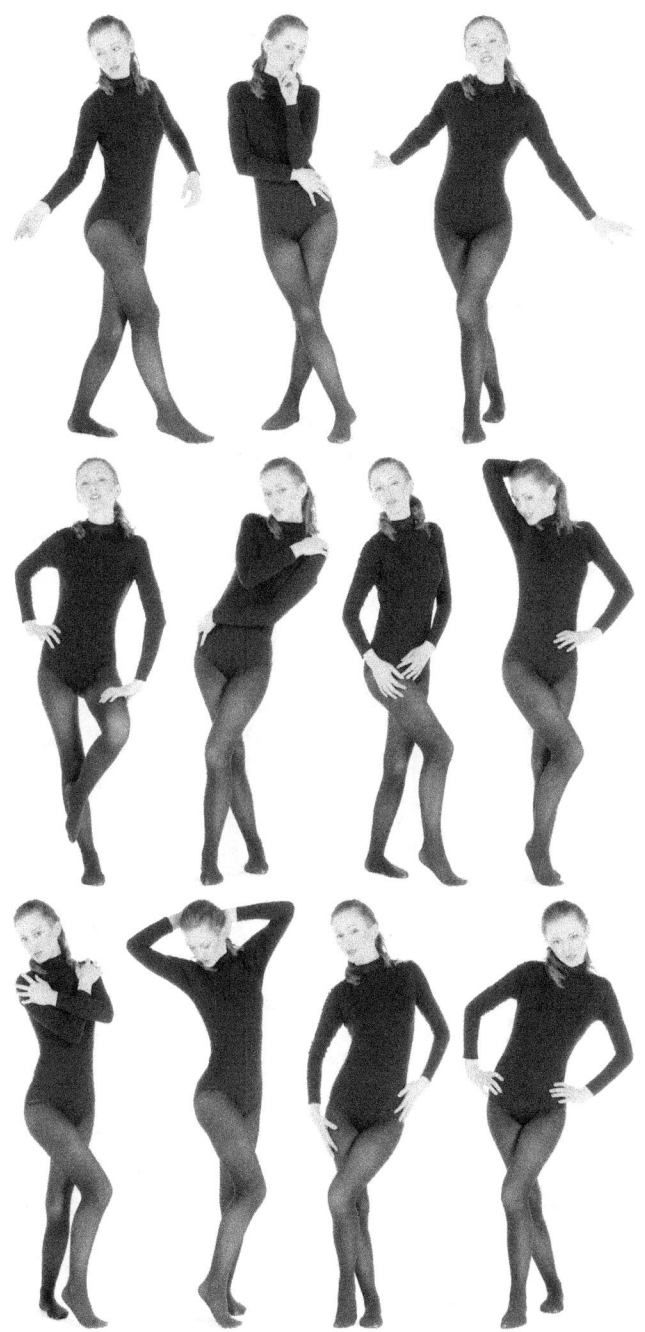

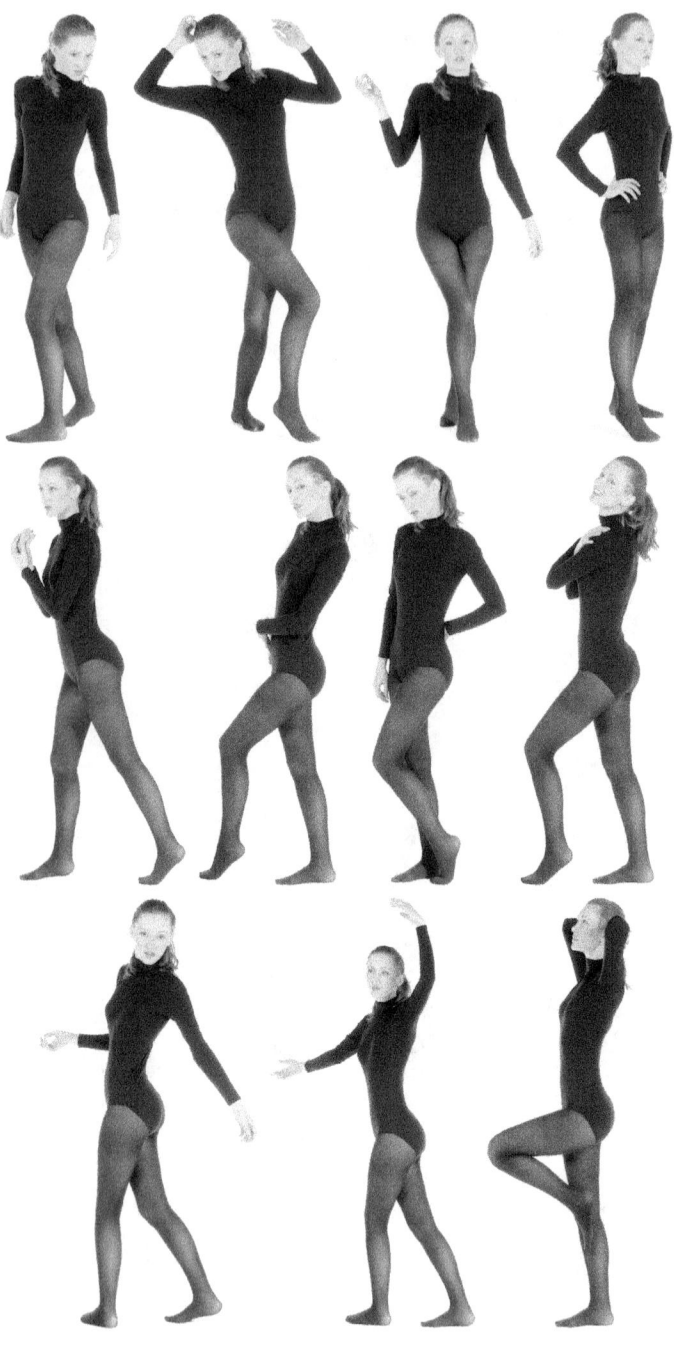

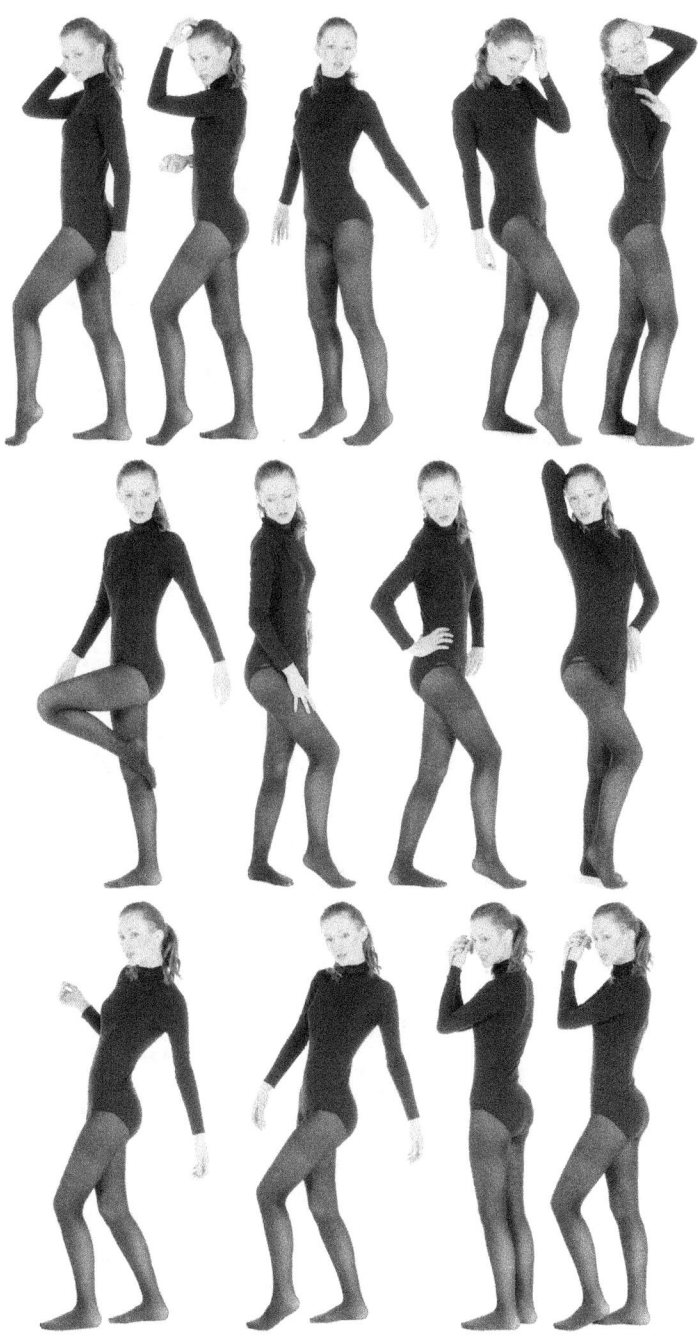

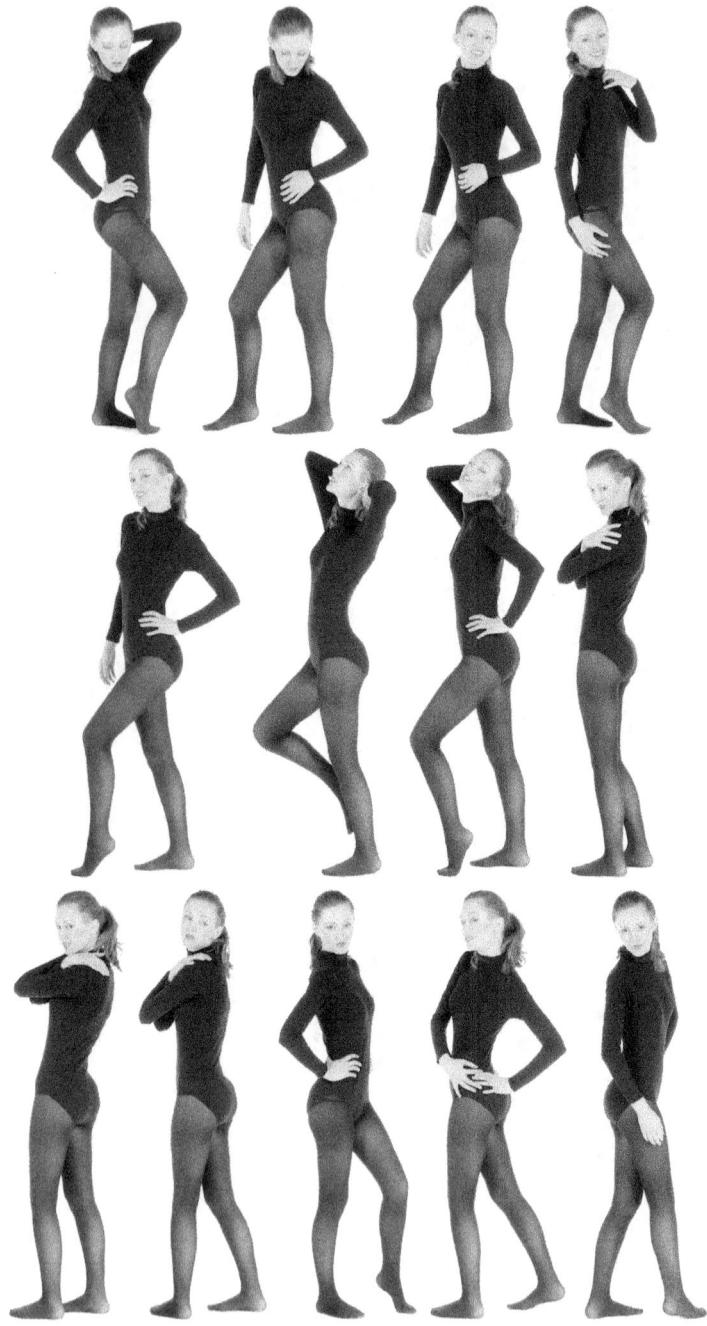

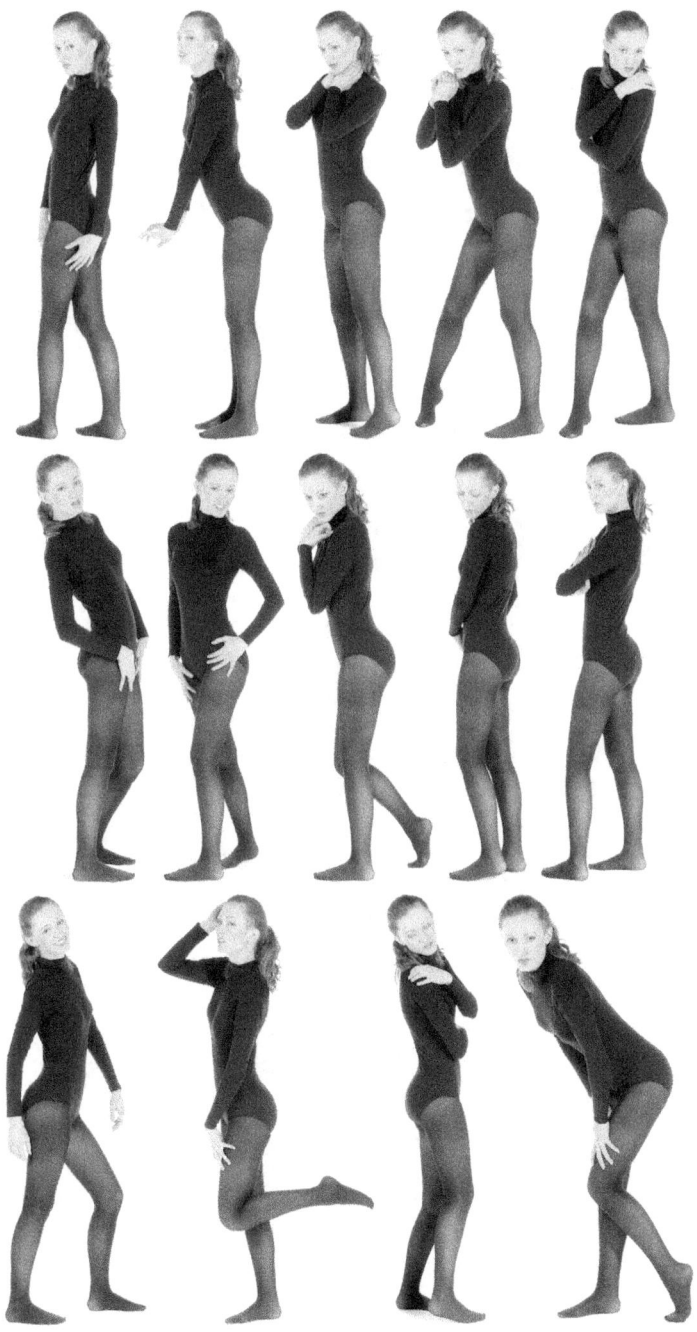

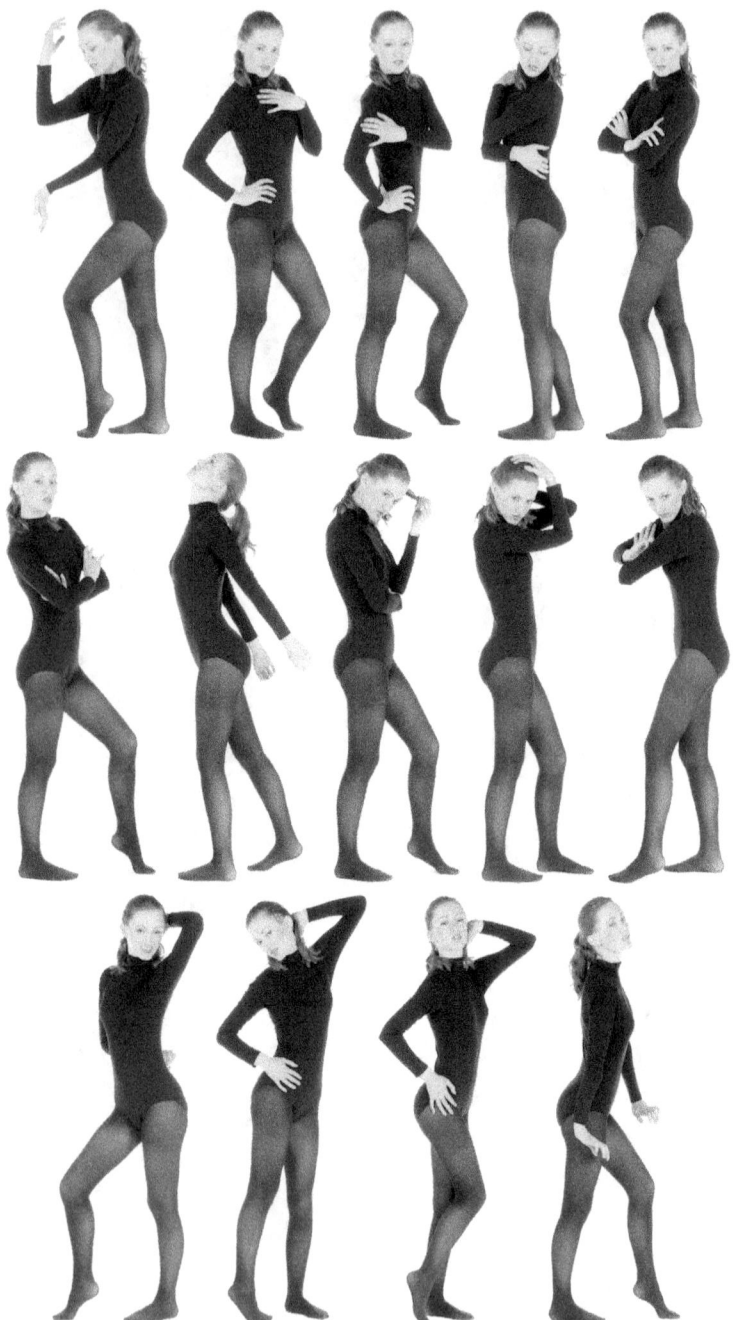

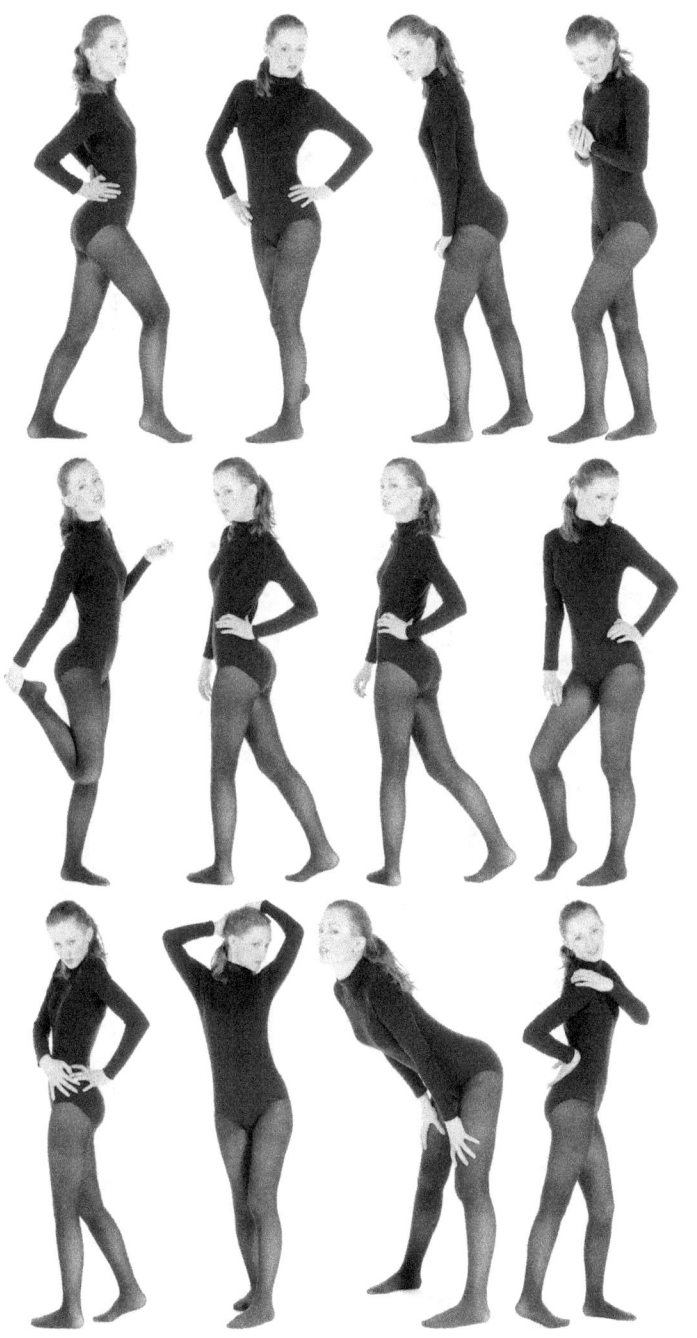

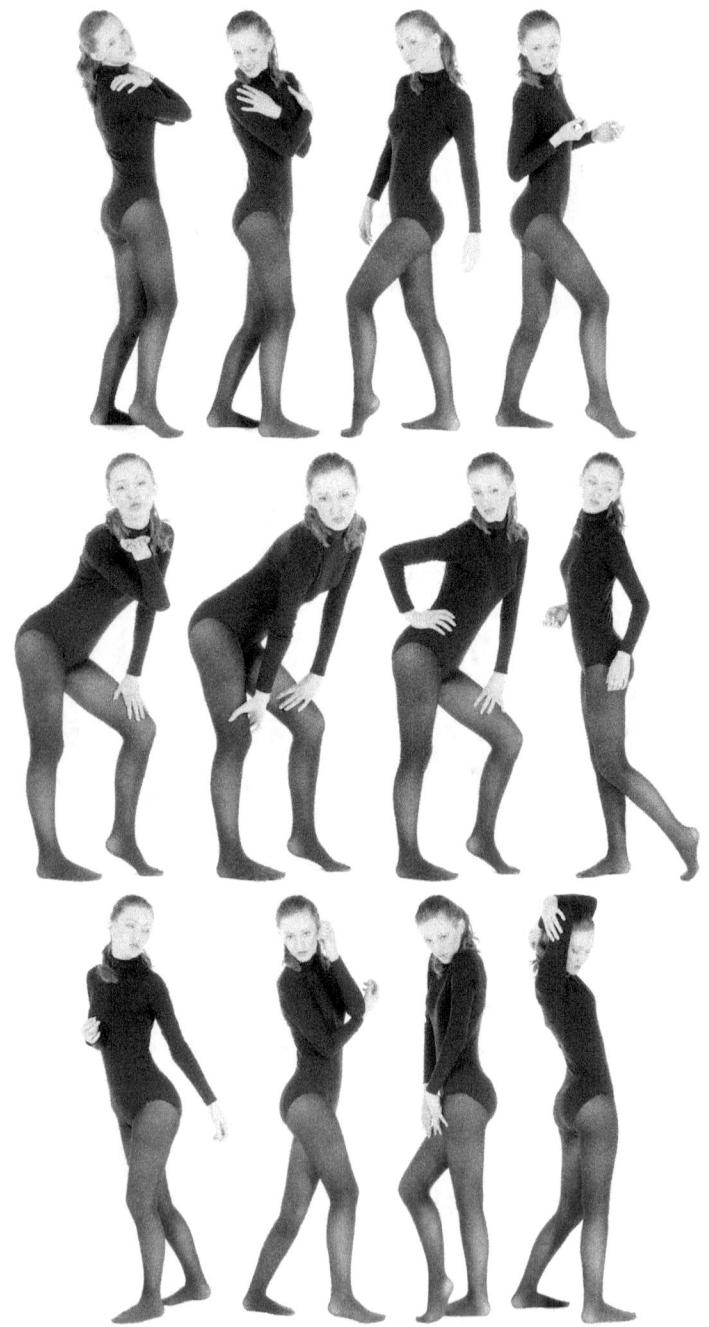

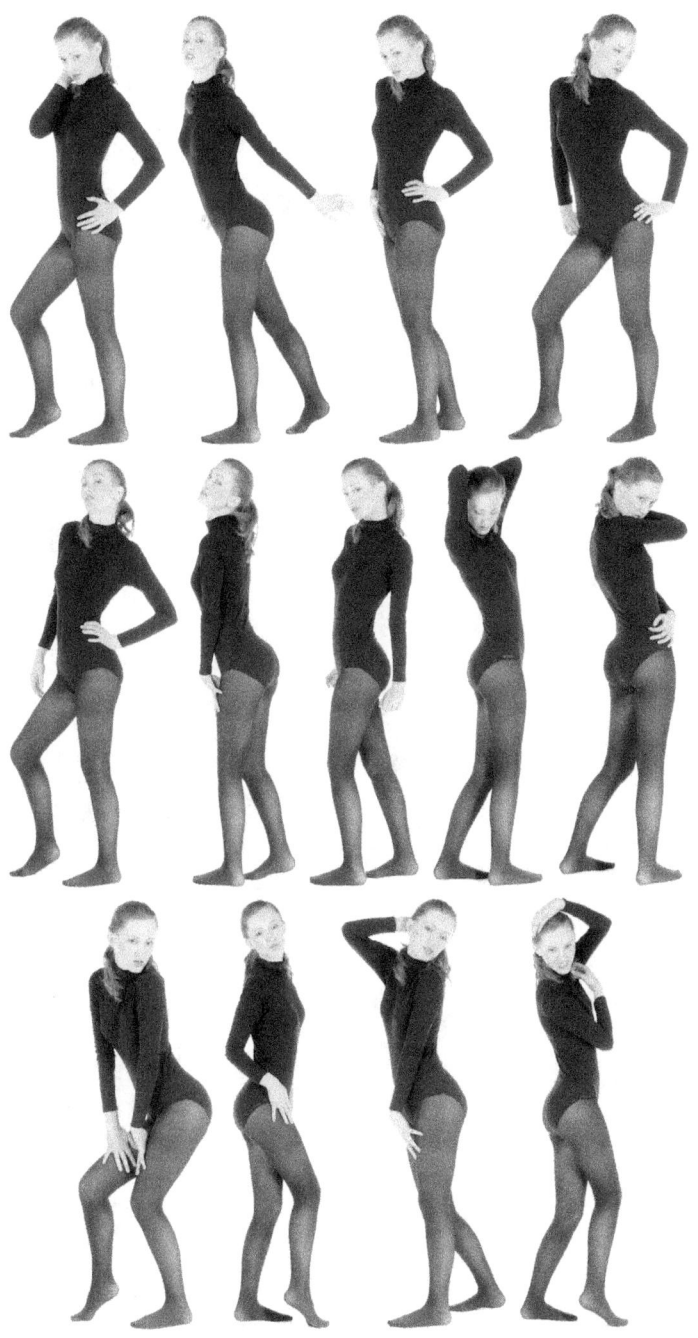

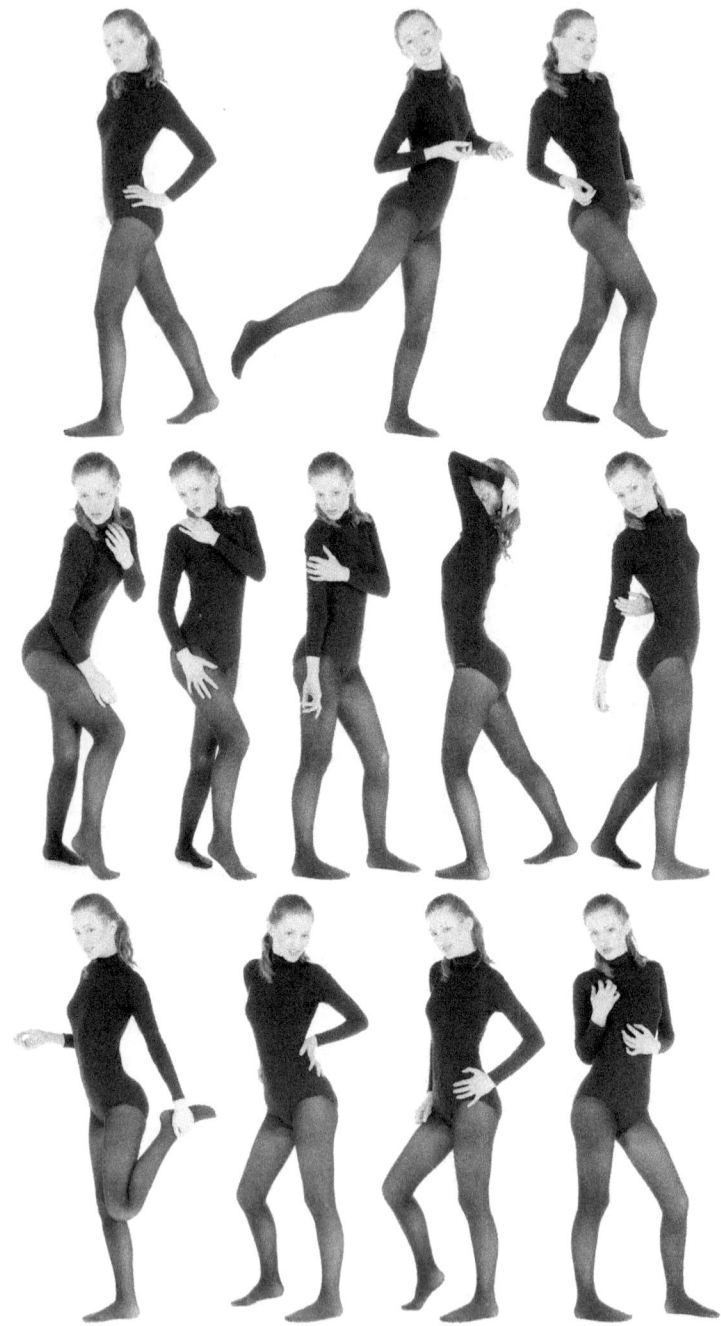

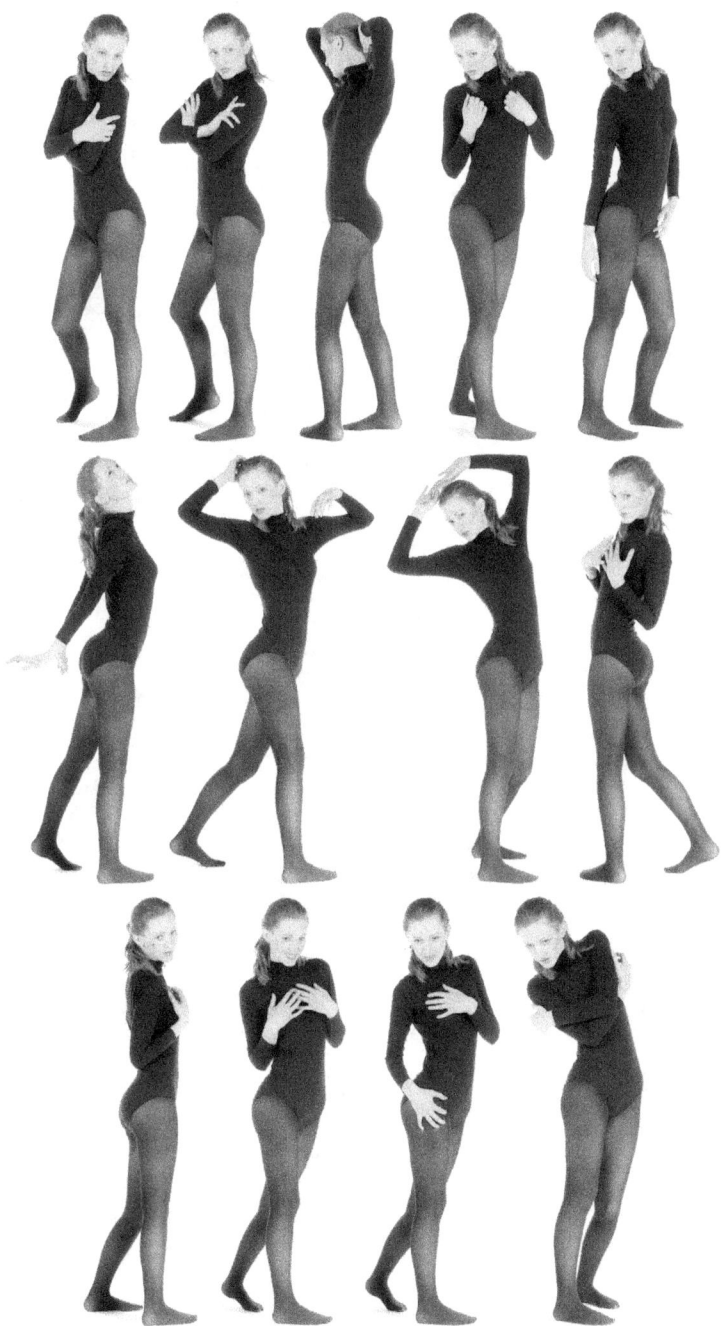

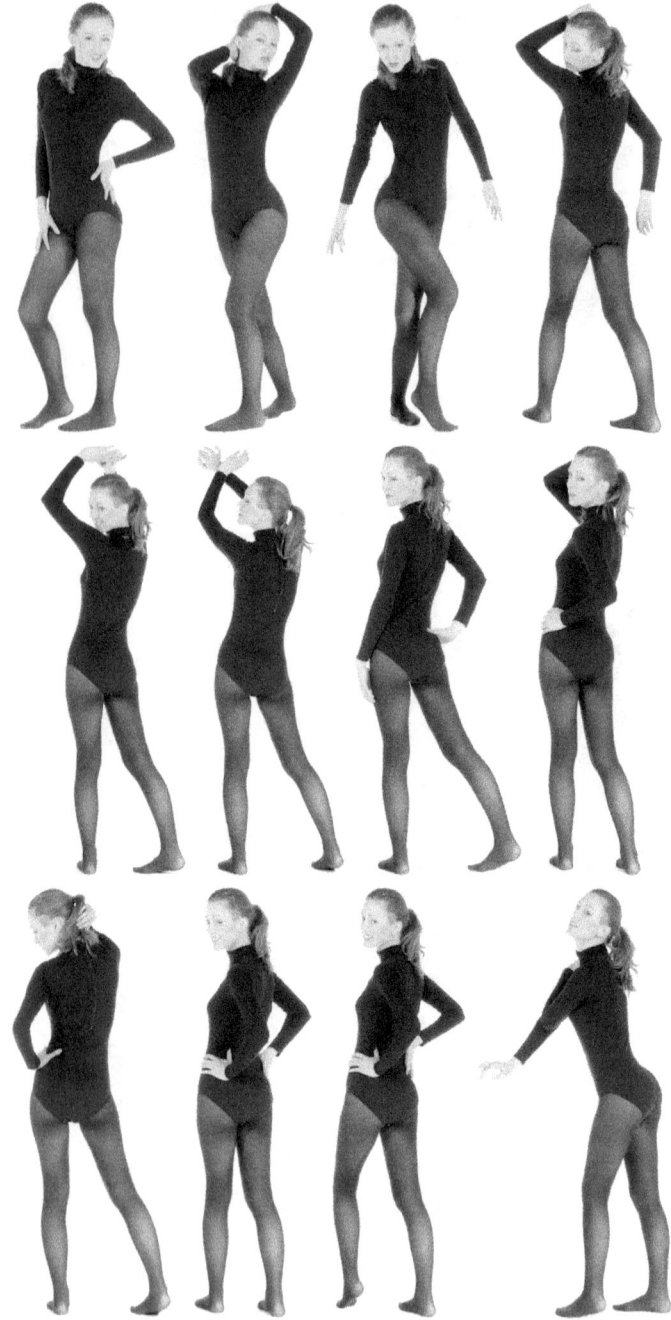

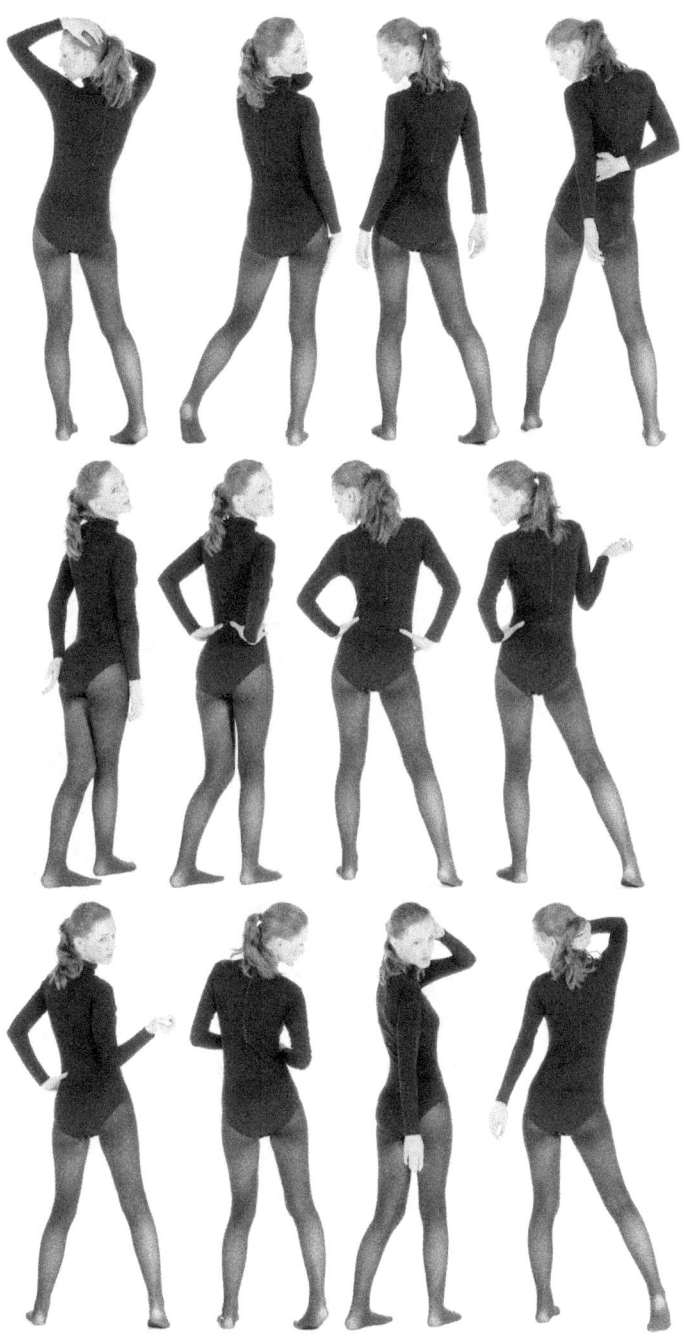

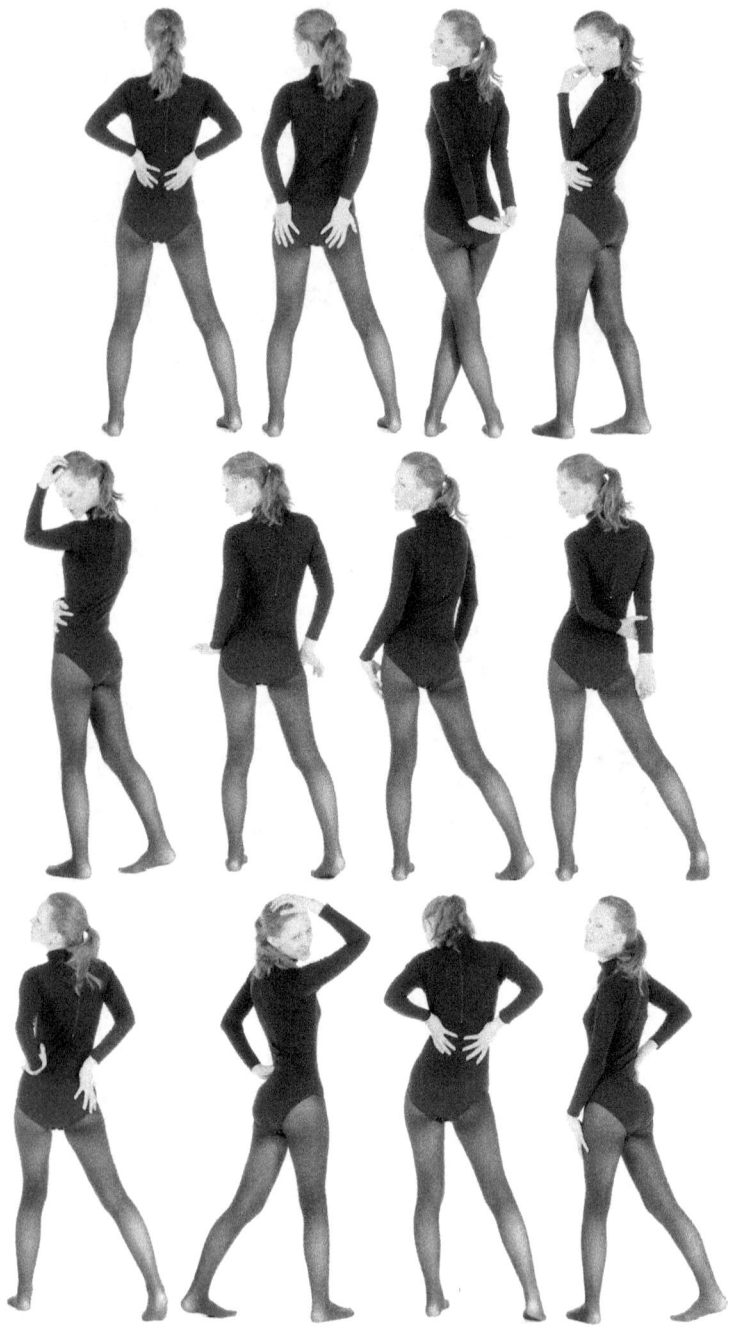

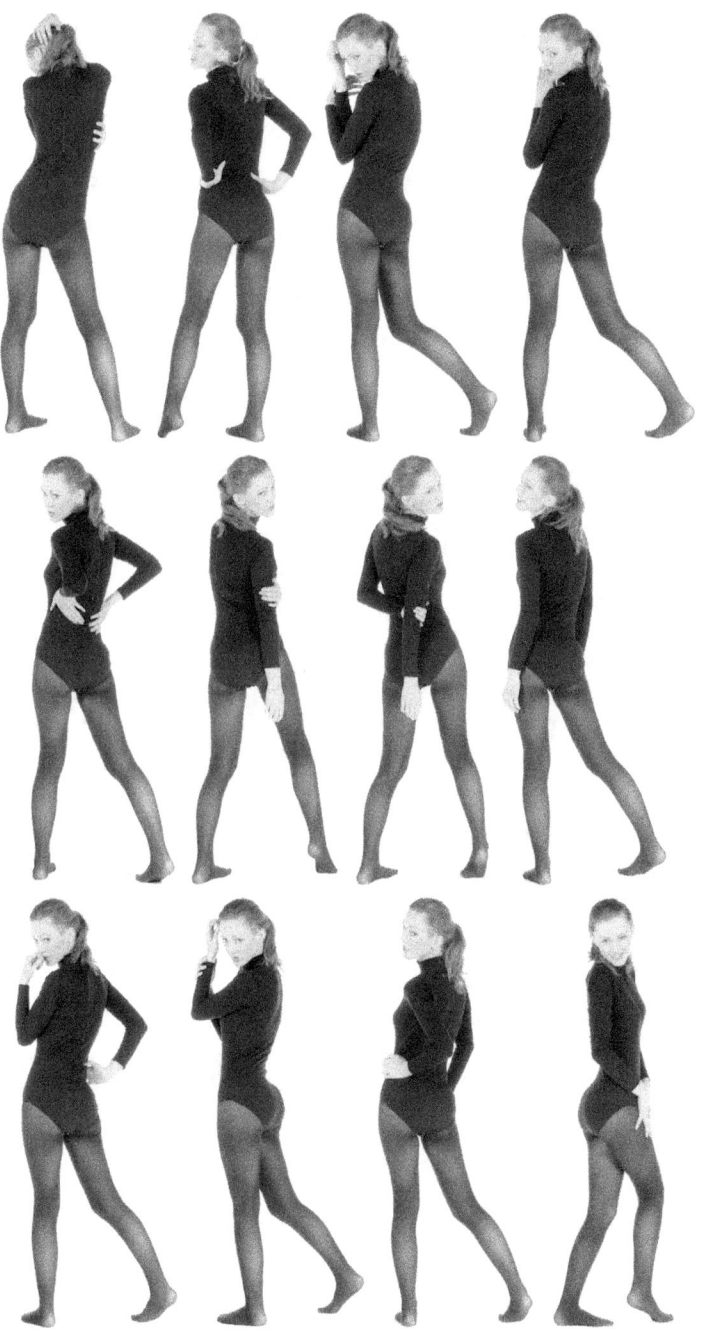

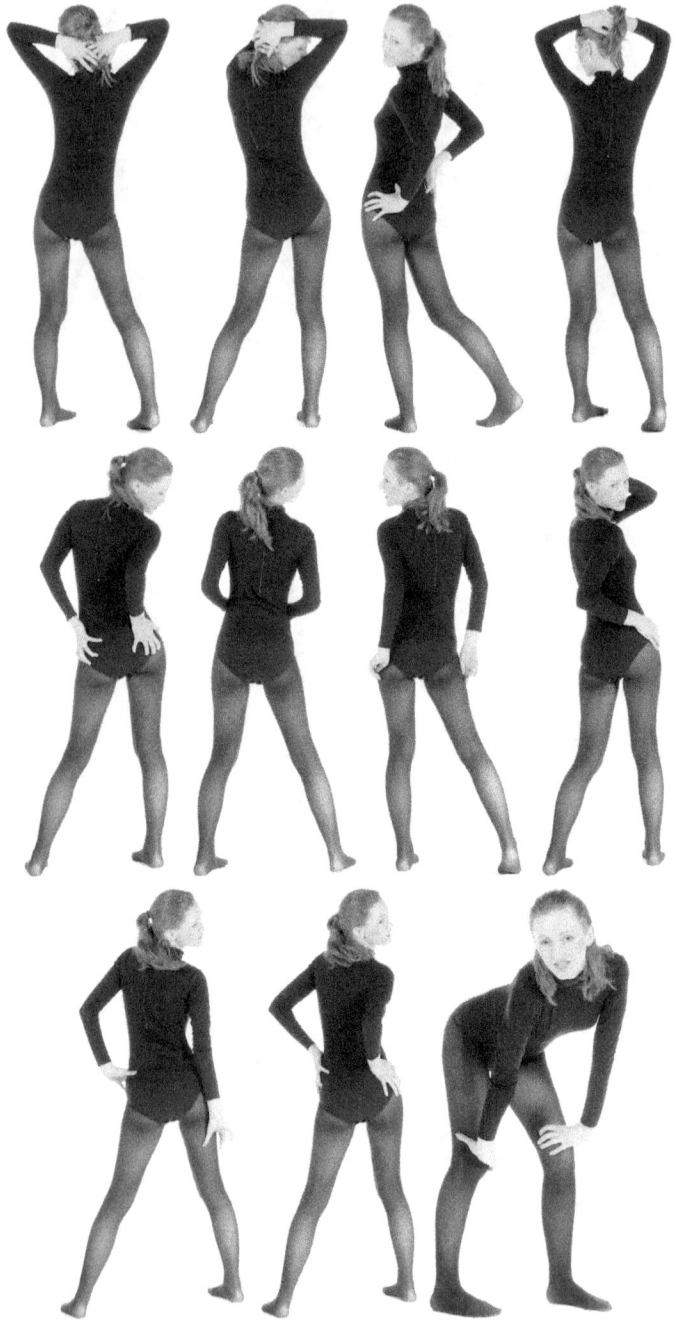

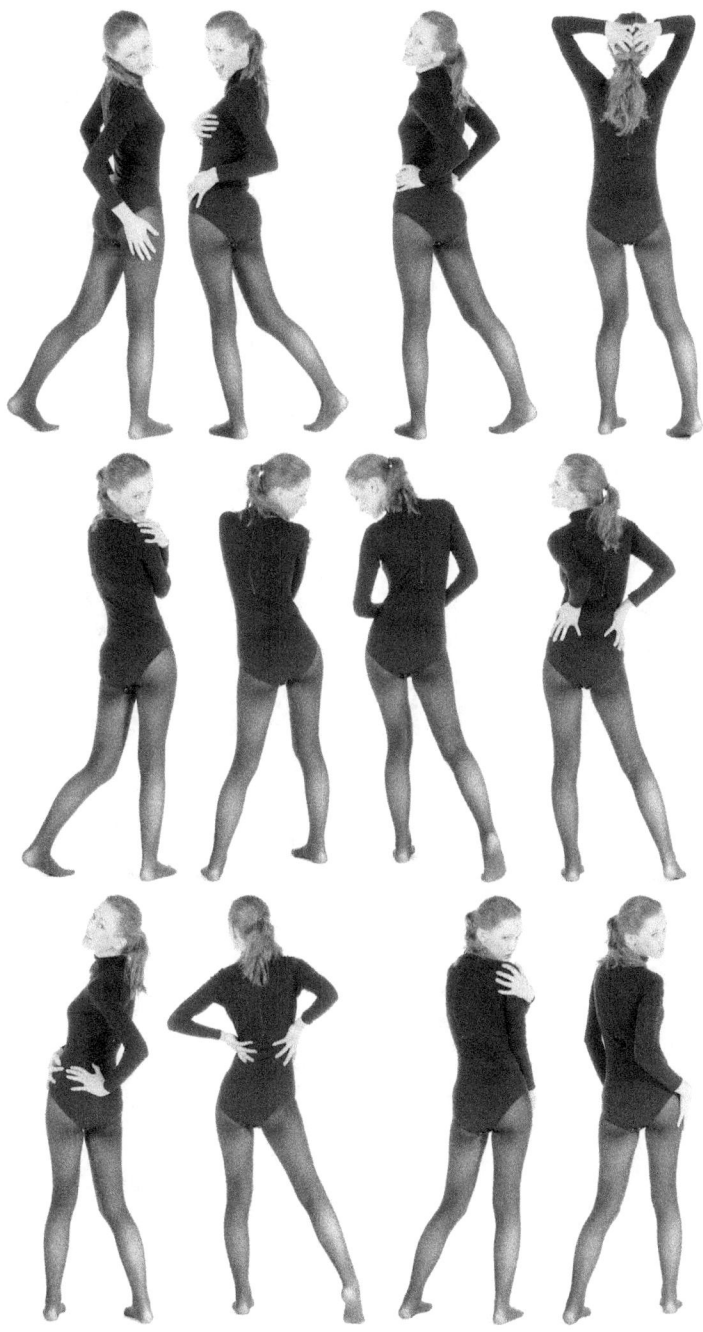

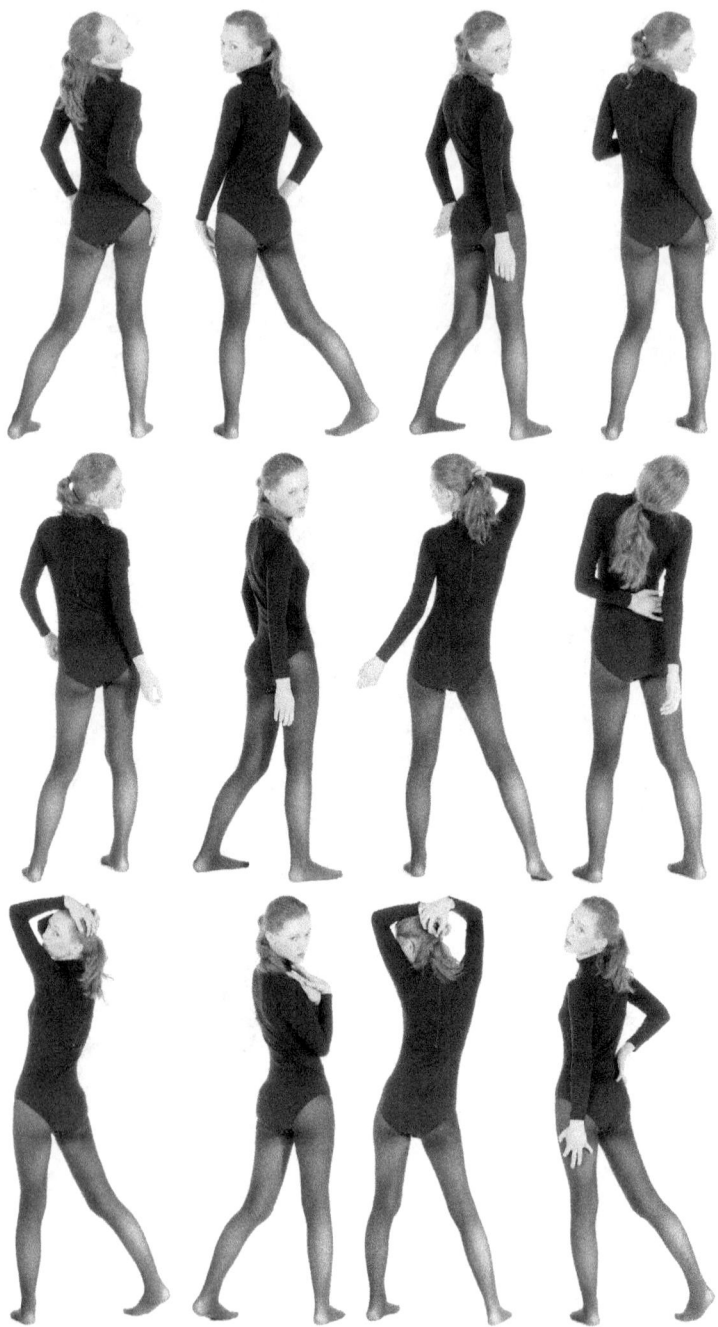

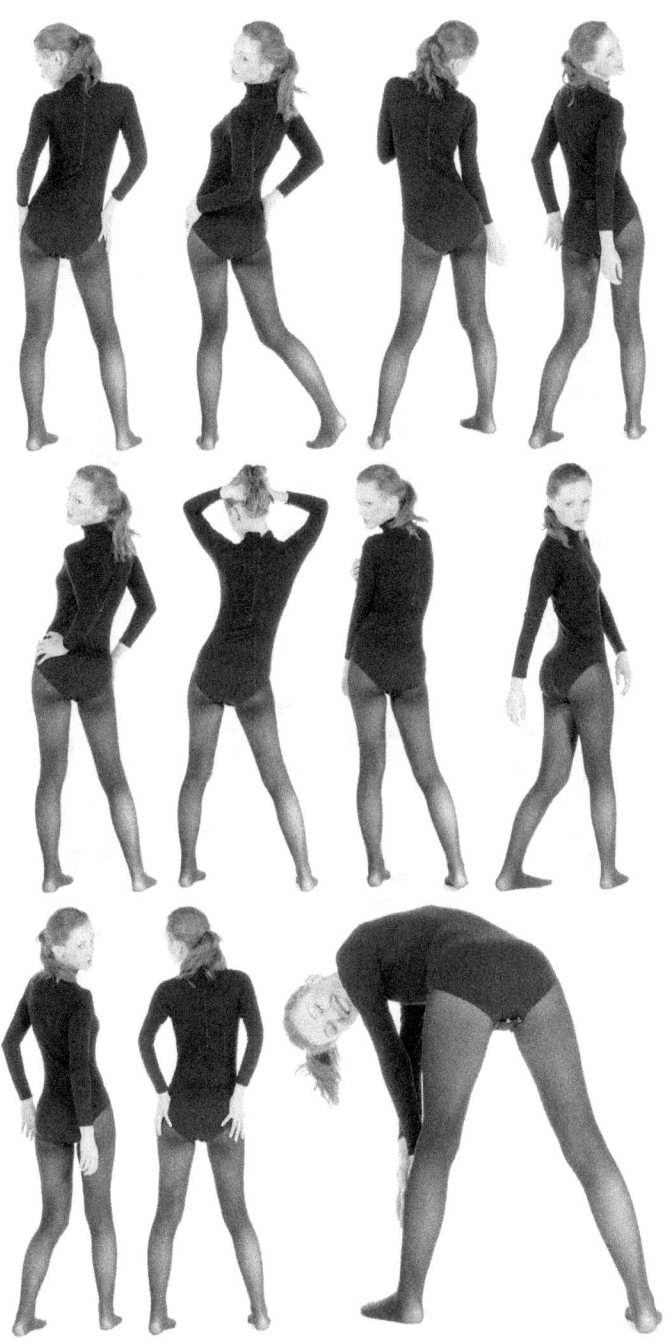

SITTING POSES

Common in Fashion Photography, but less so than standing.

SITTING ON THE FLOOR

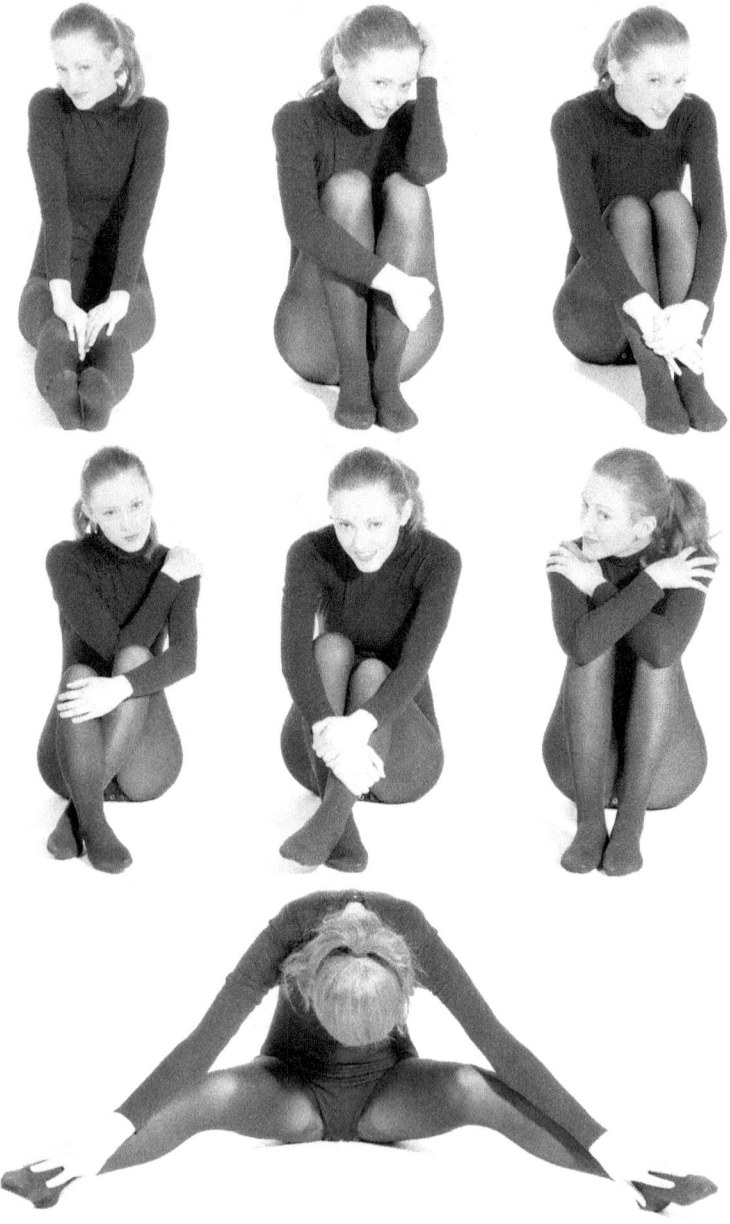

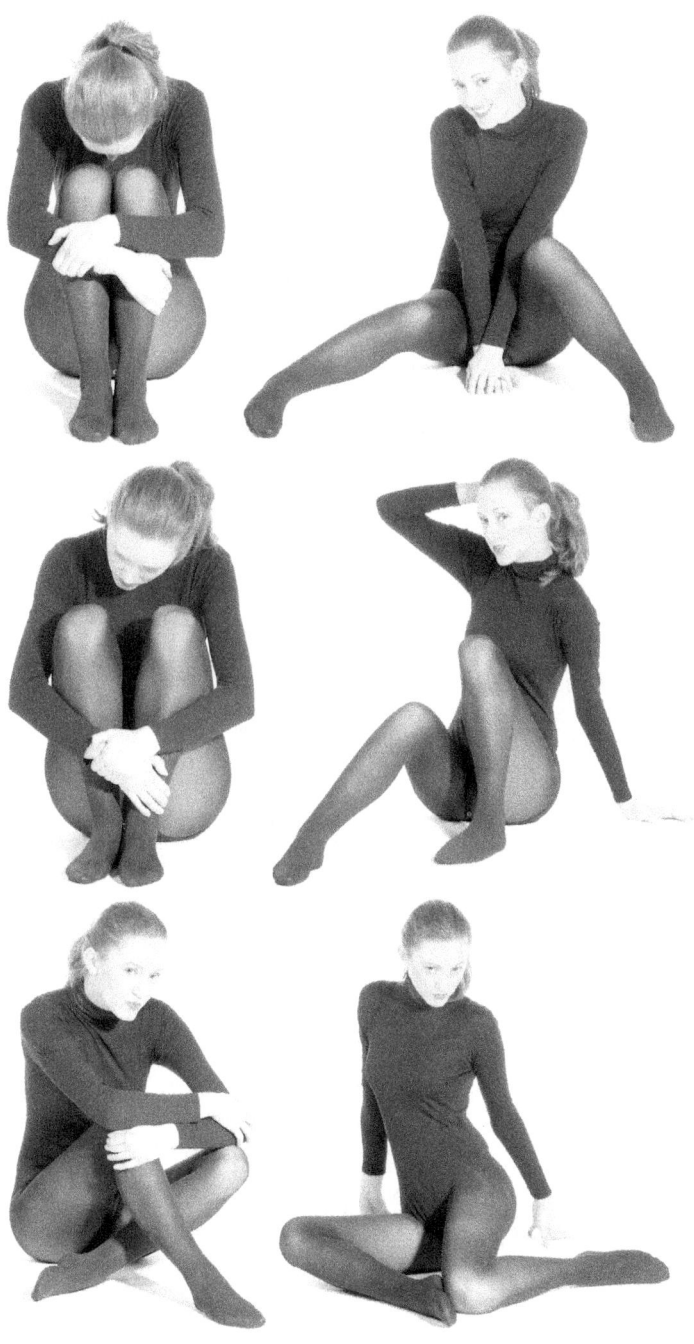

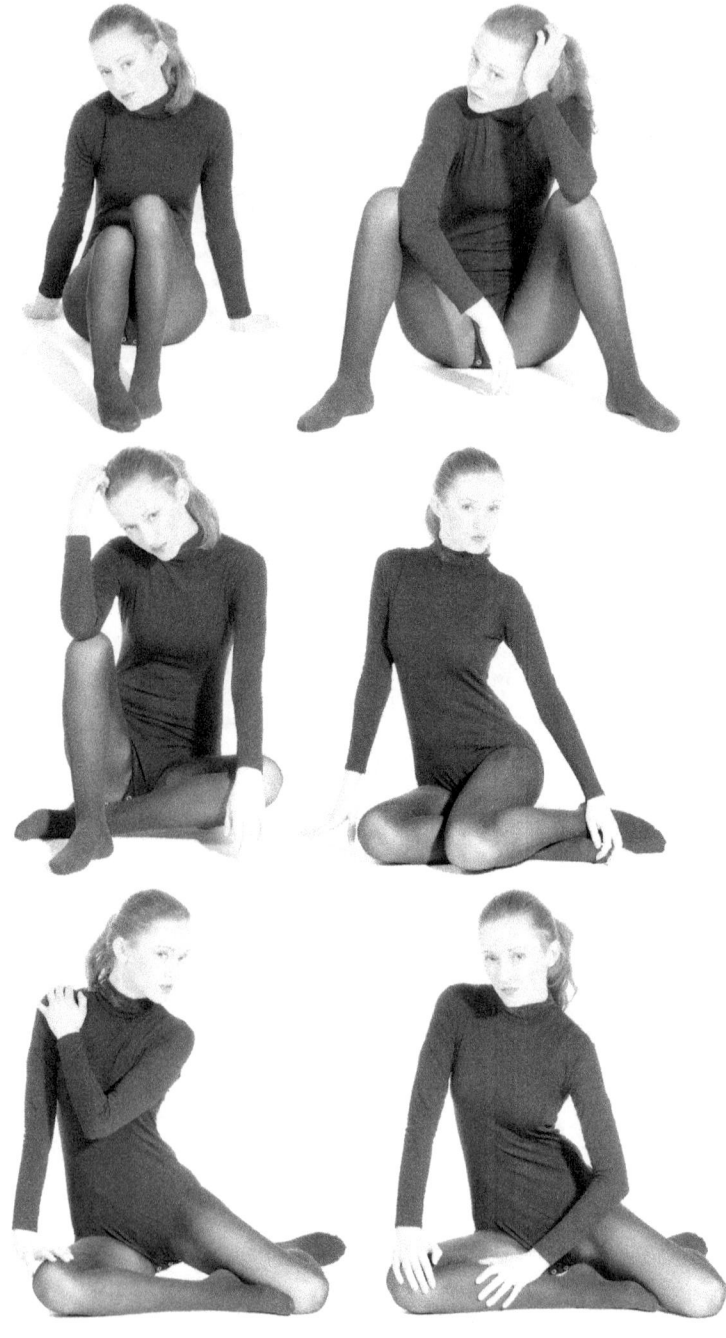

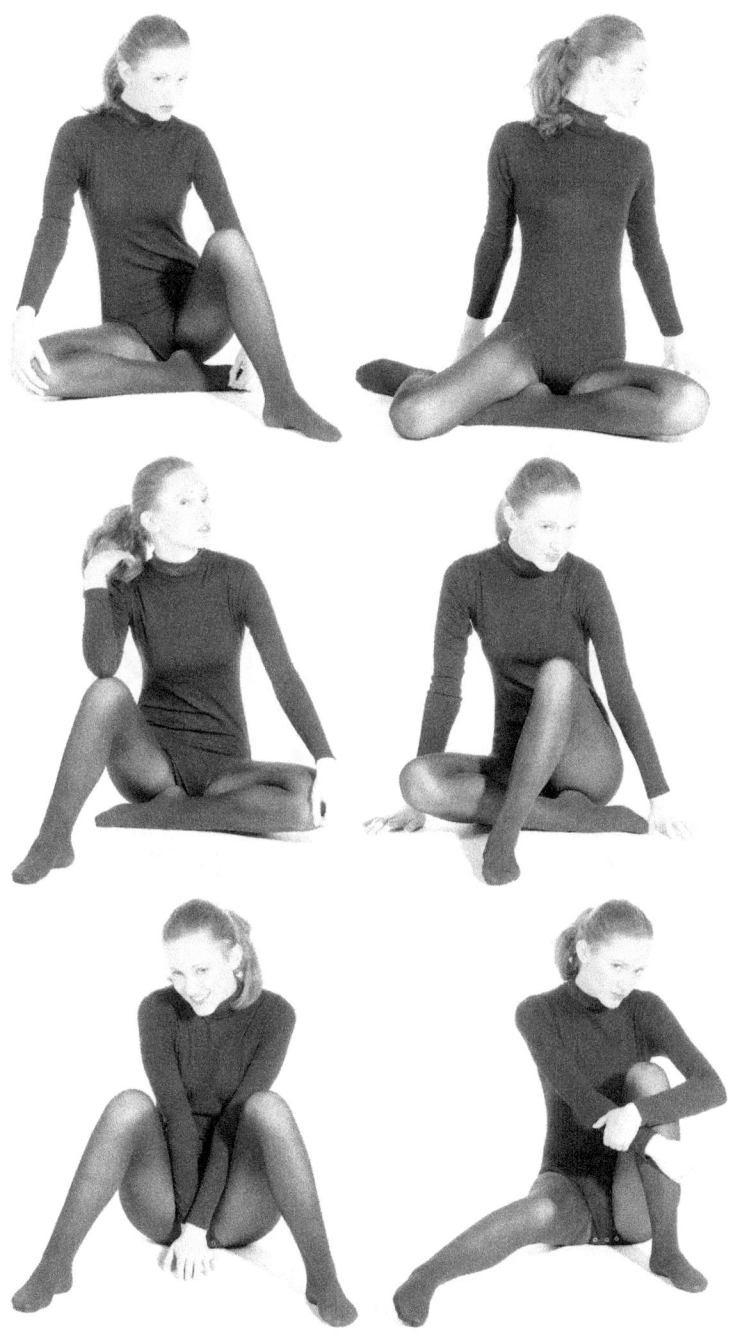

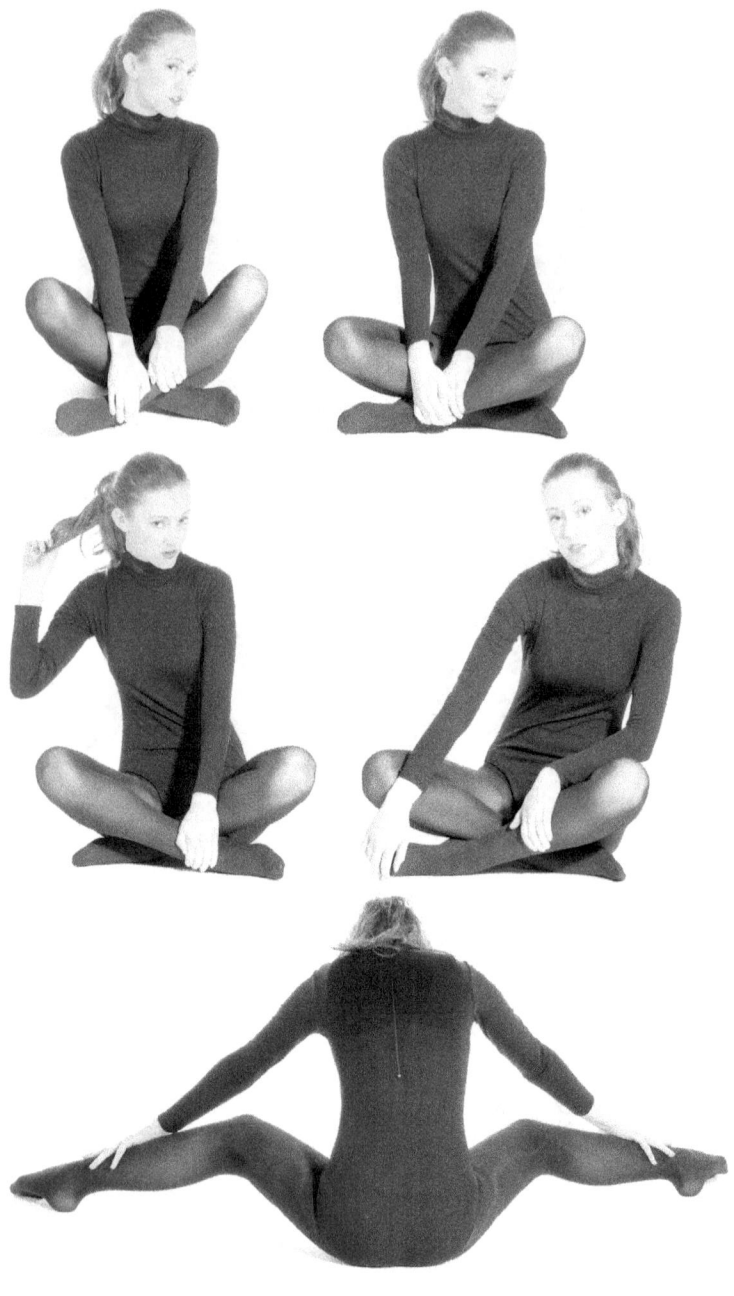

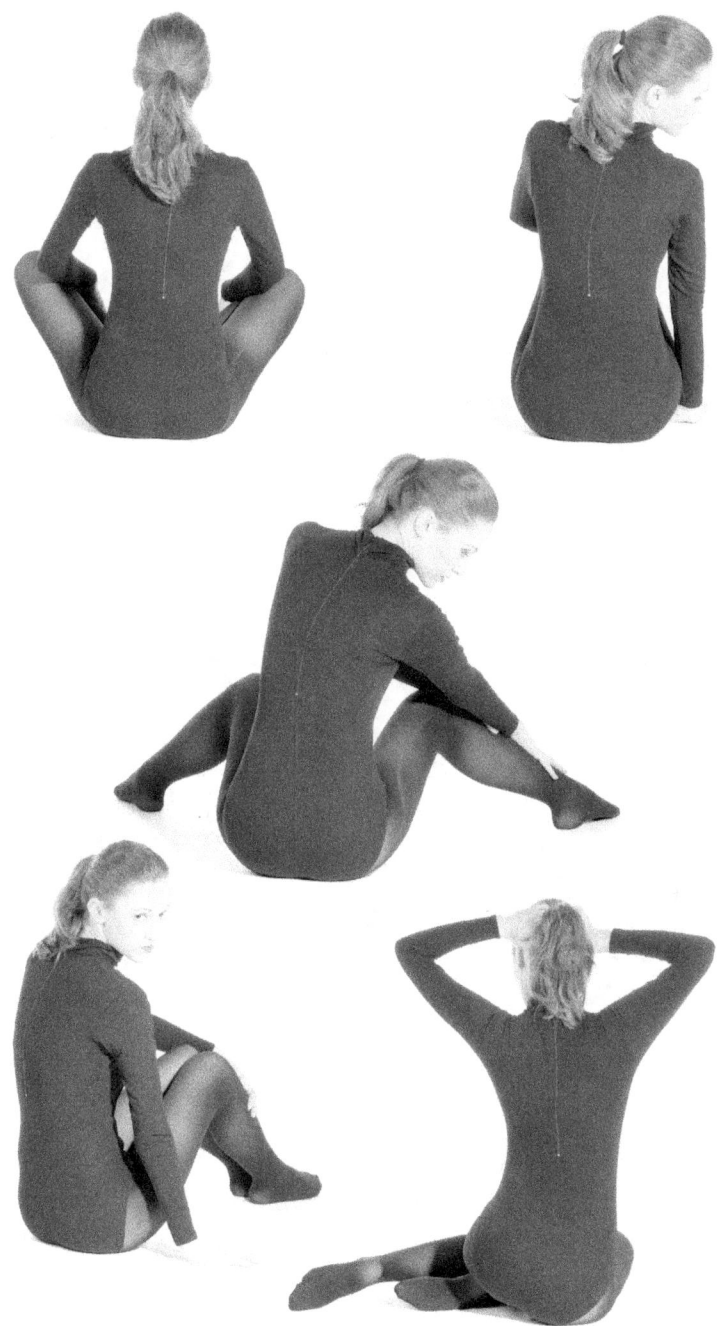

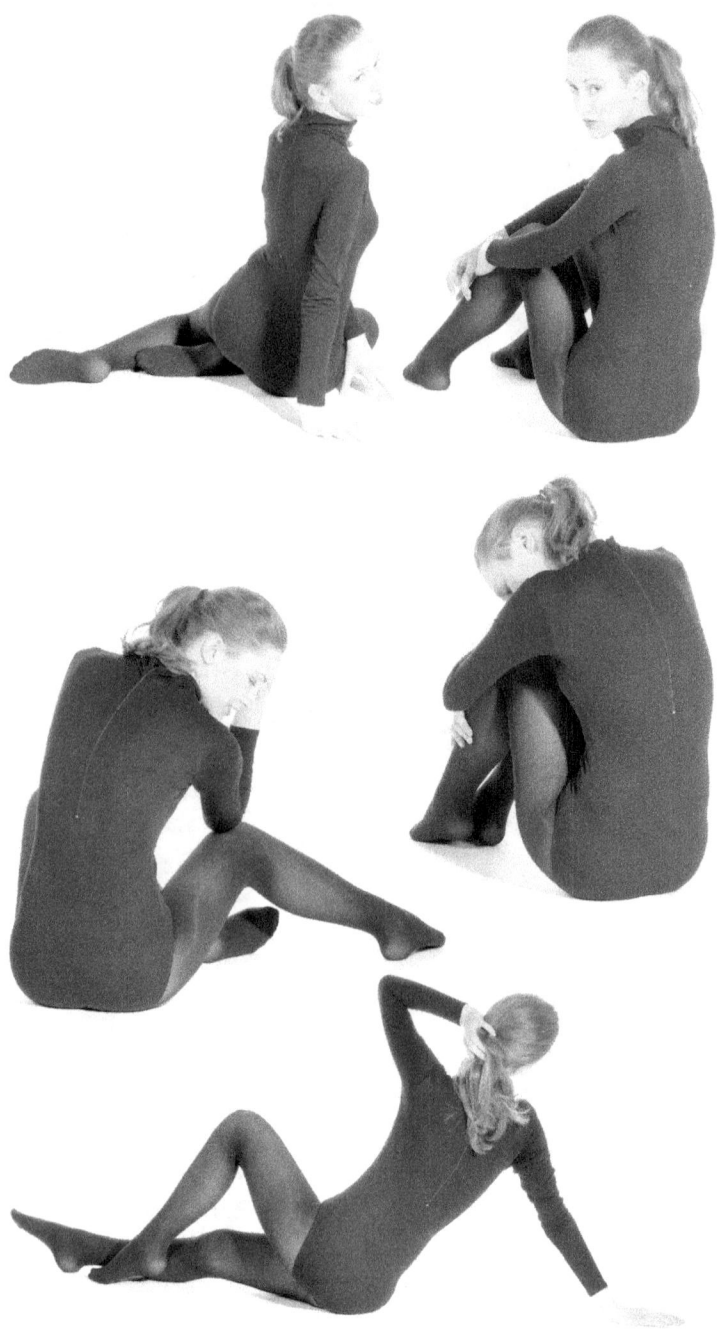

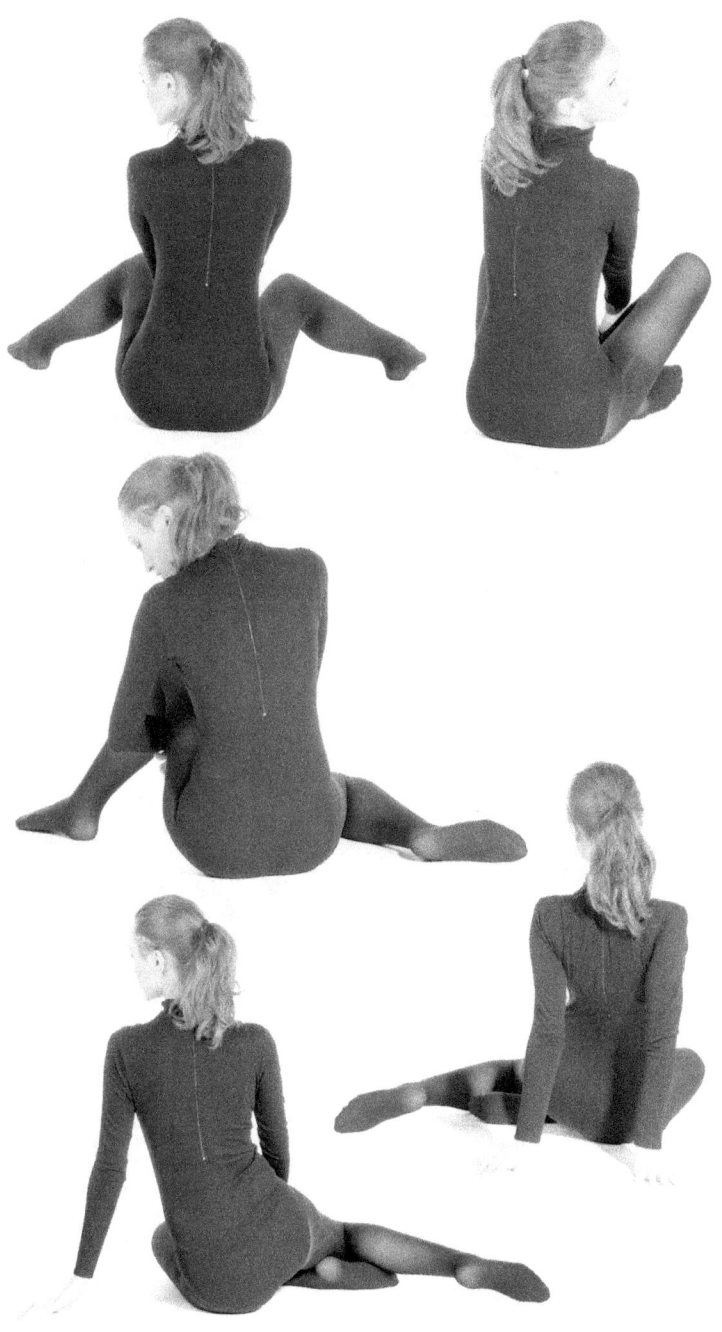

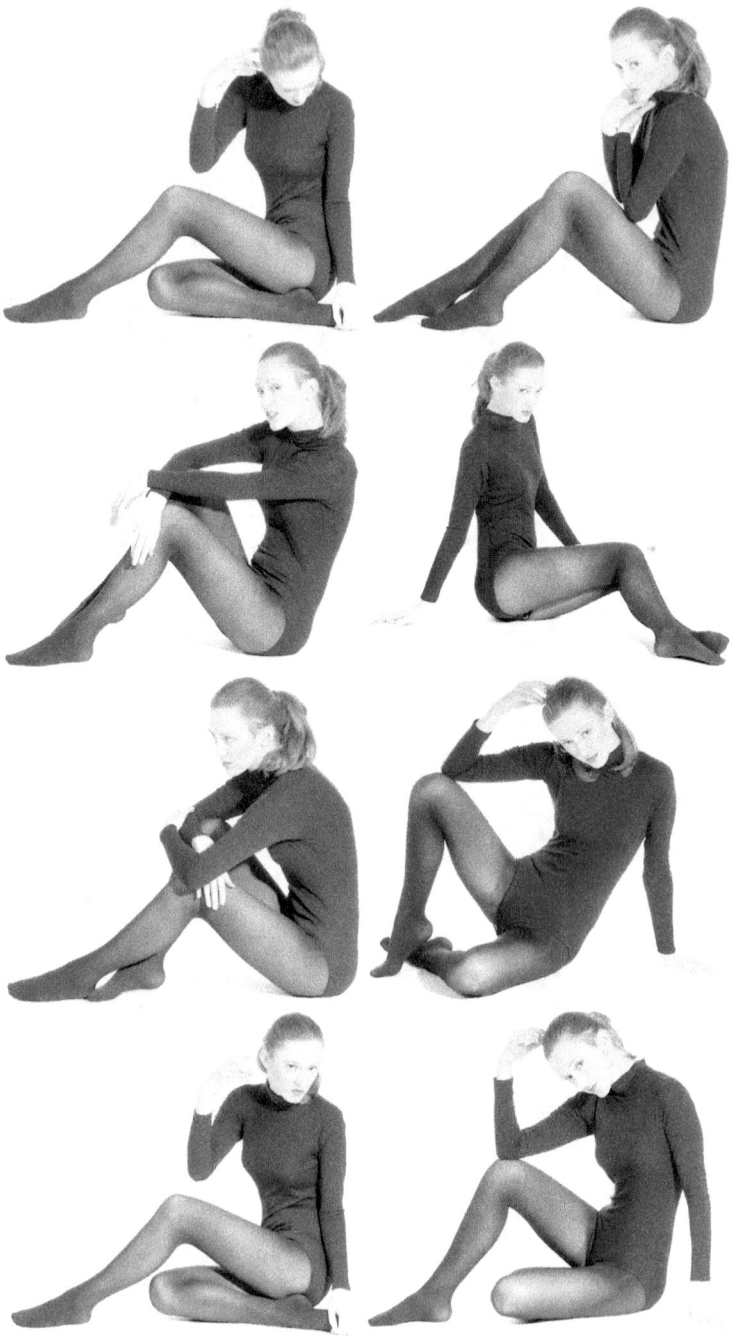

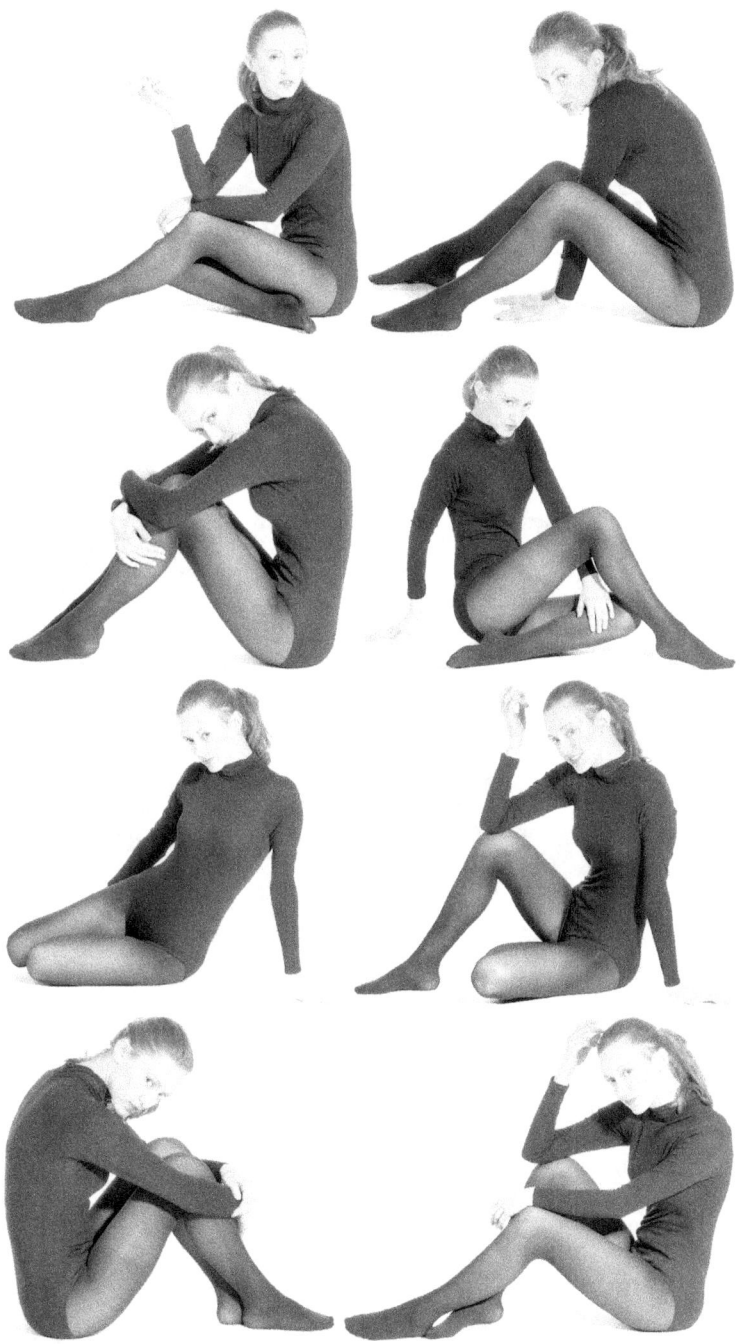

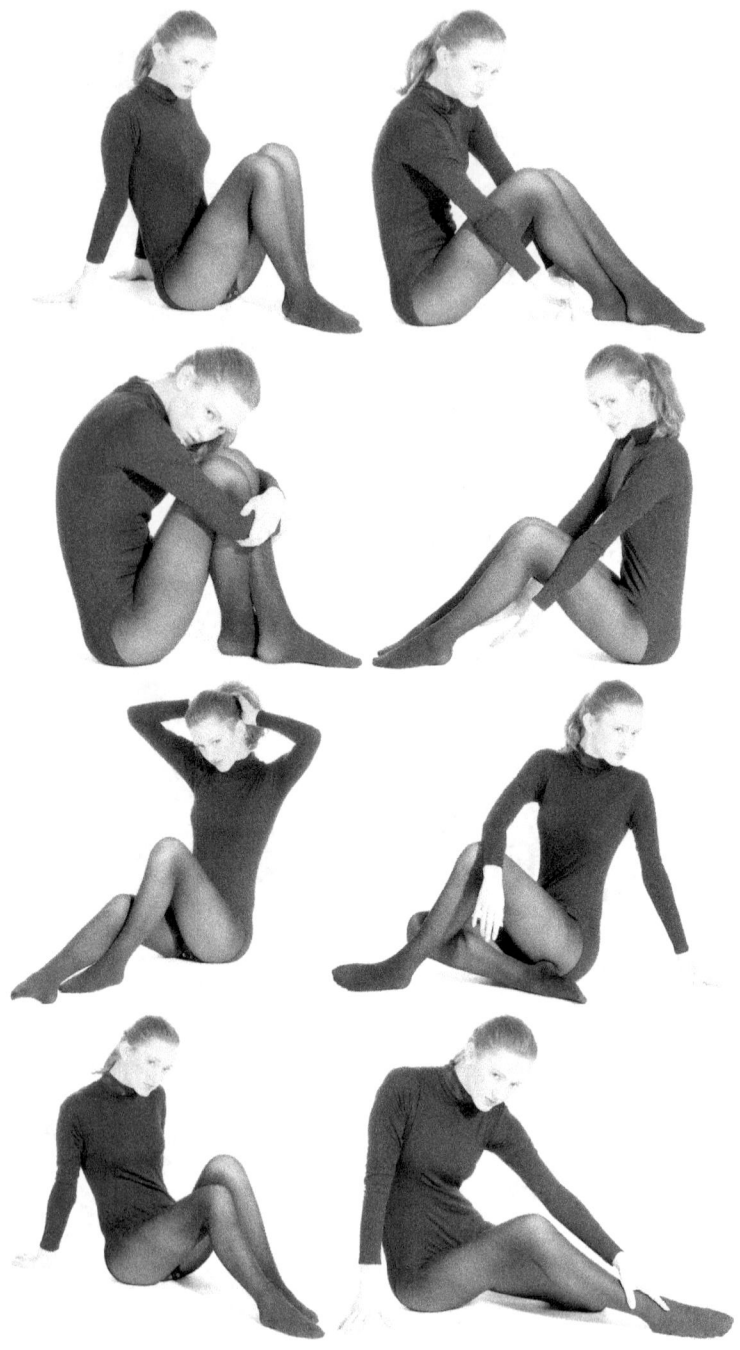

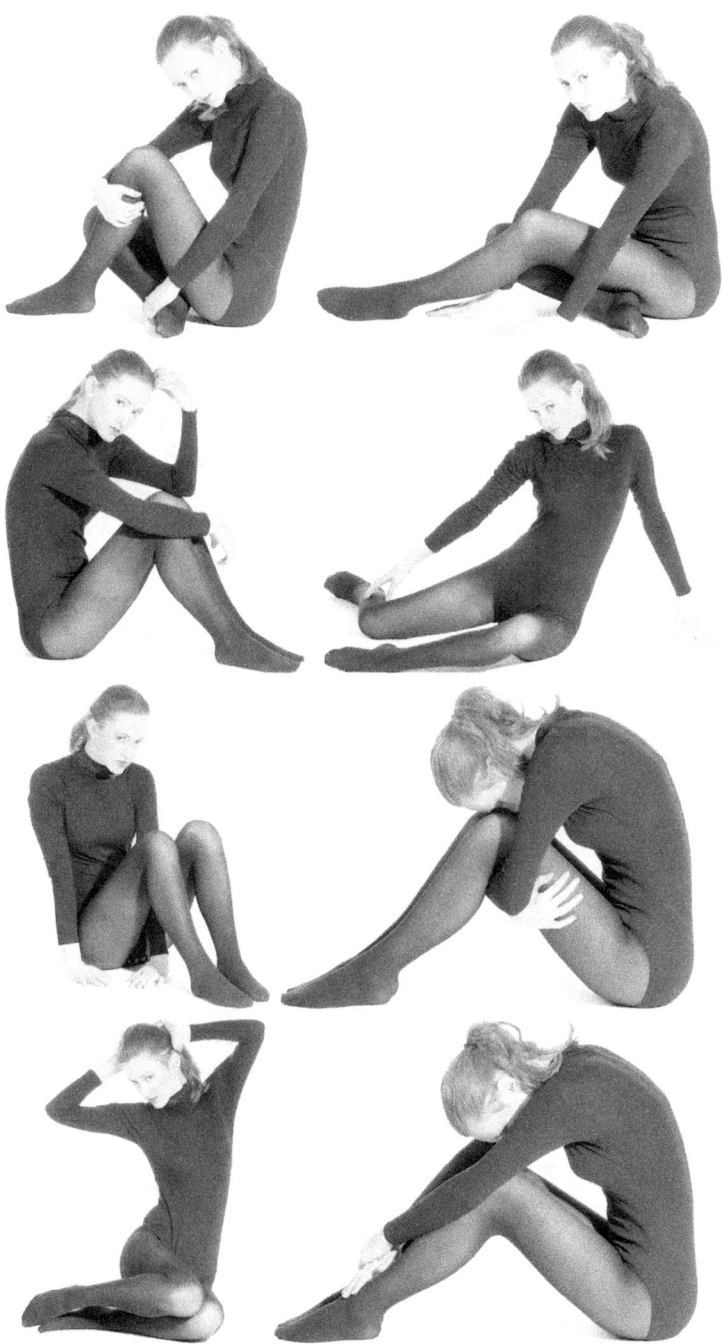

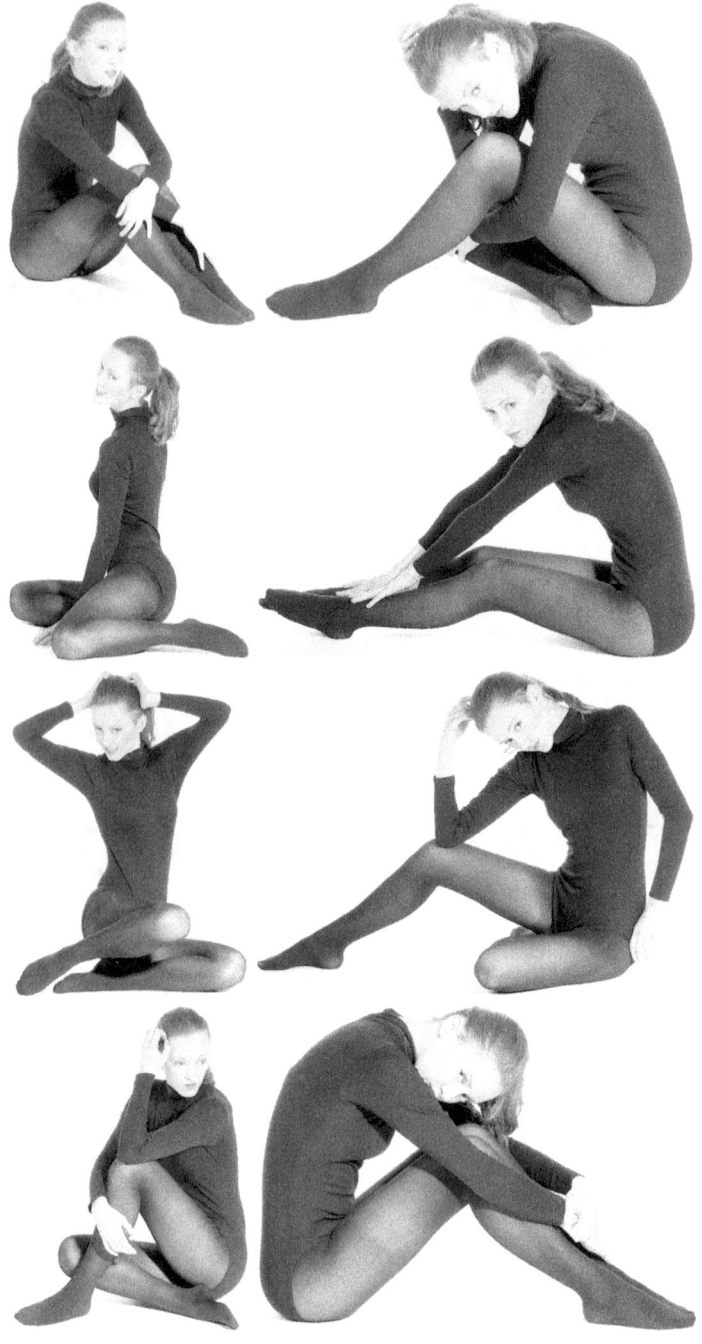

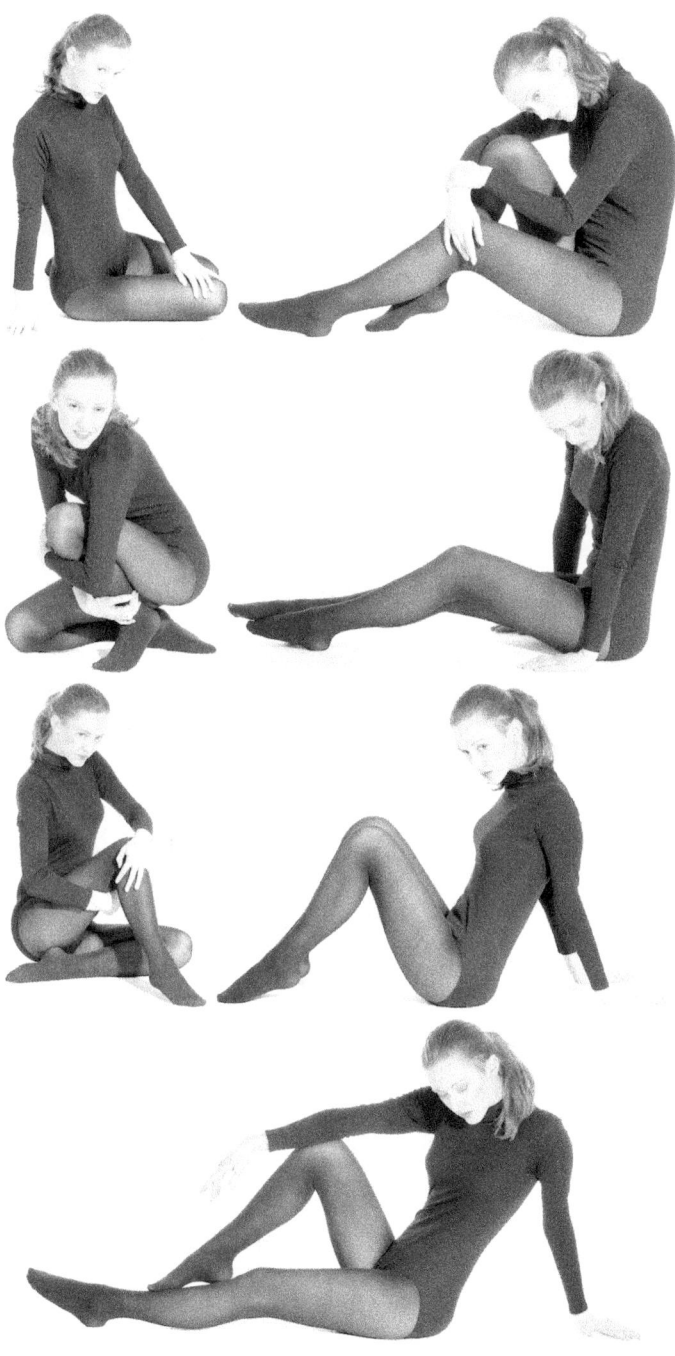

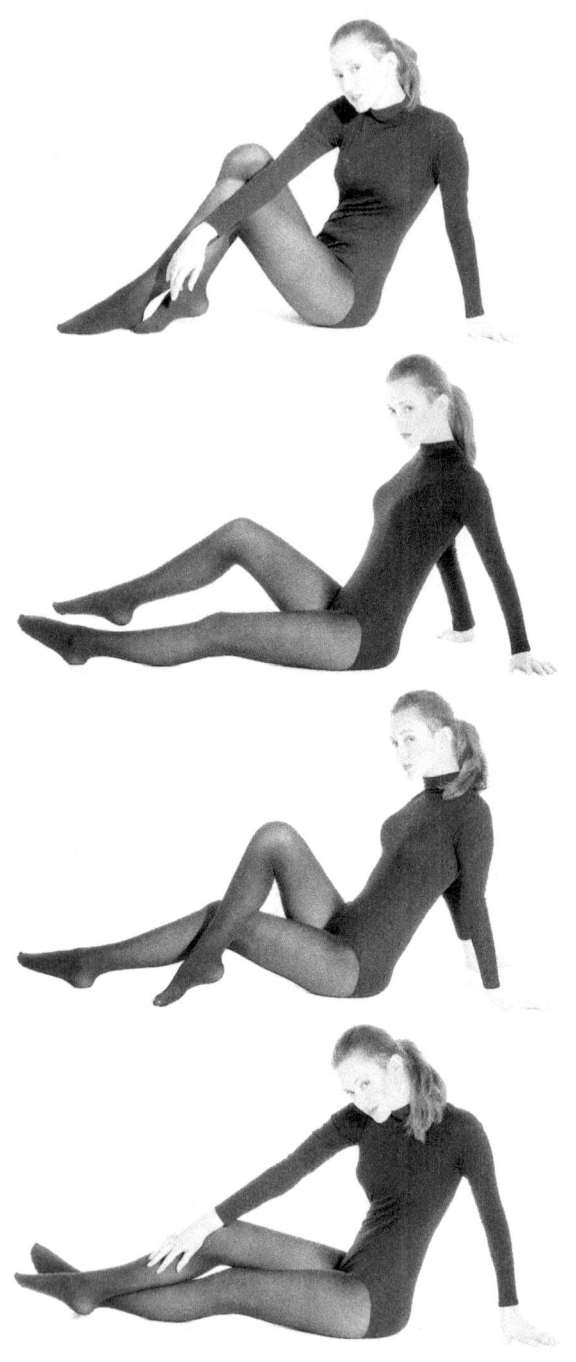

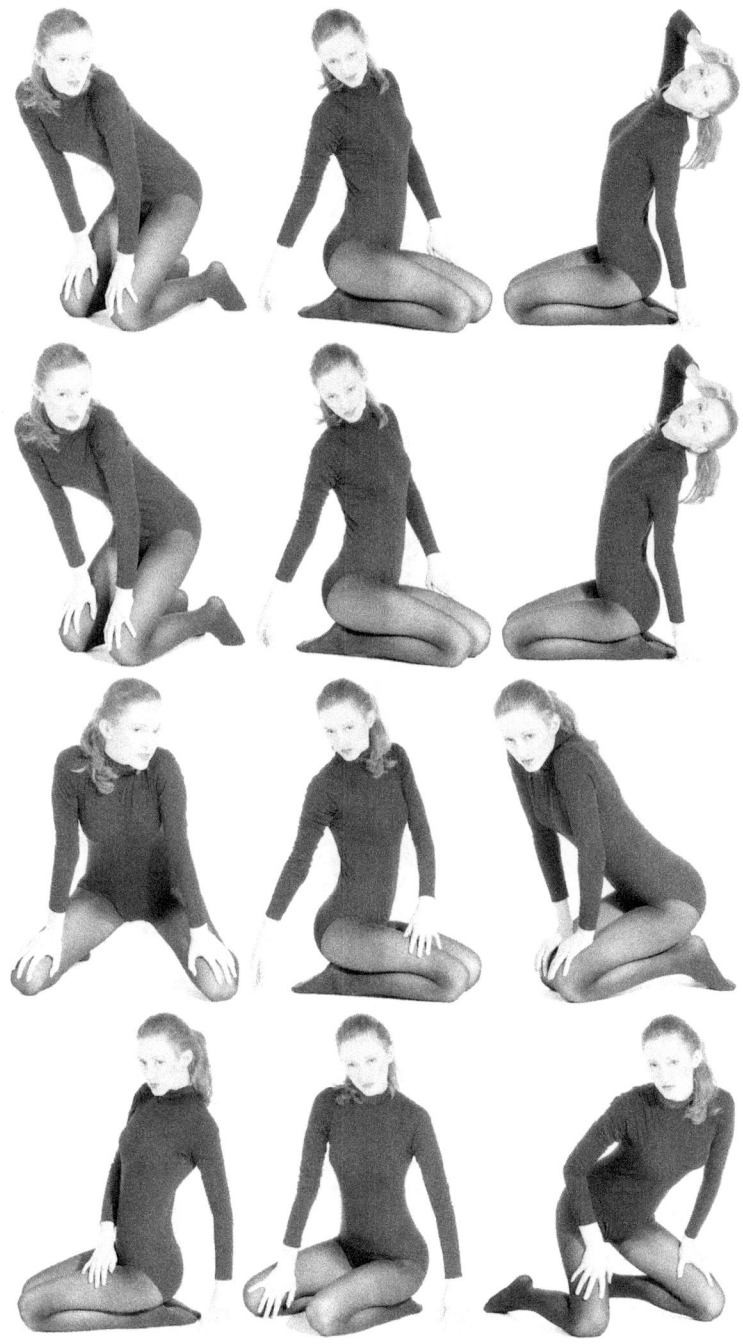

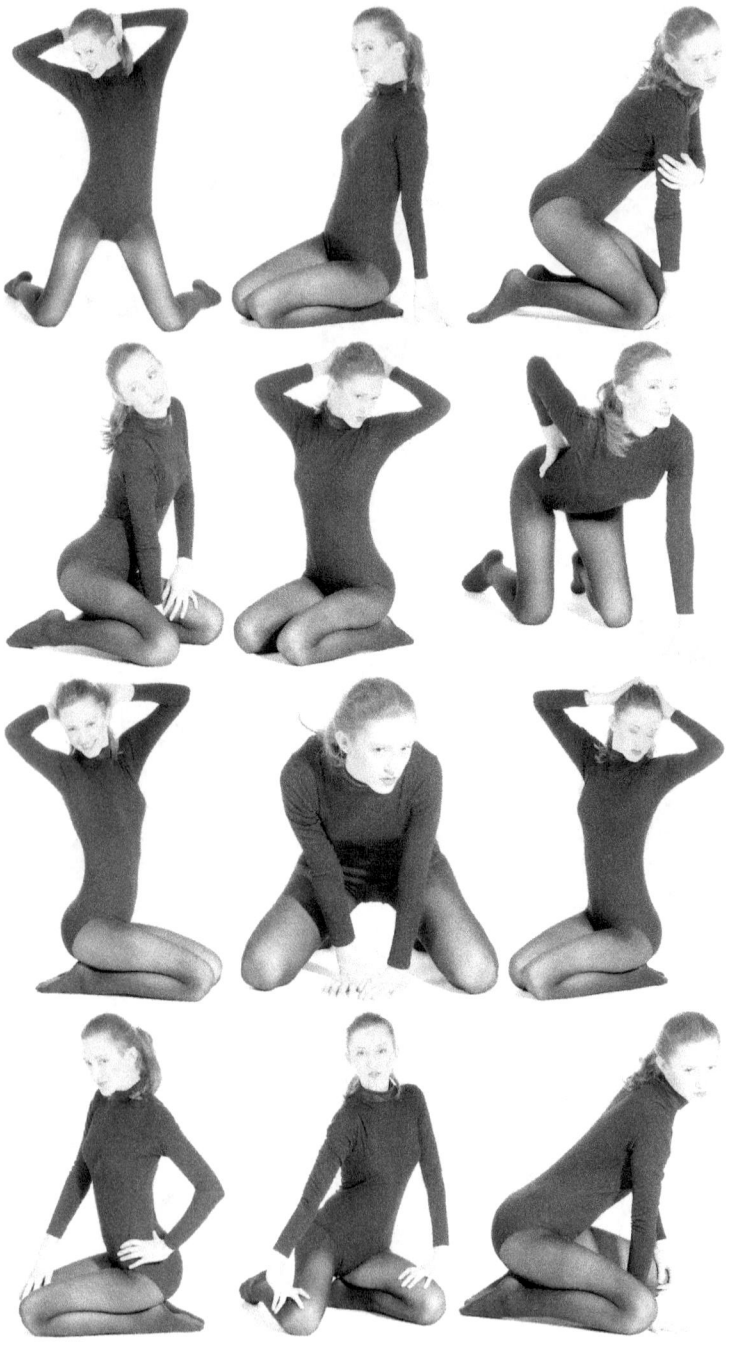

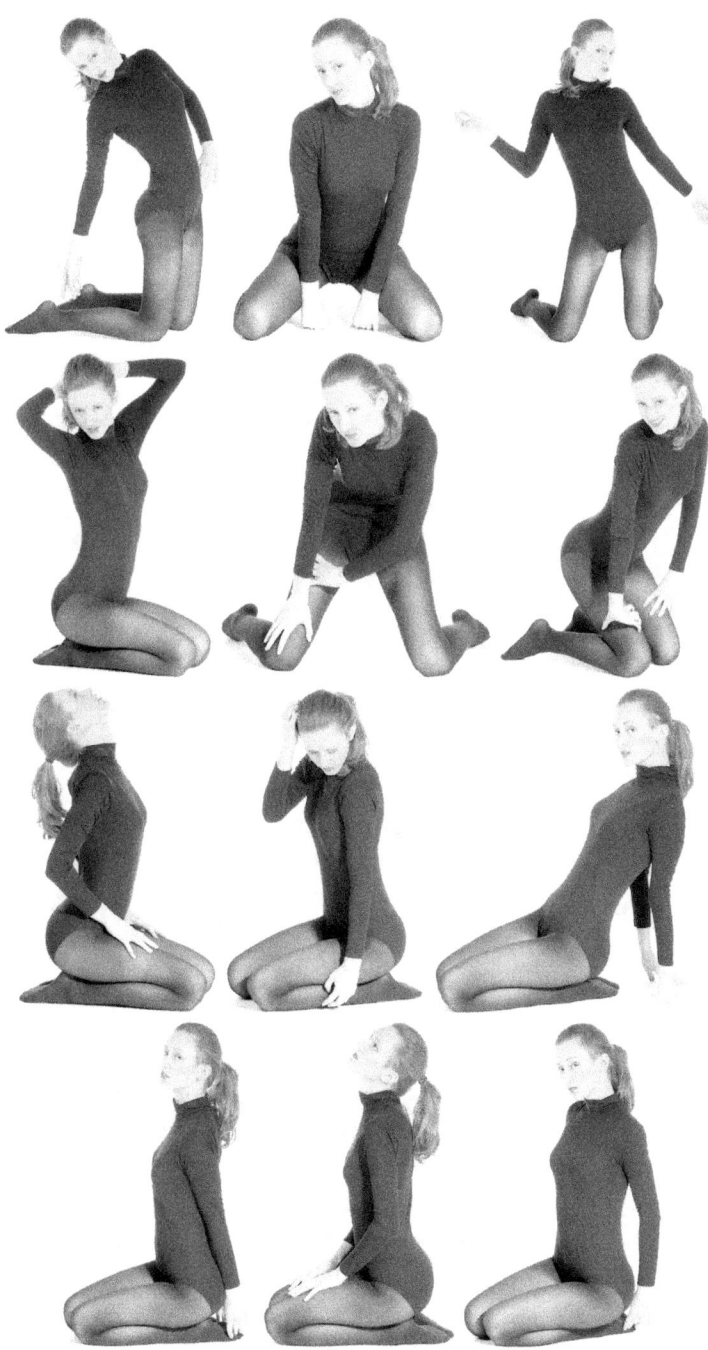

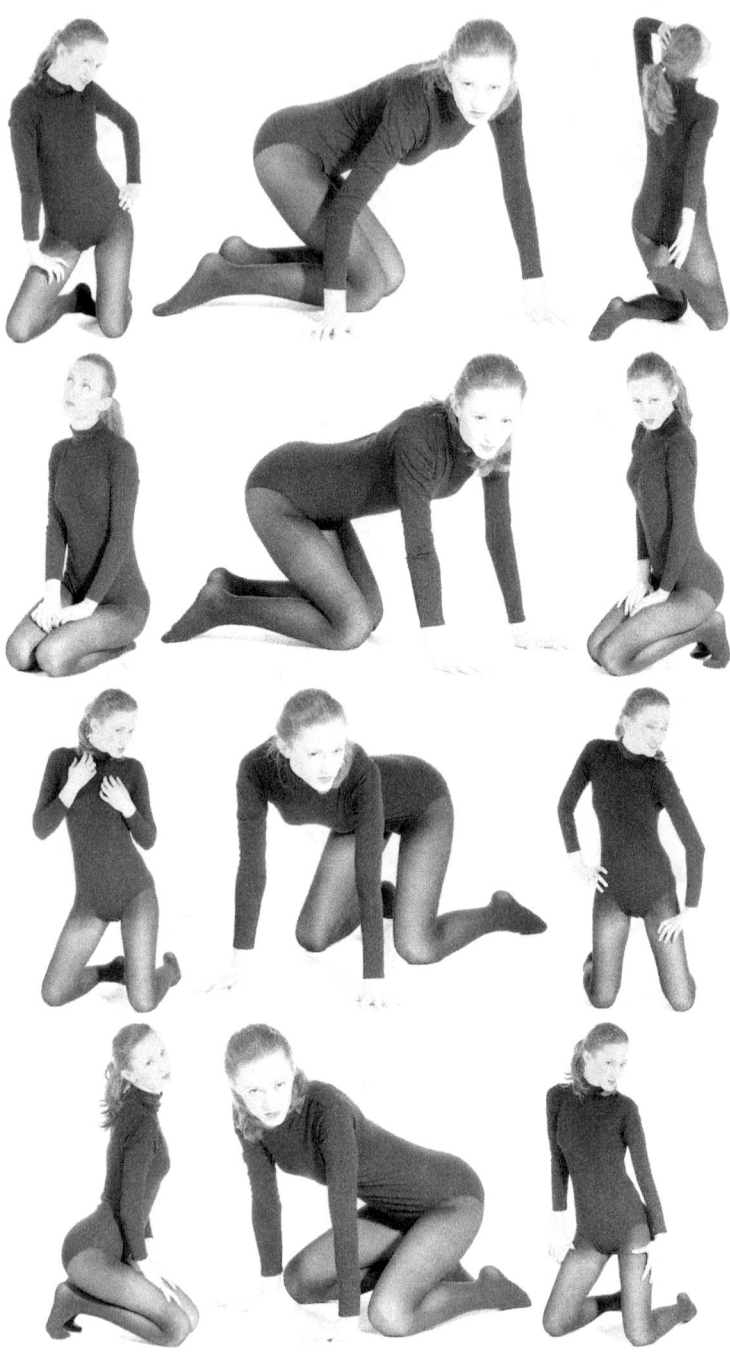

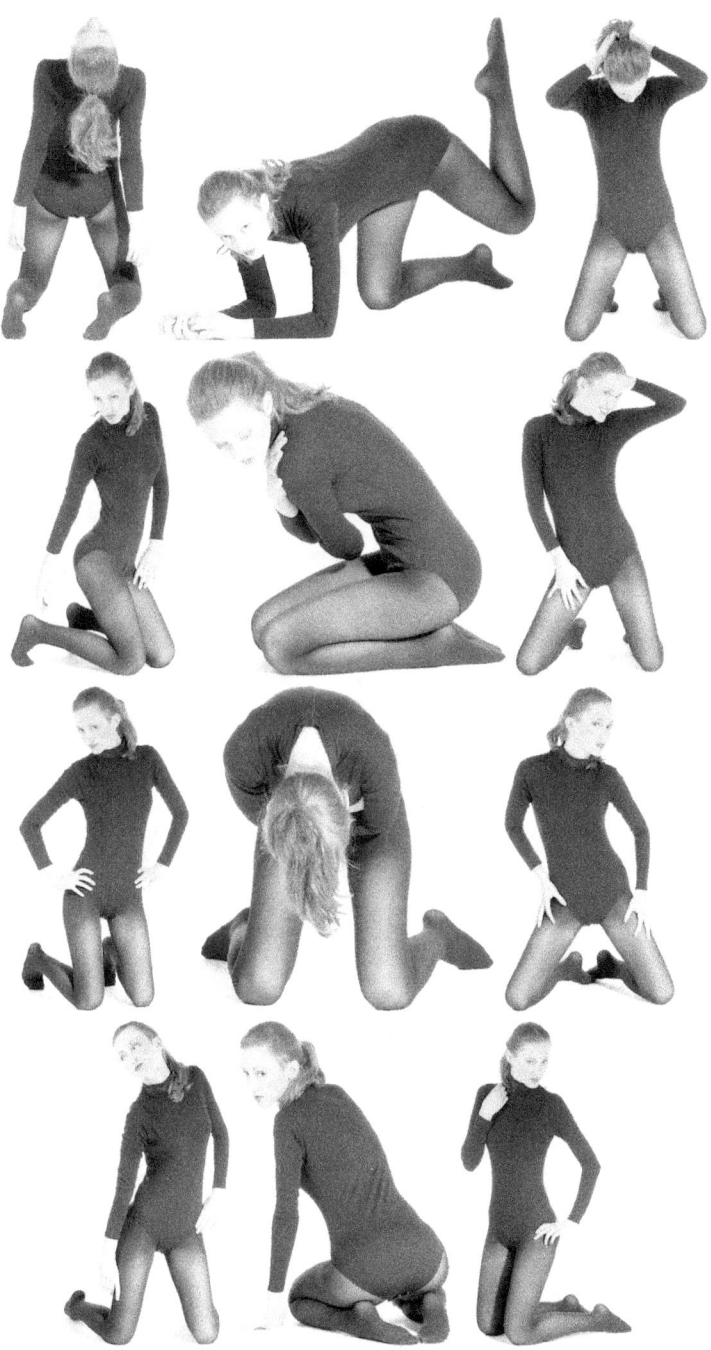

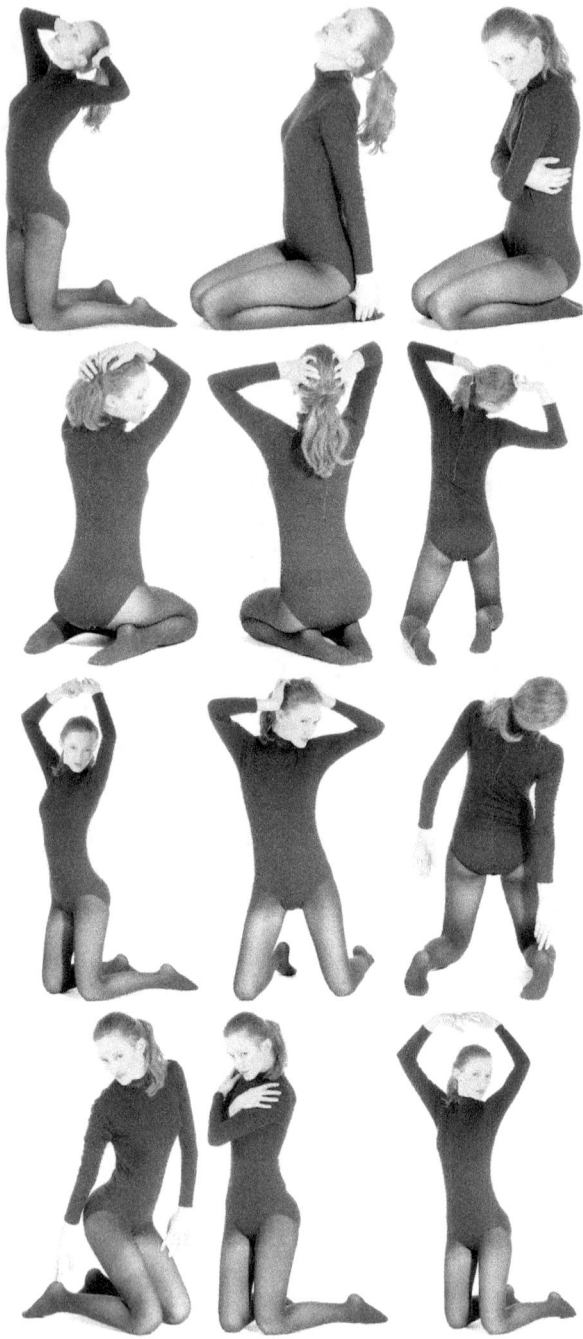

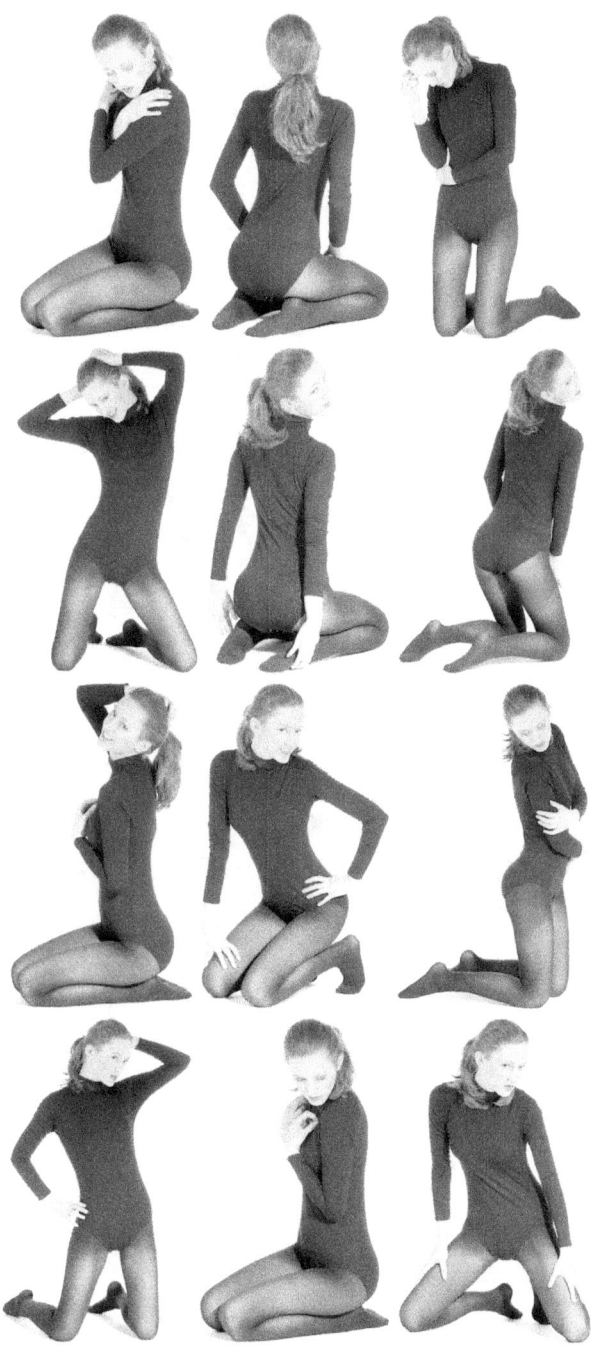

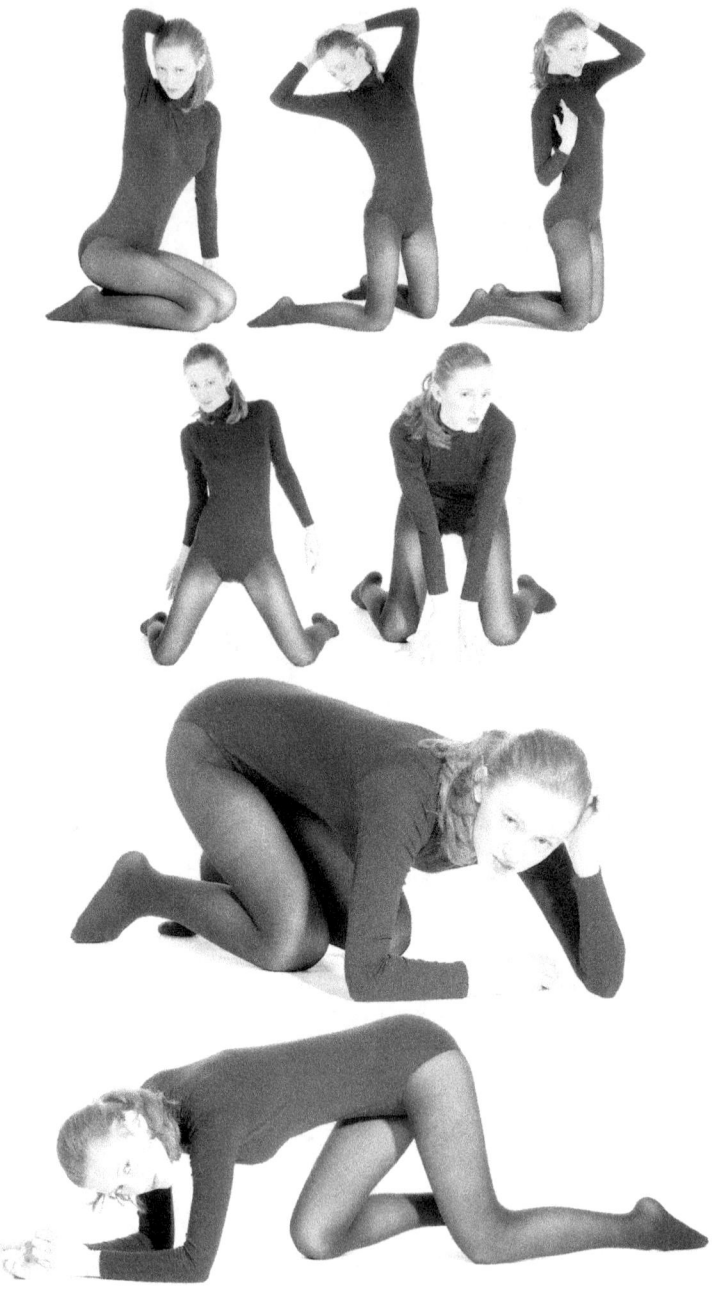

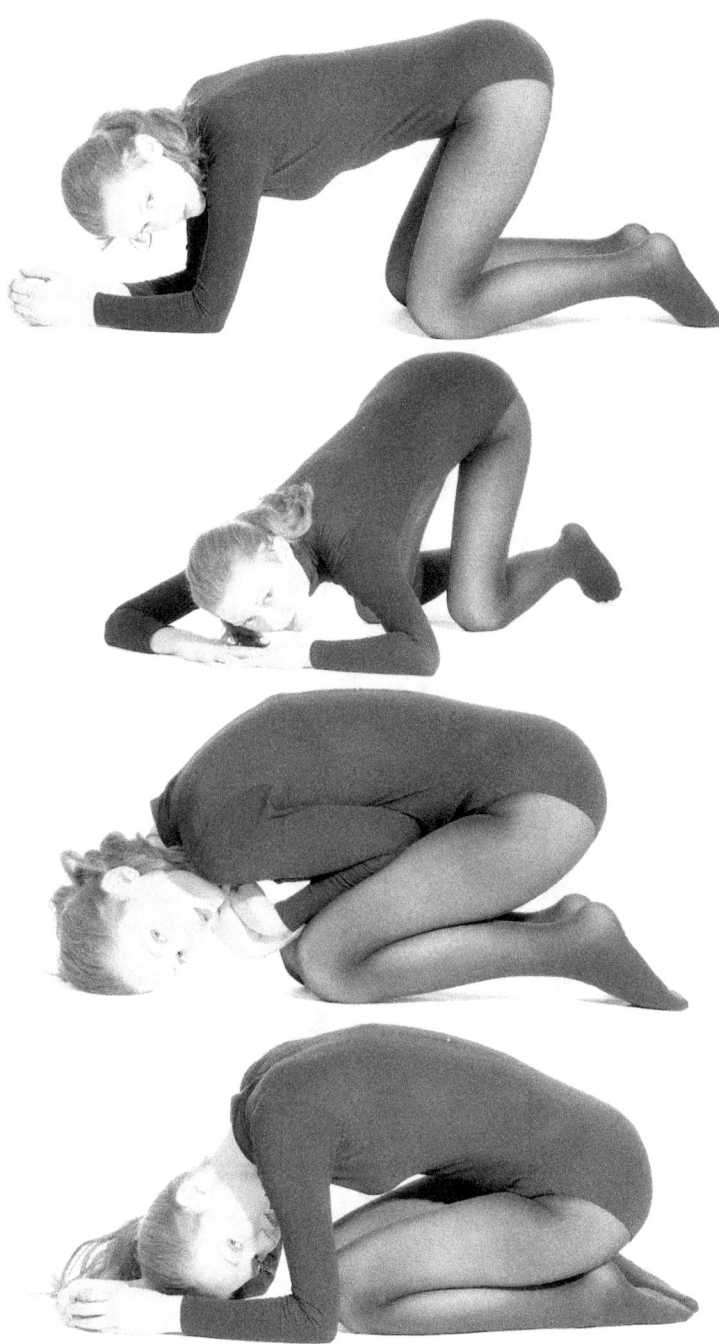

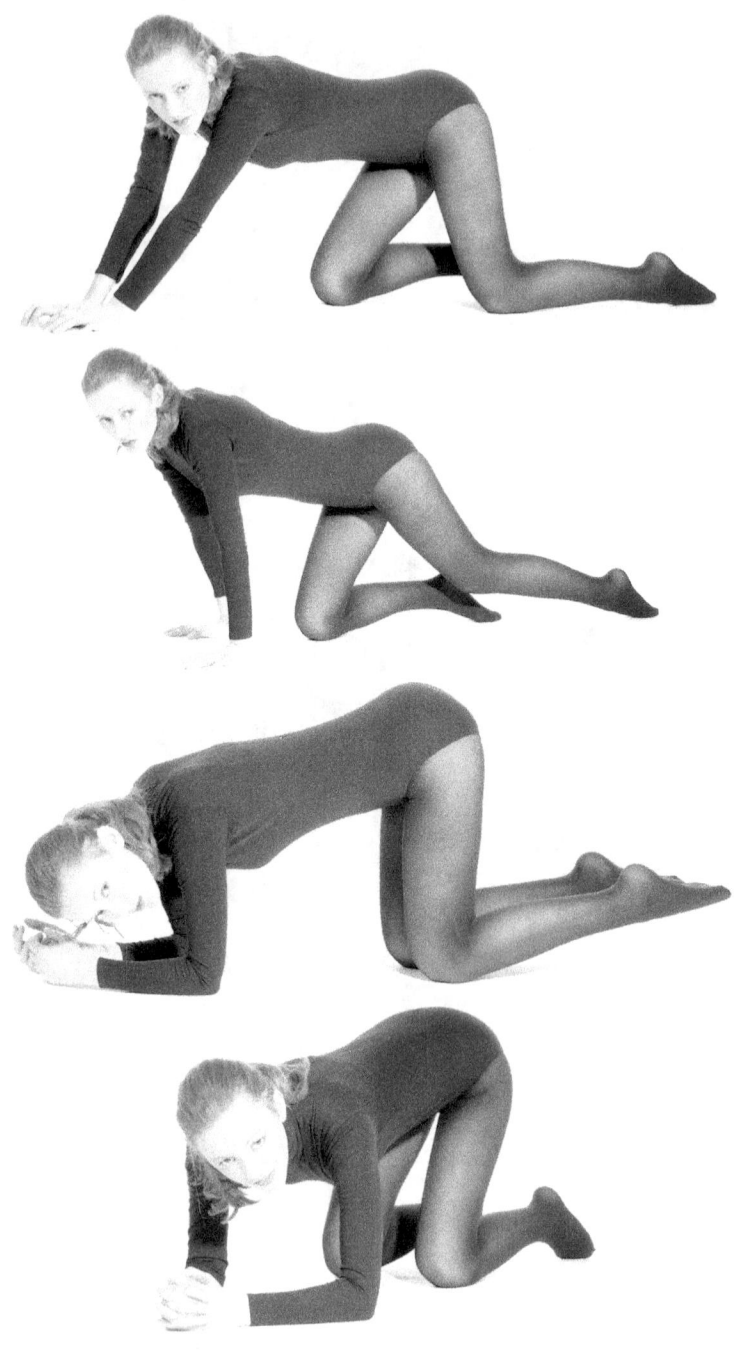

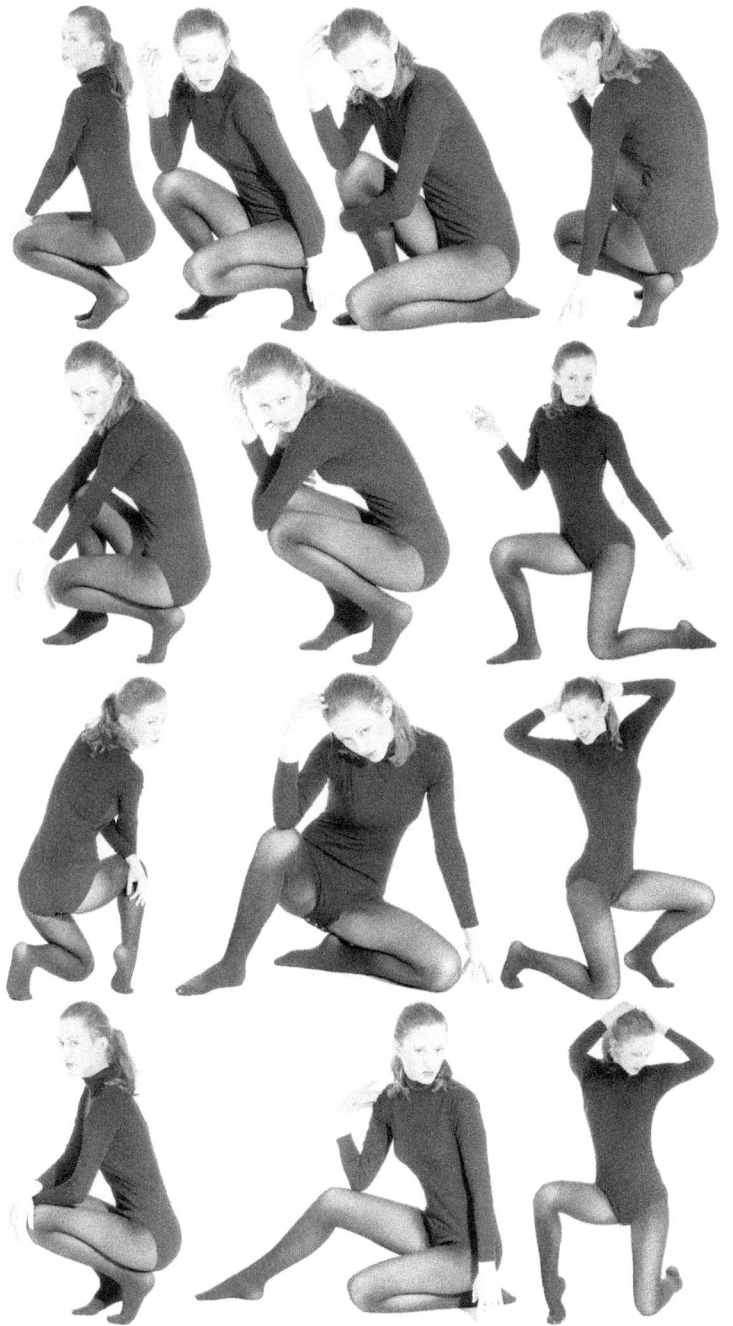

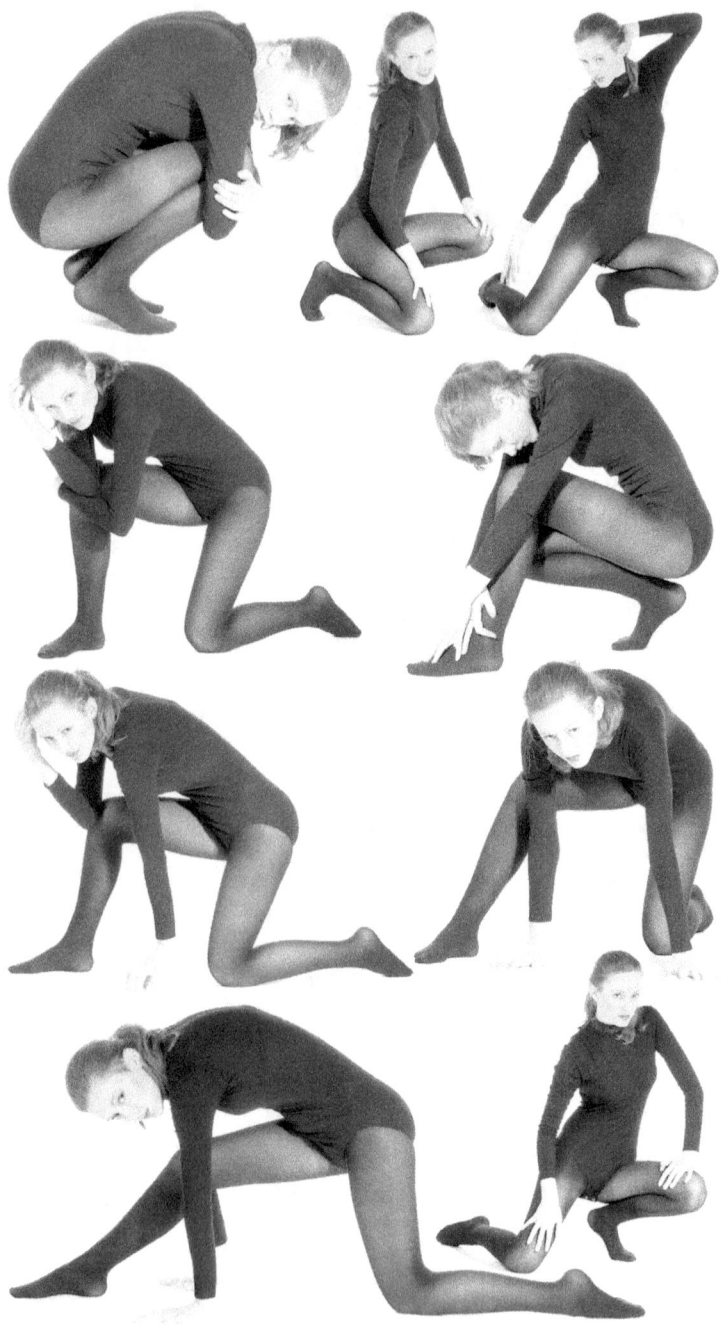

SITTING ON CHAIRS, STOOLS OR OTHER PROPS

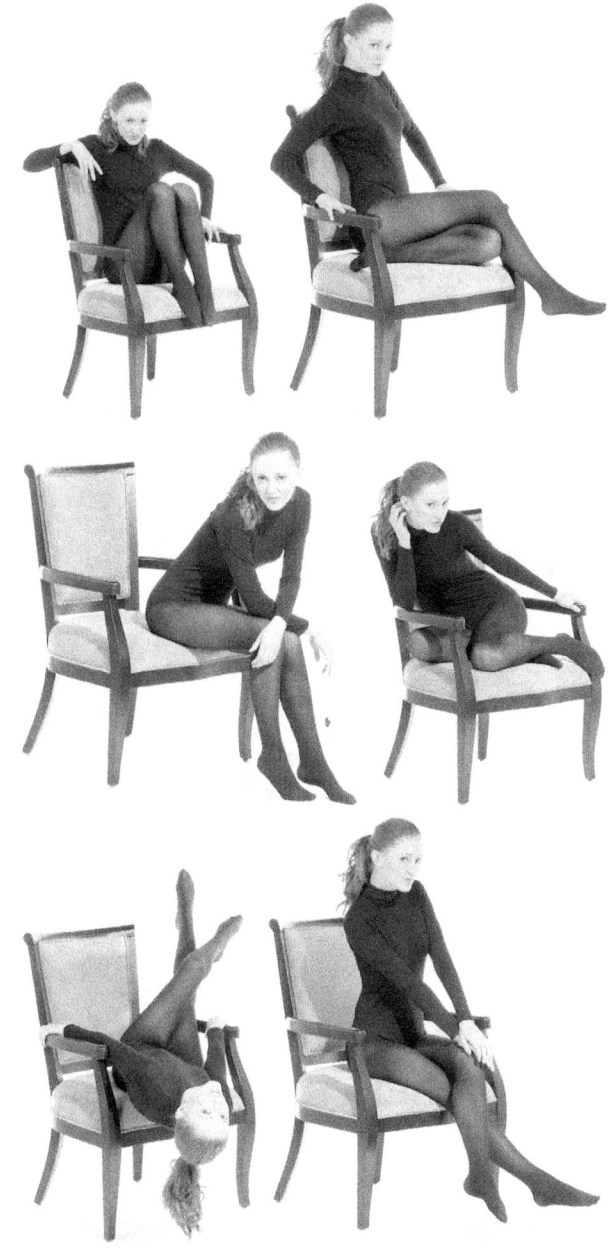

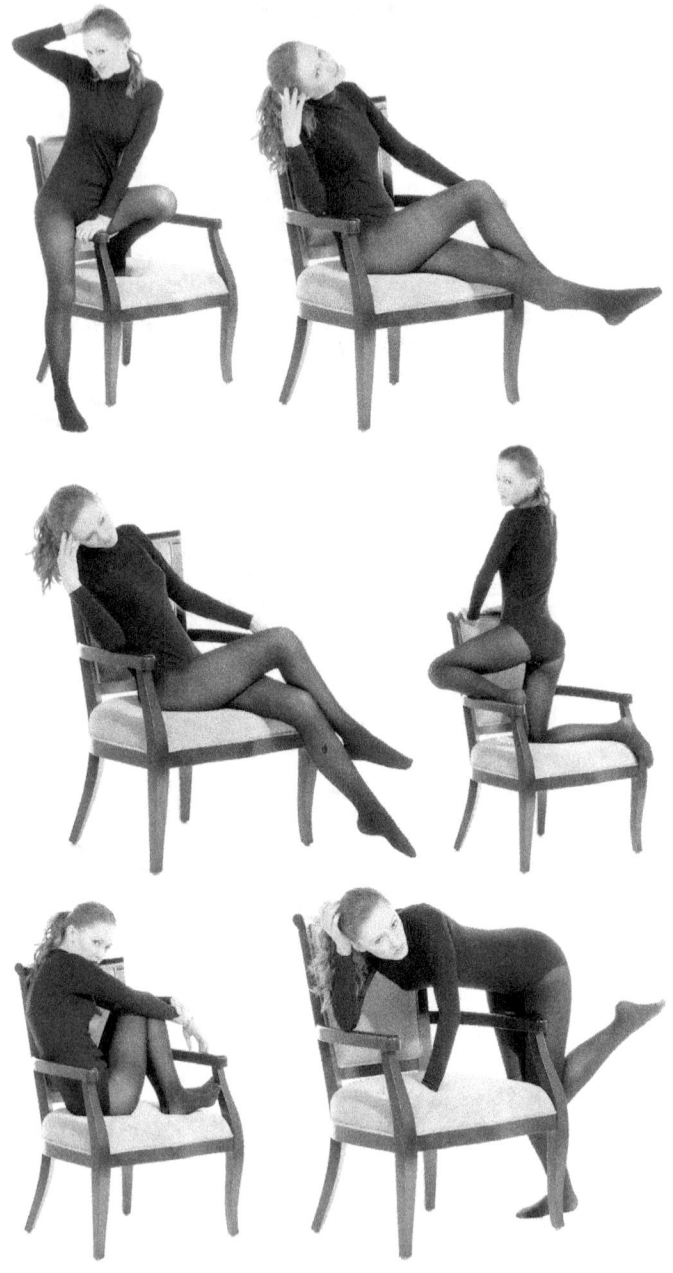

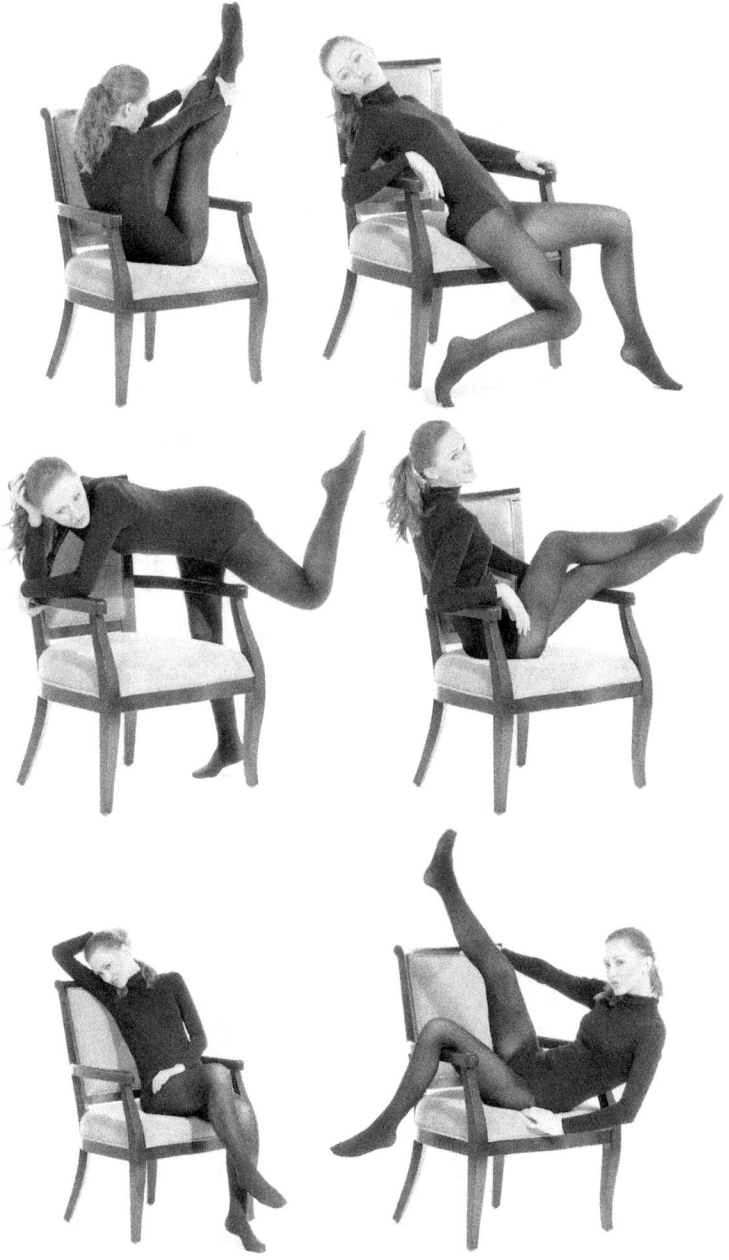

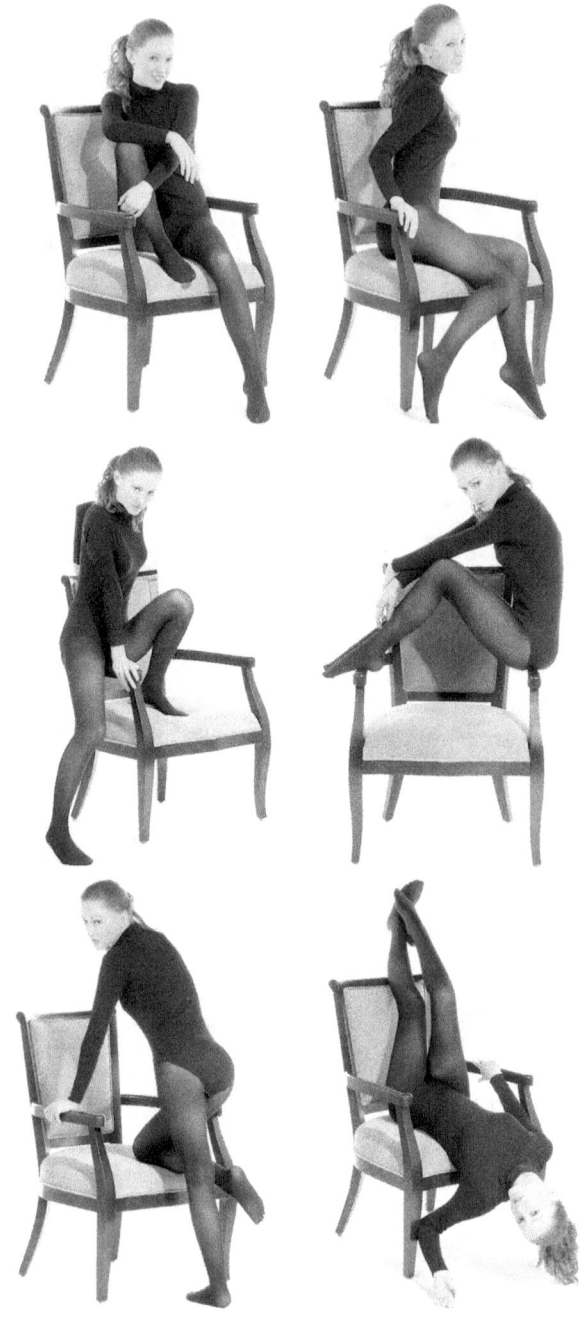

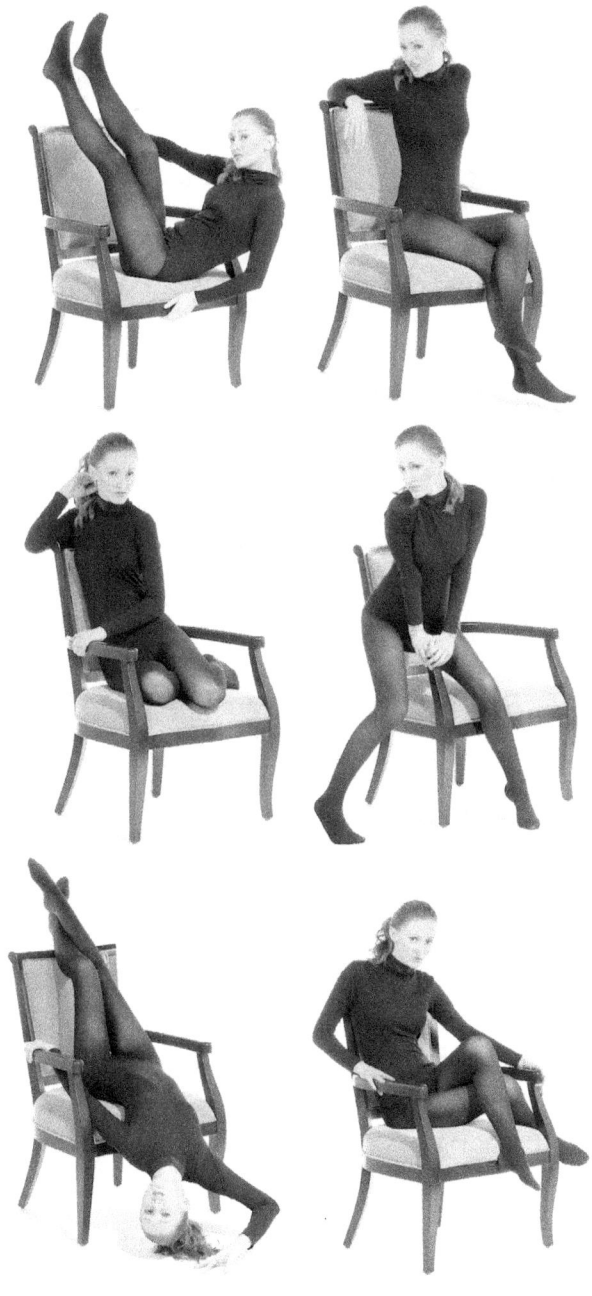

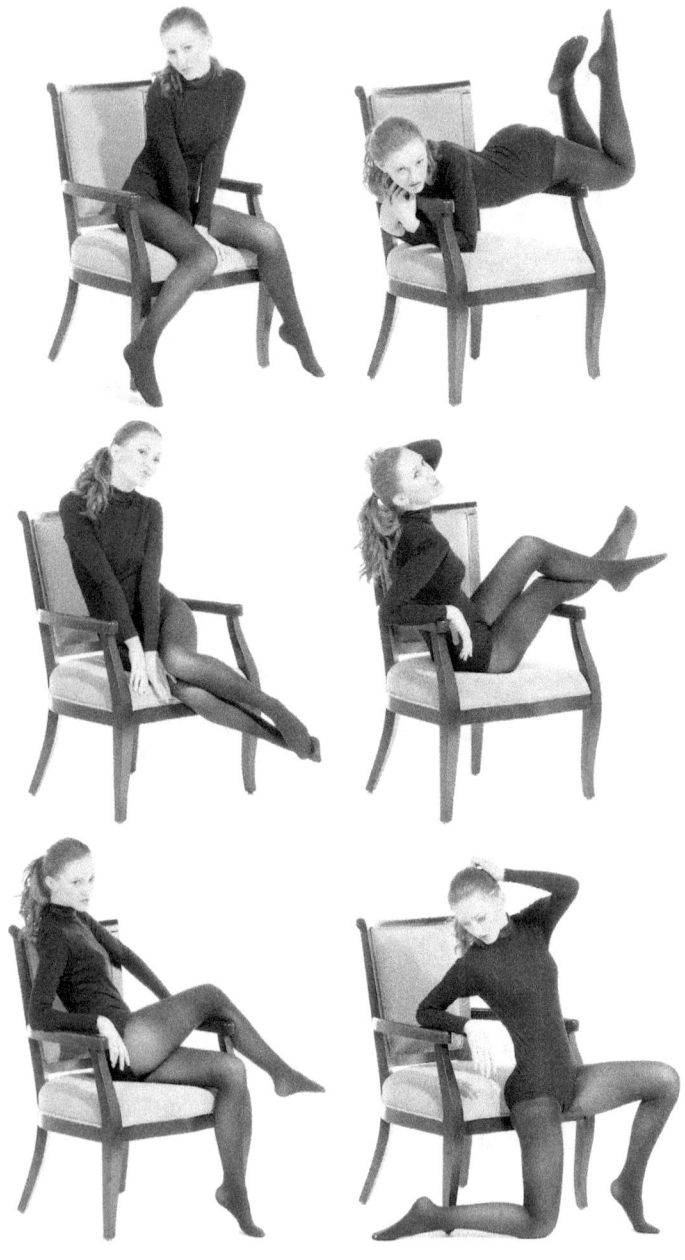

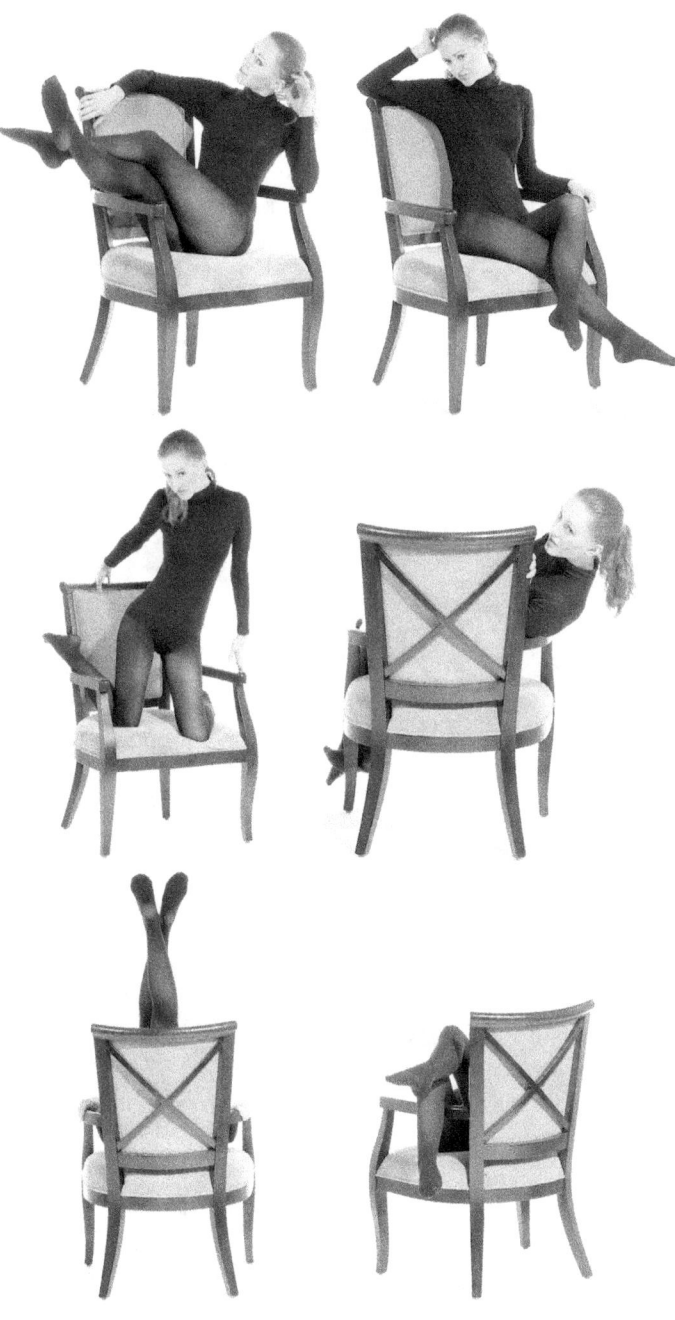

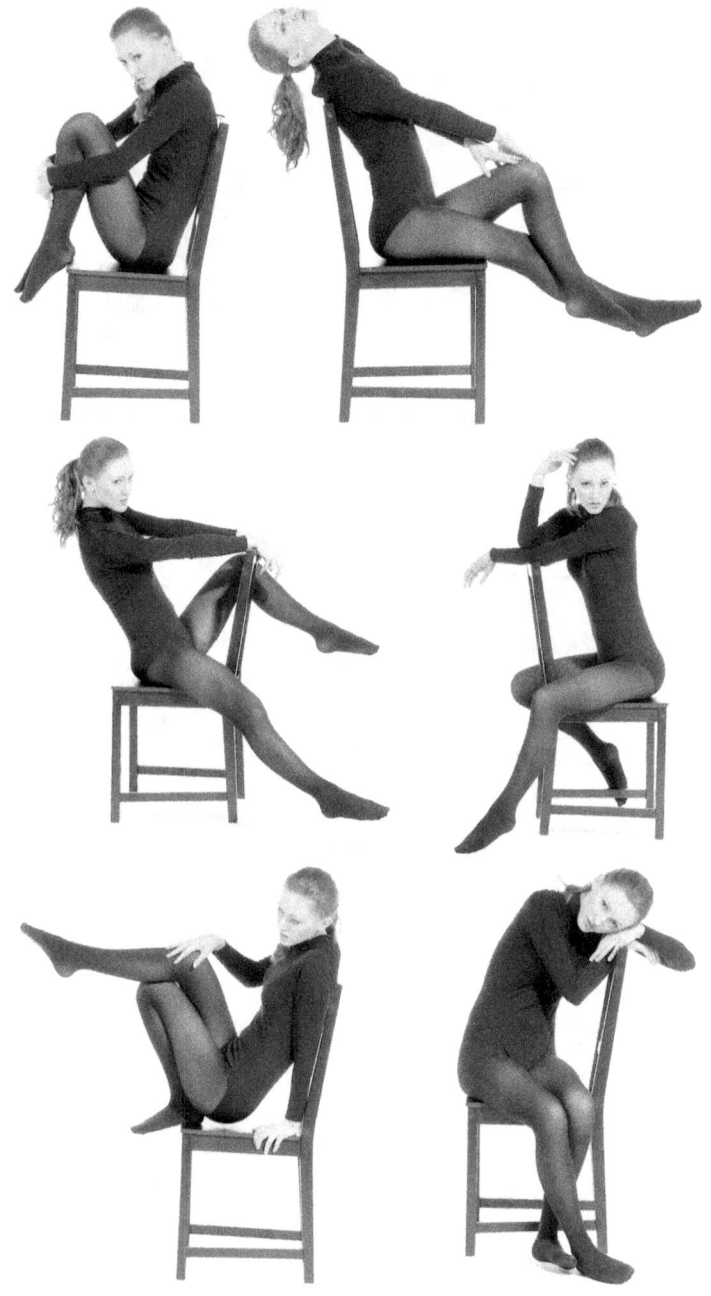

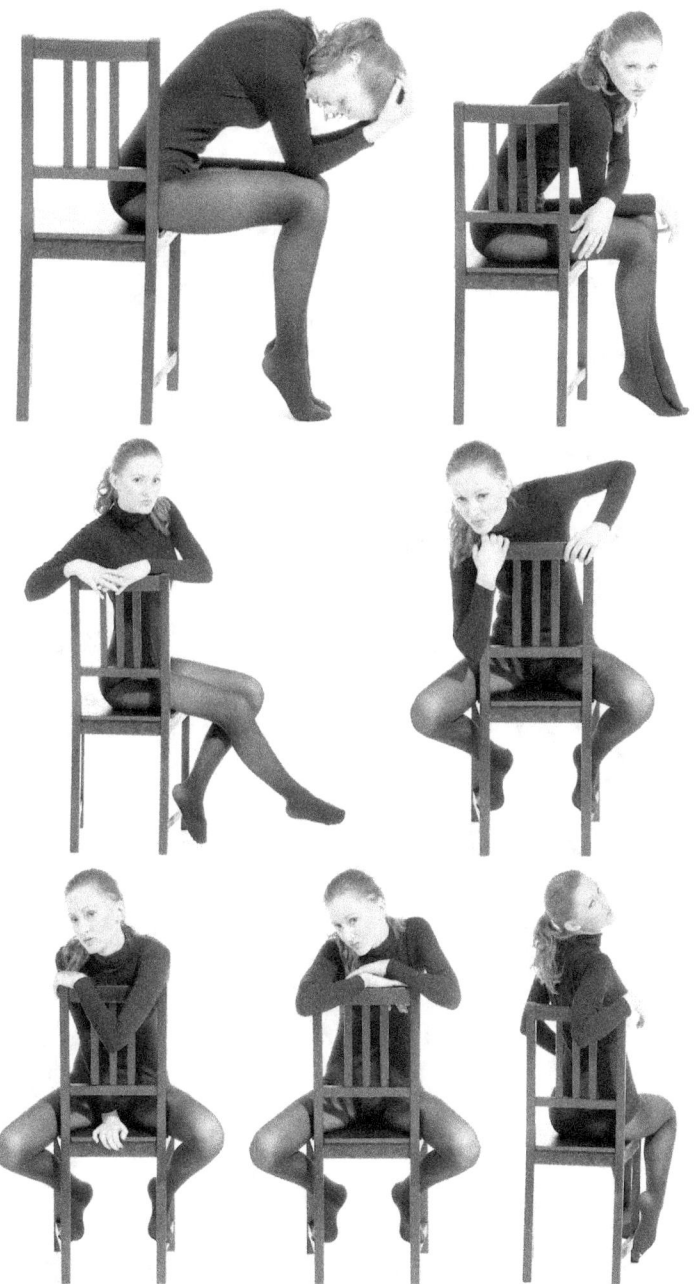

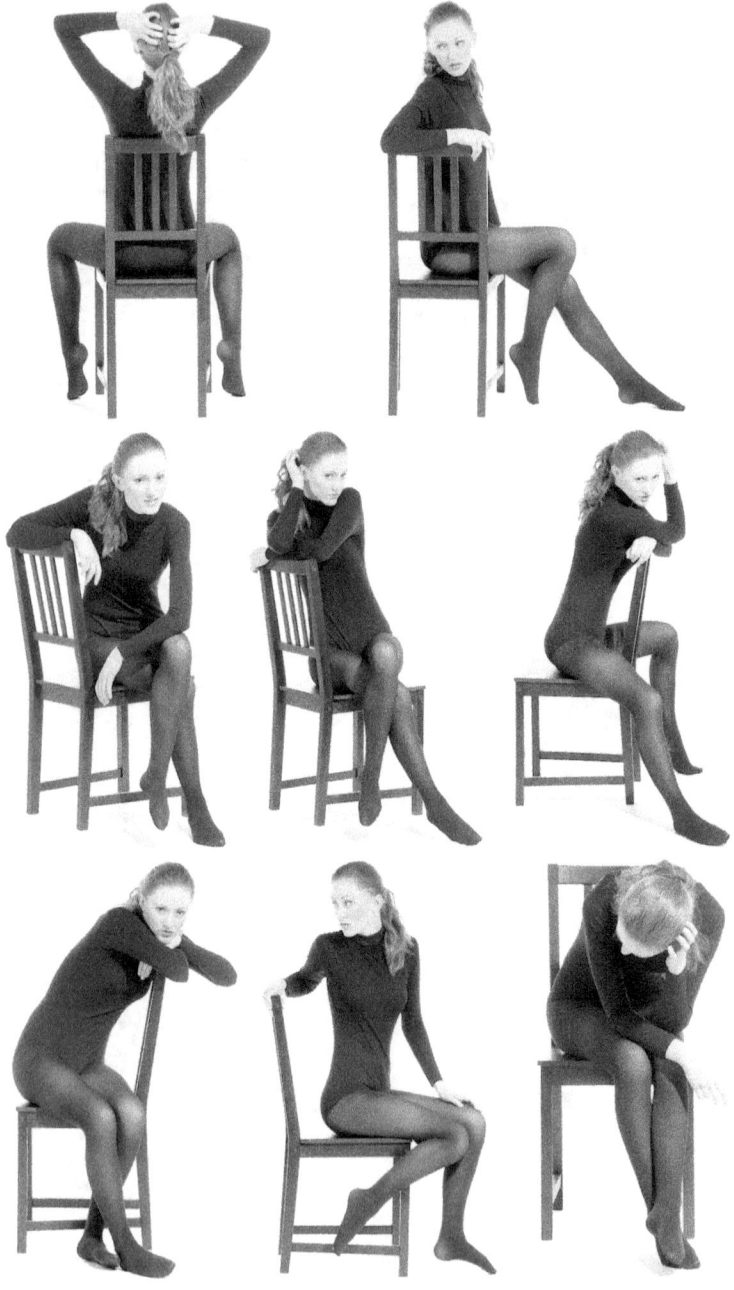

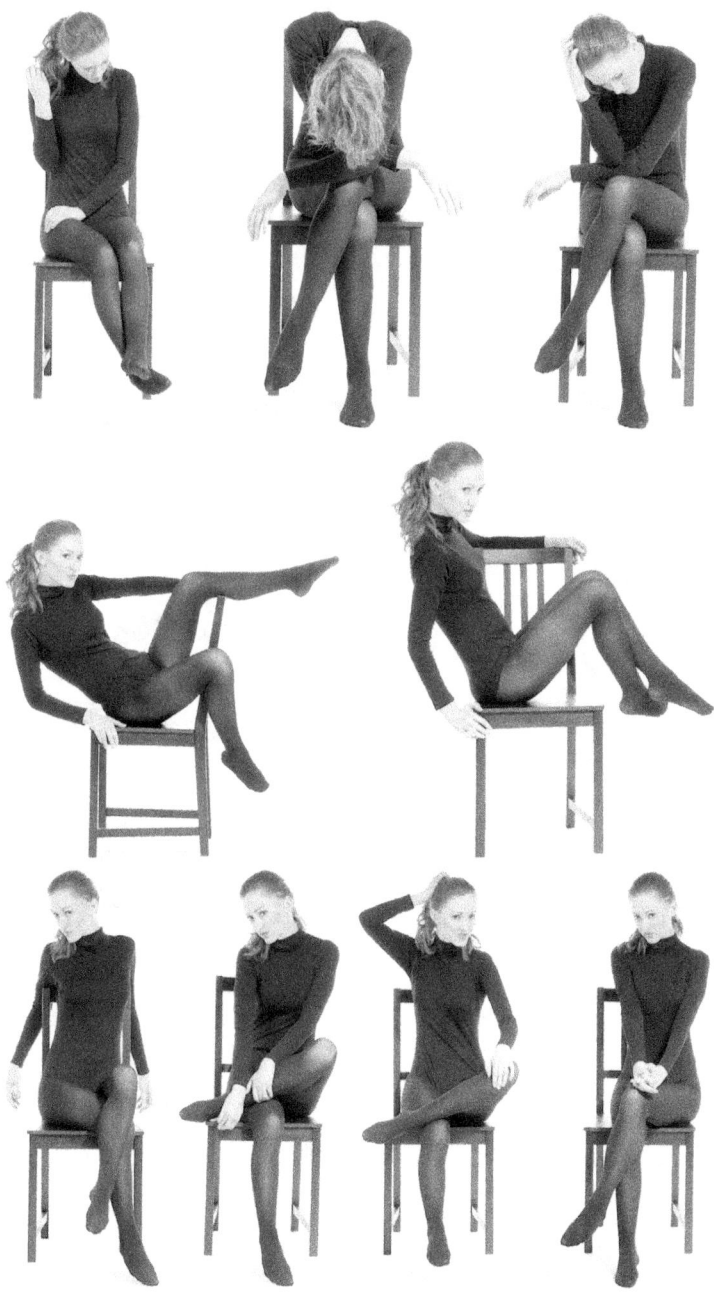

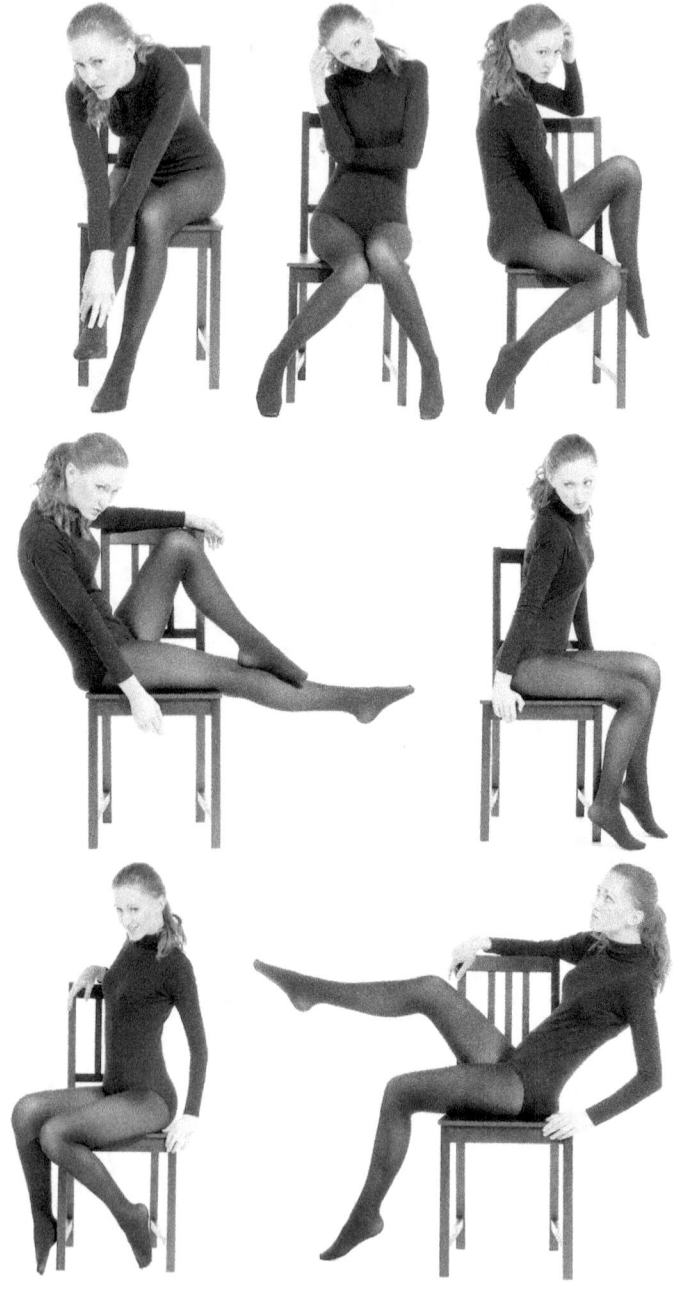

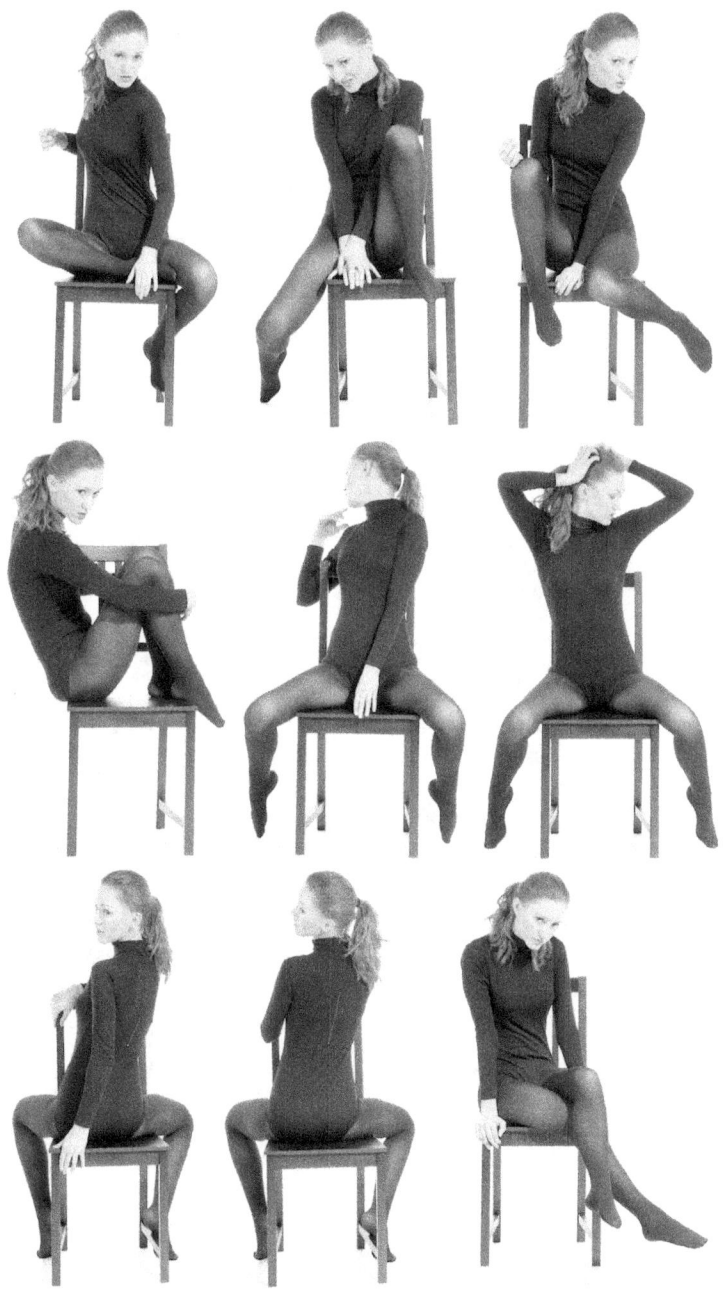

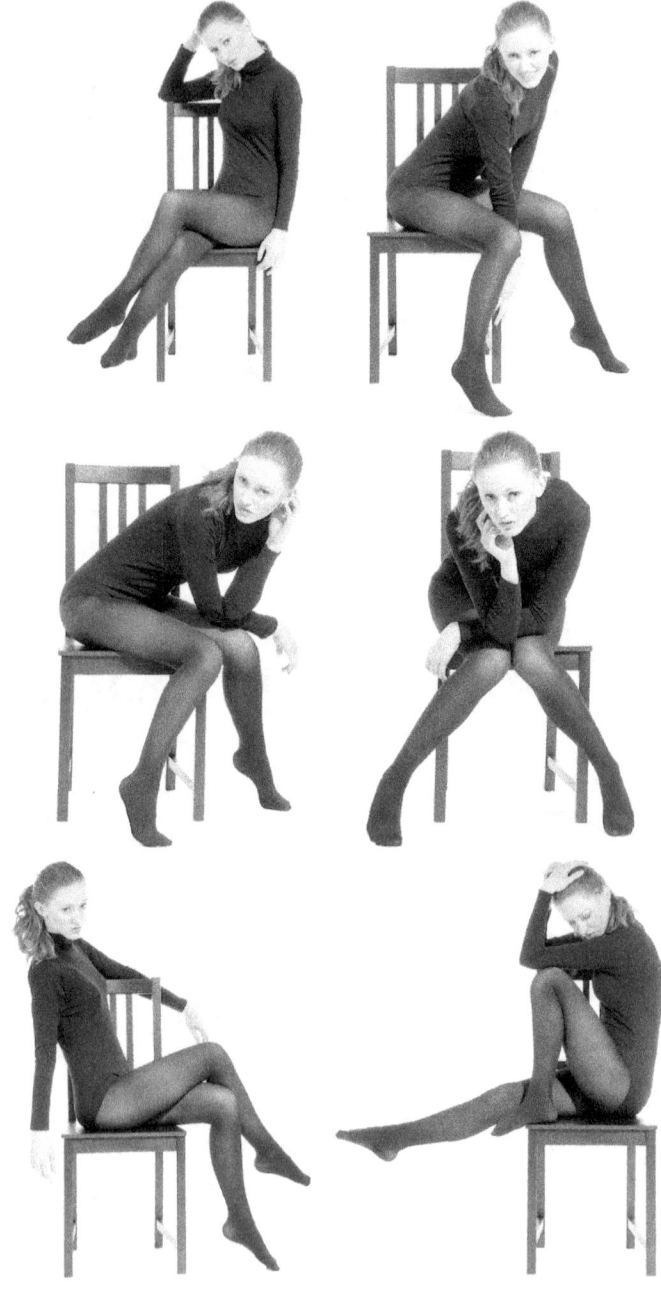

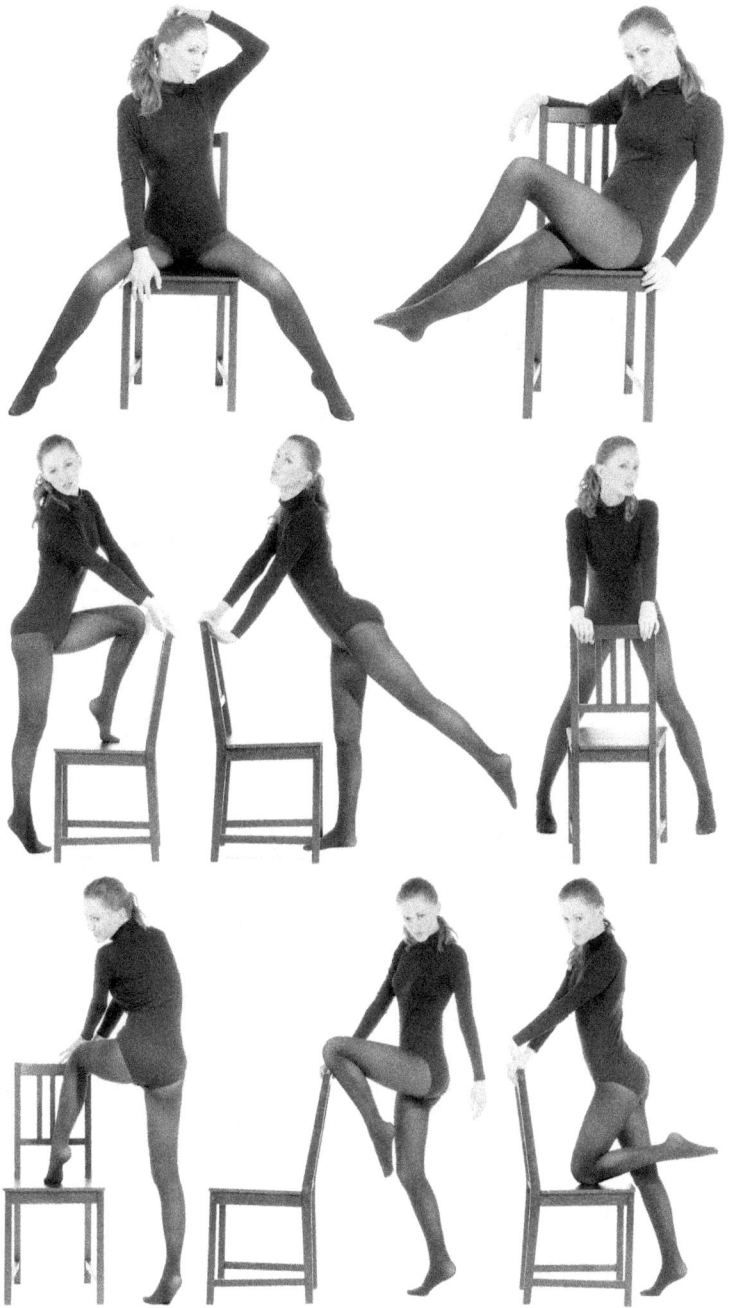

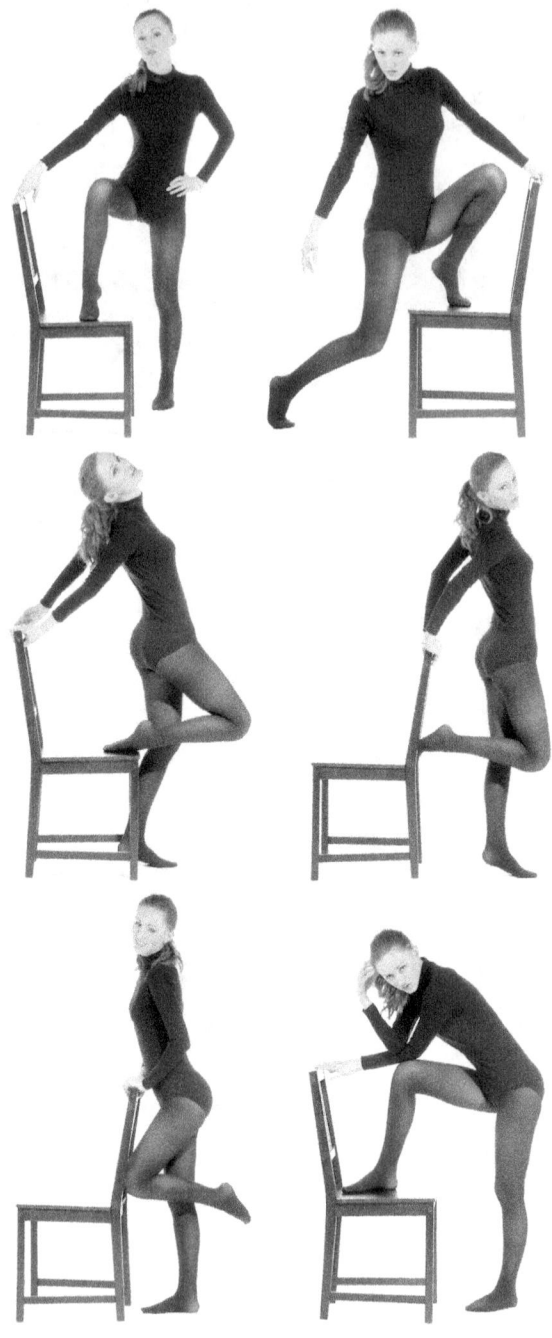

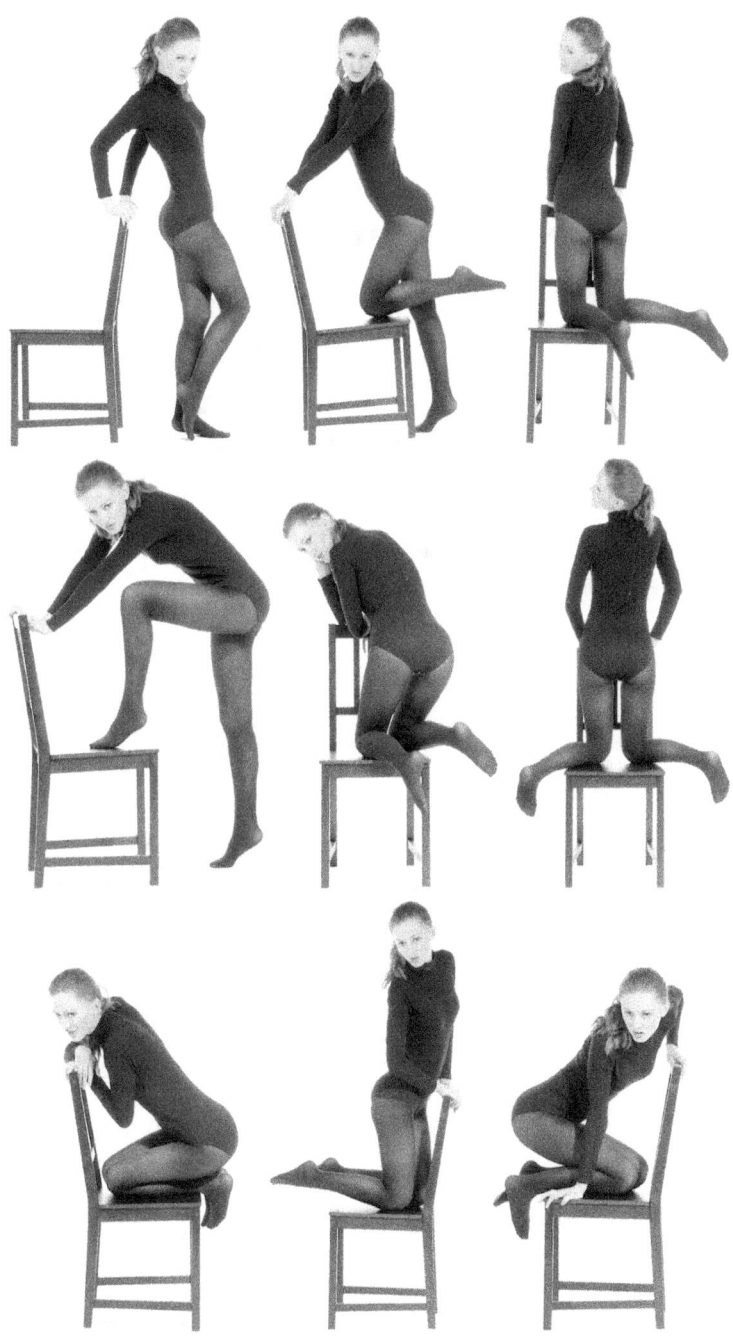

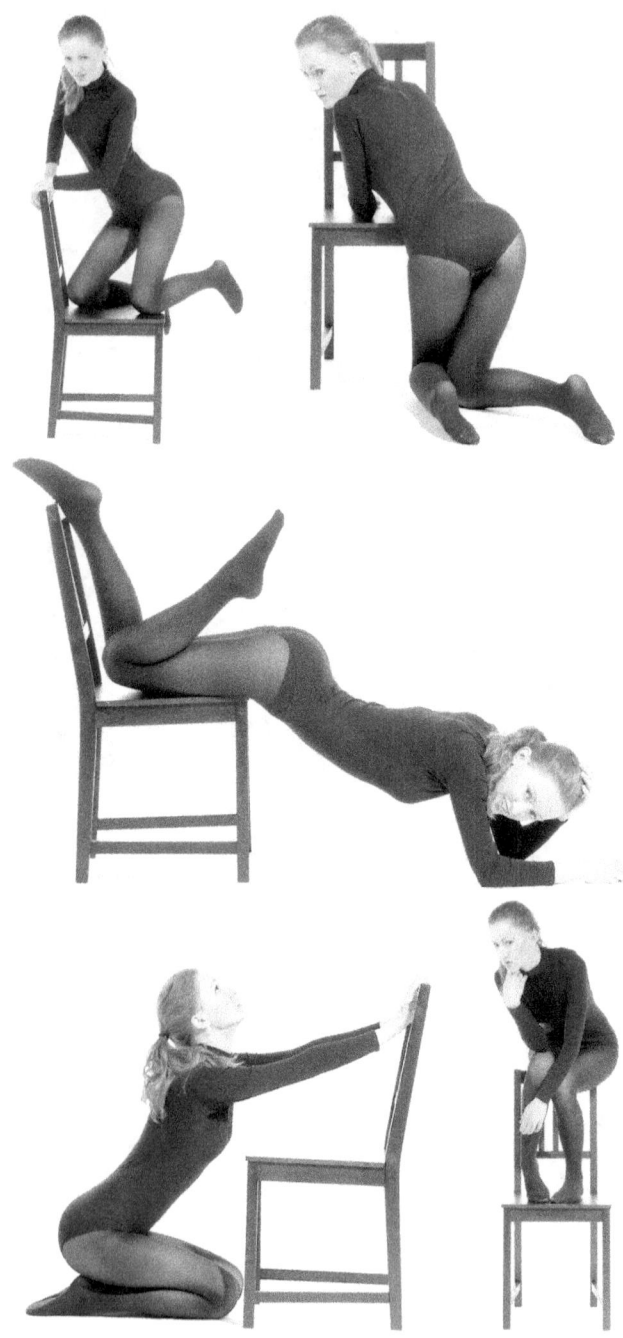

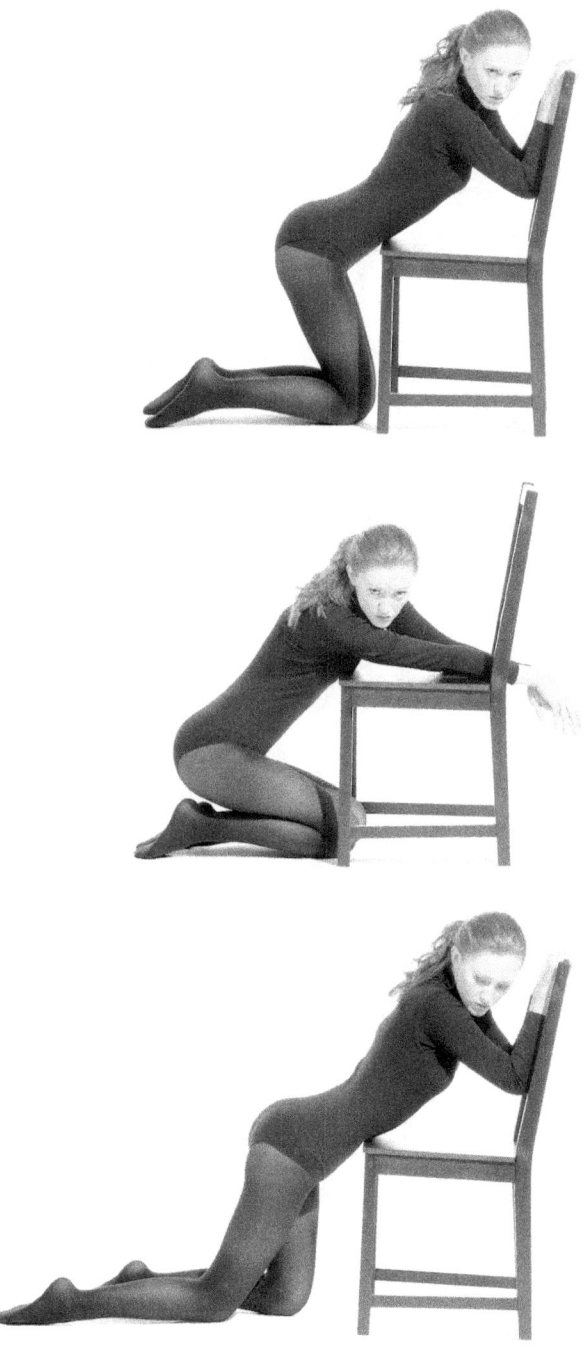

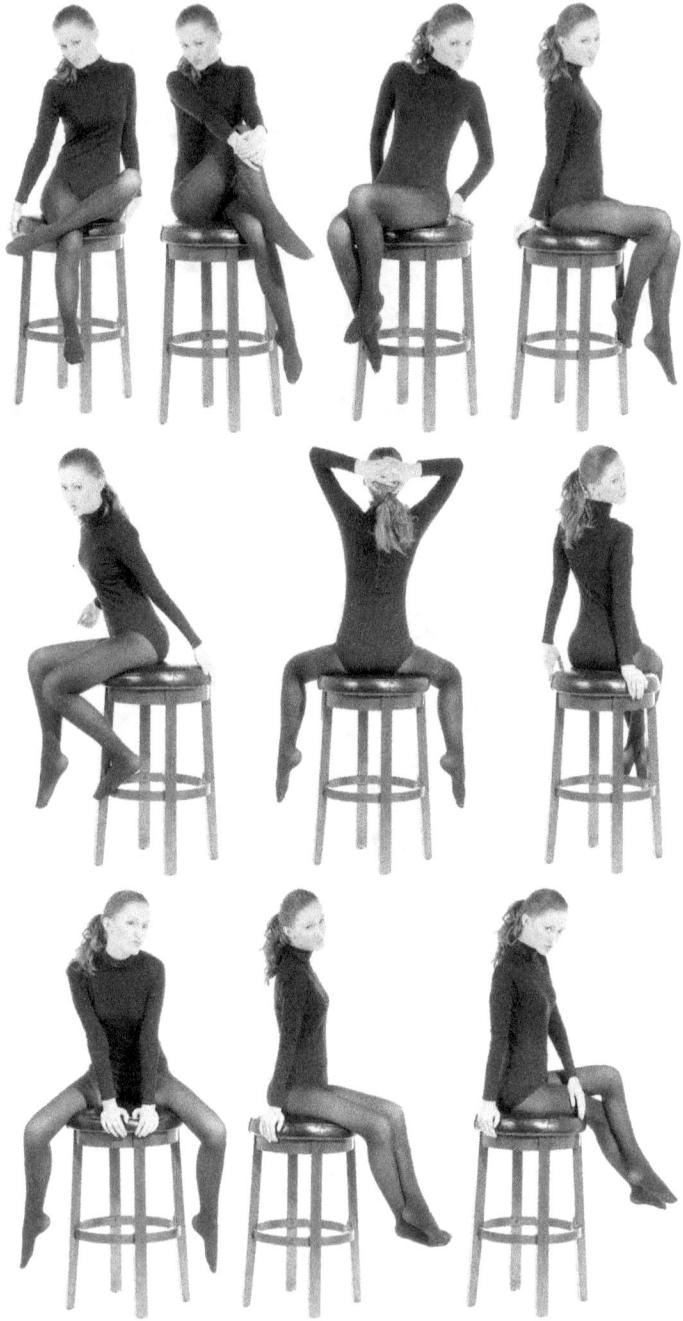

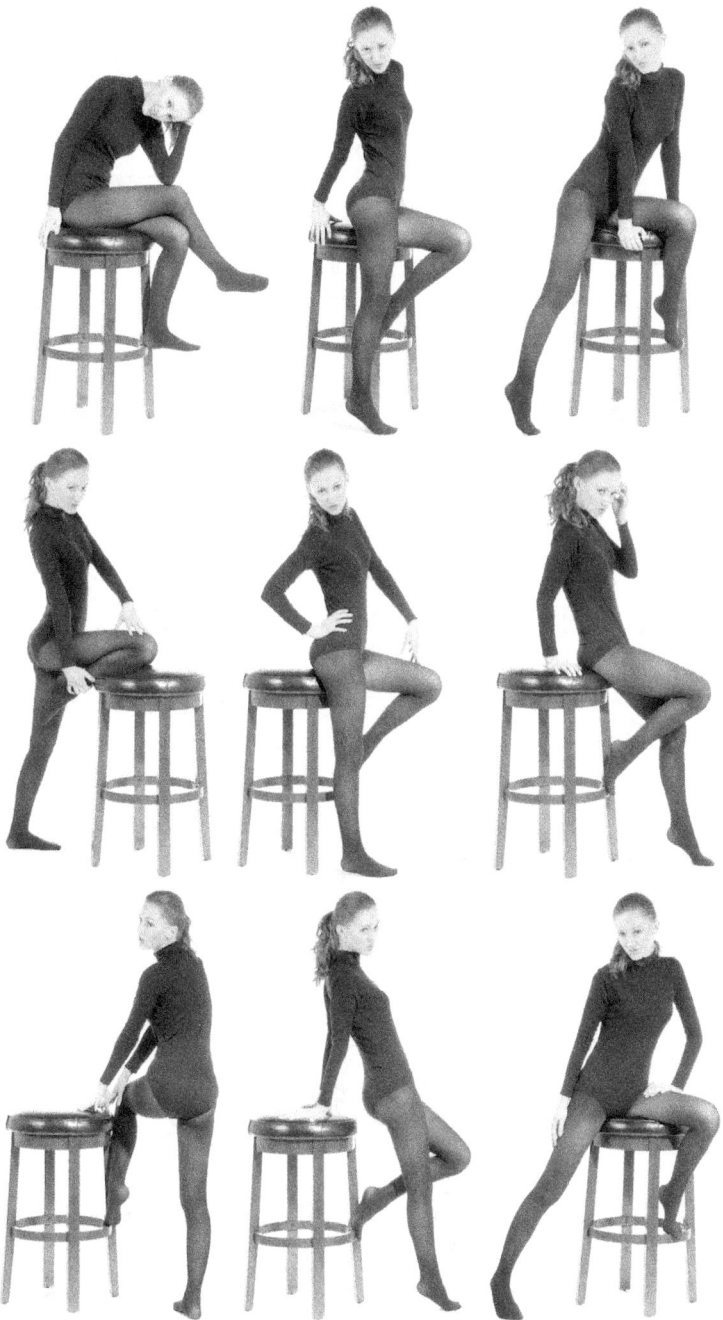

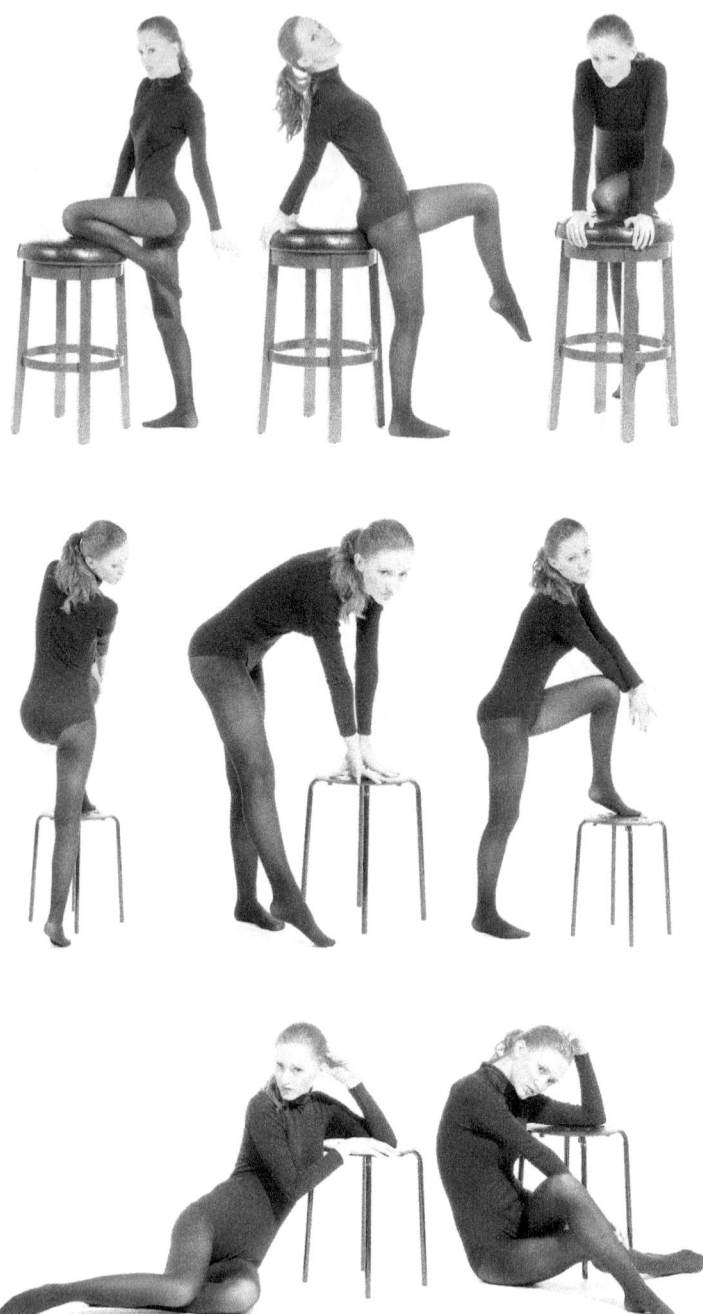

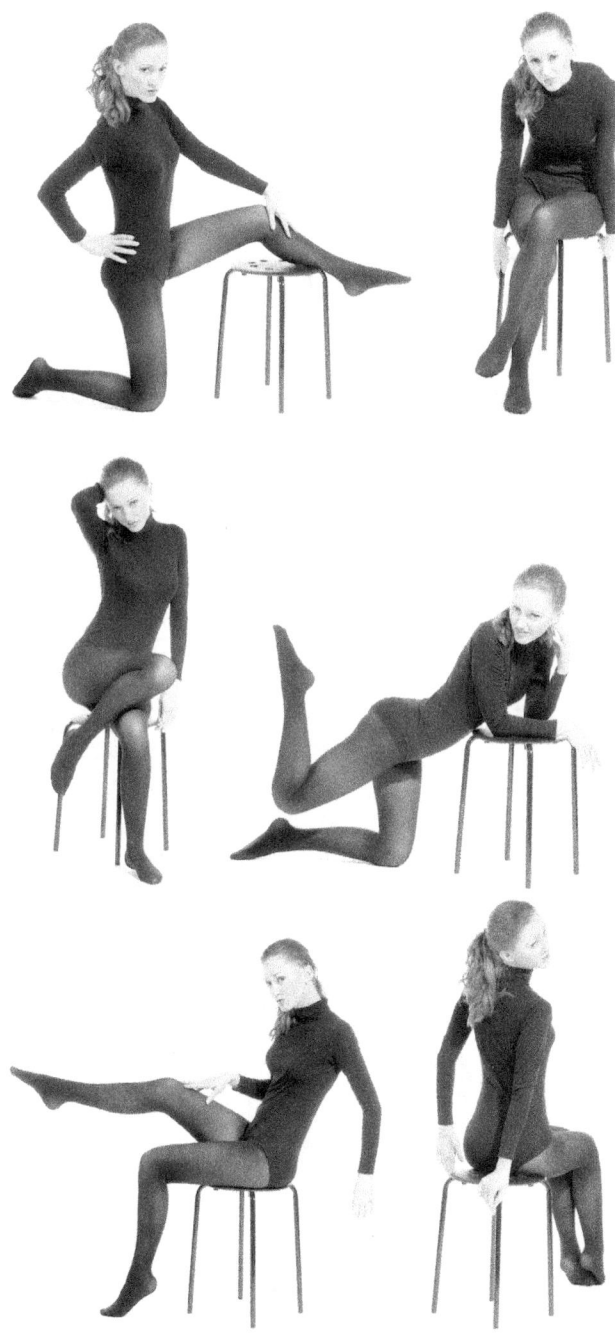

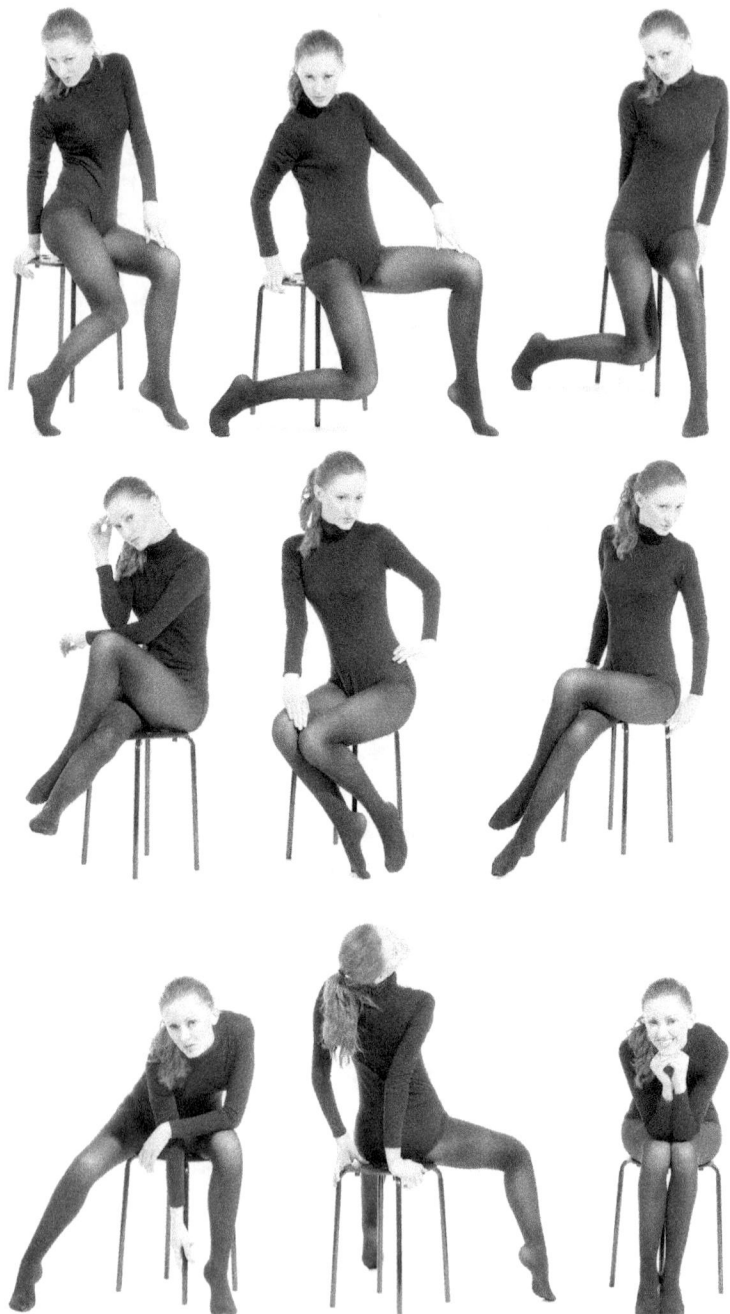

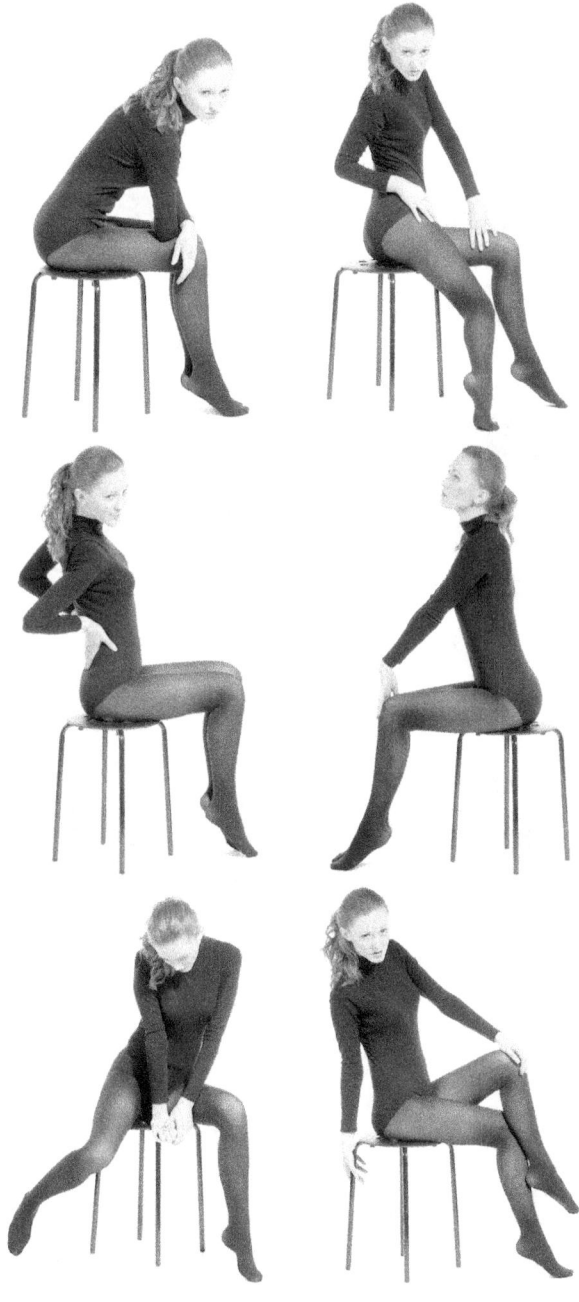

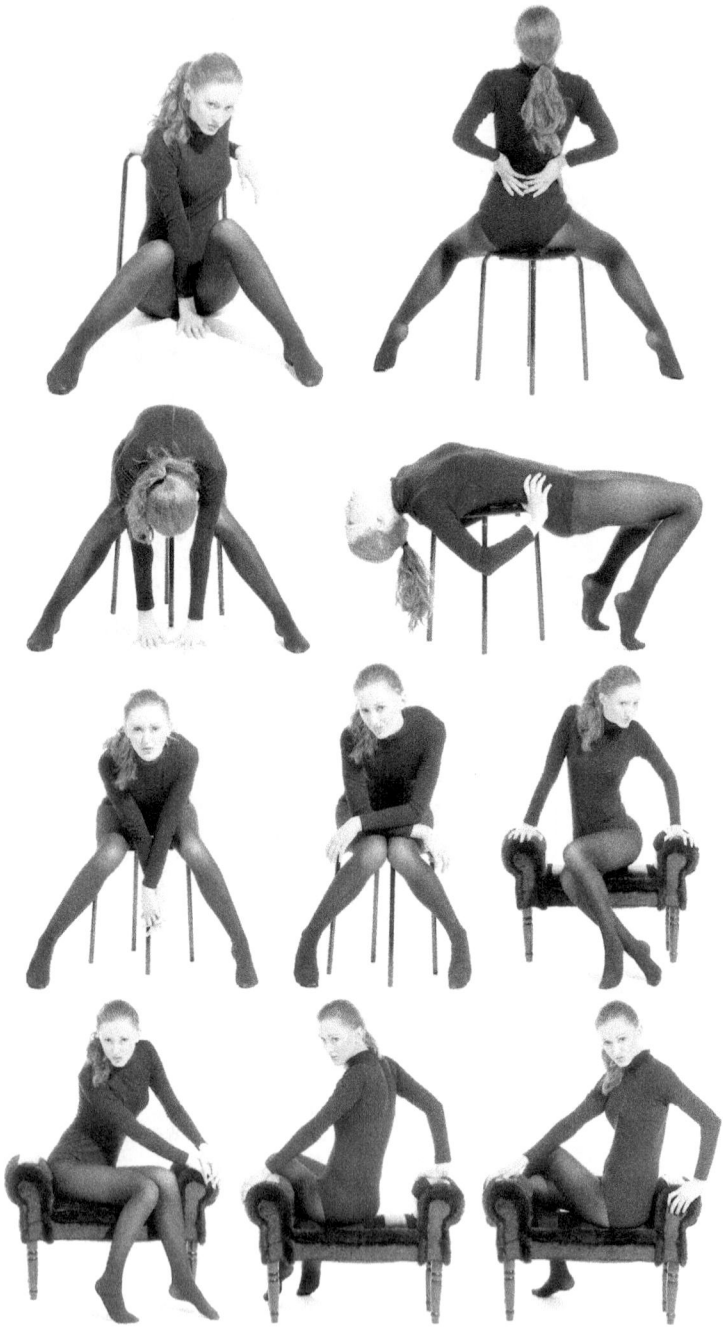

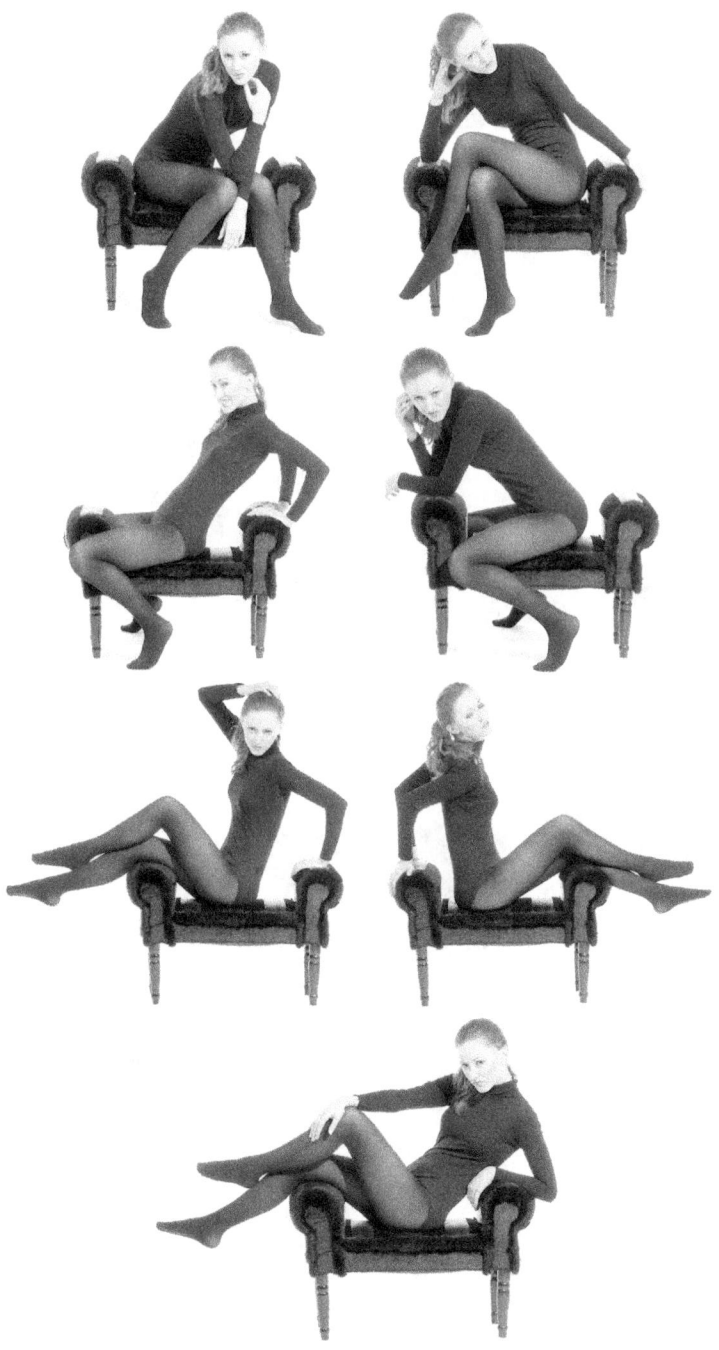

LAYING DOWN

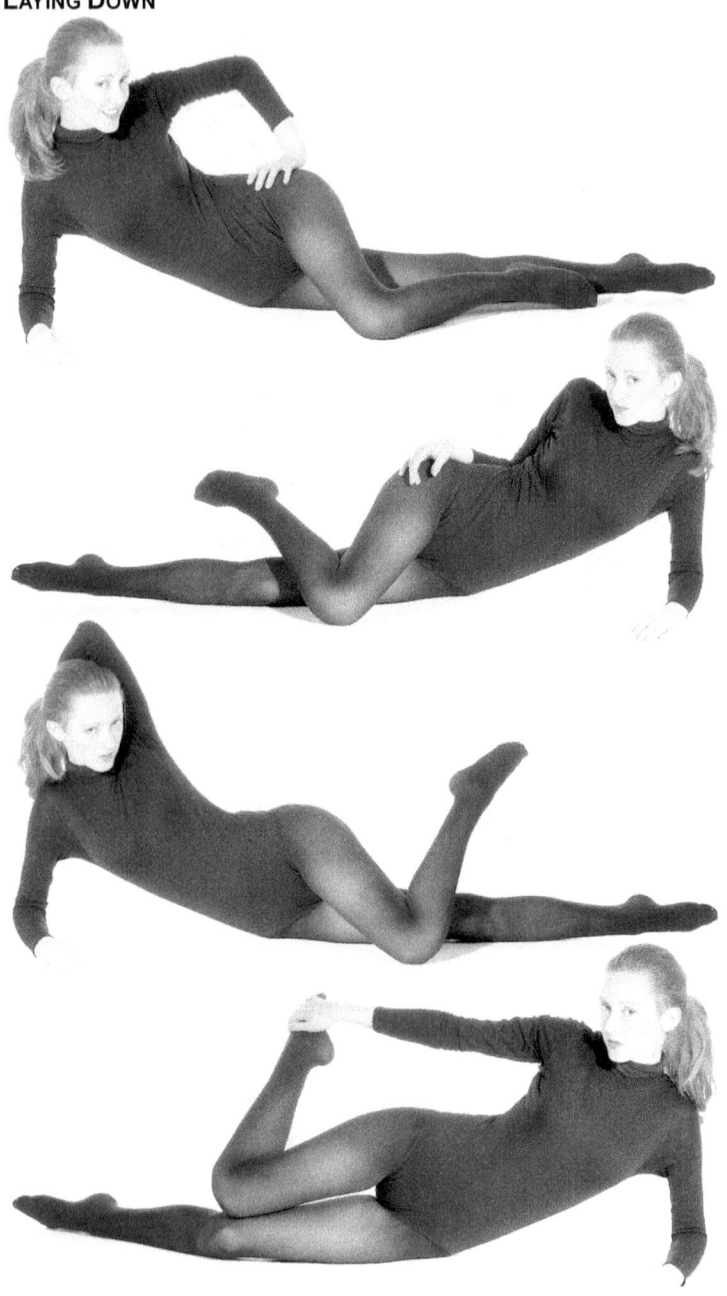

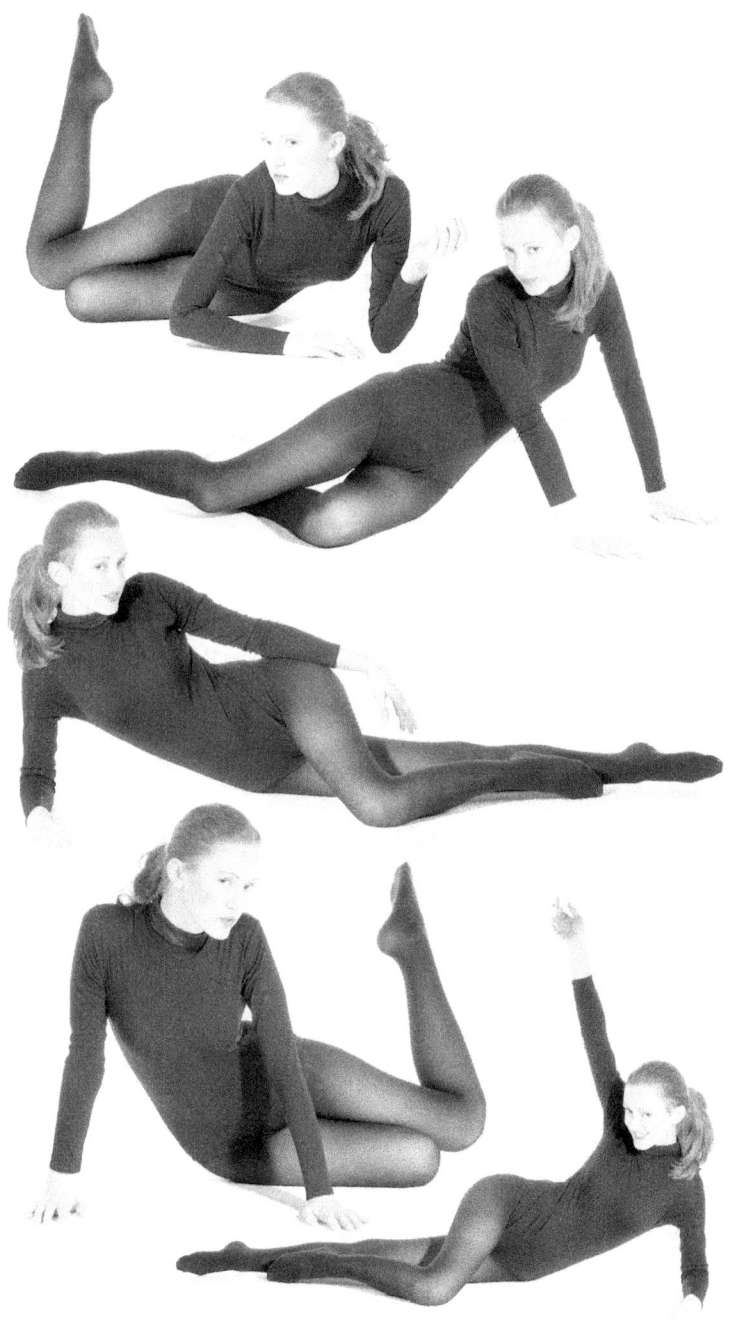

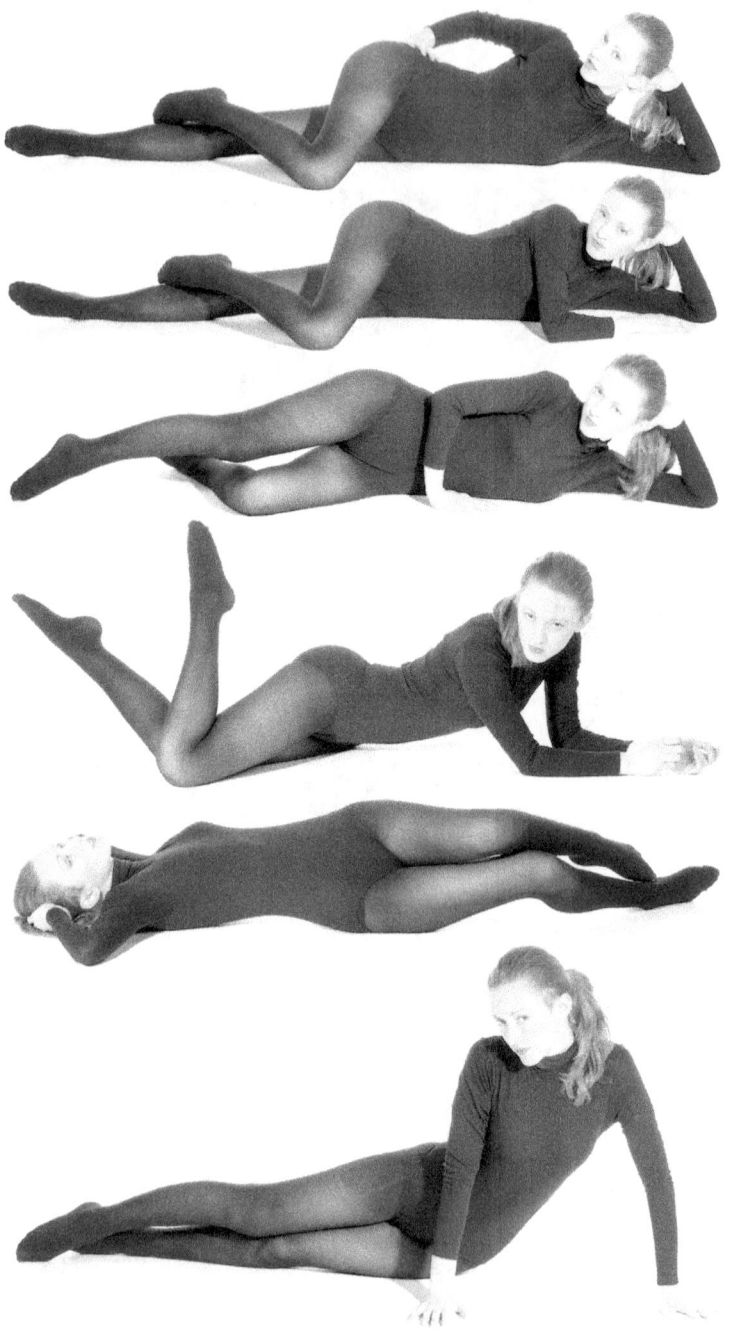

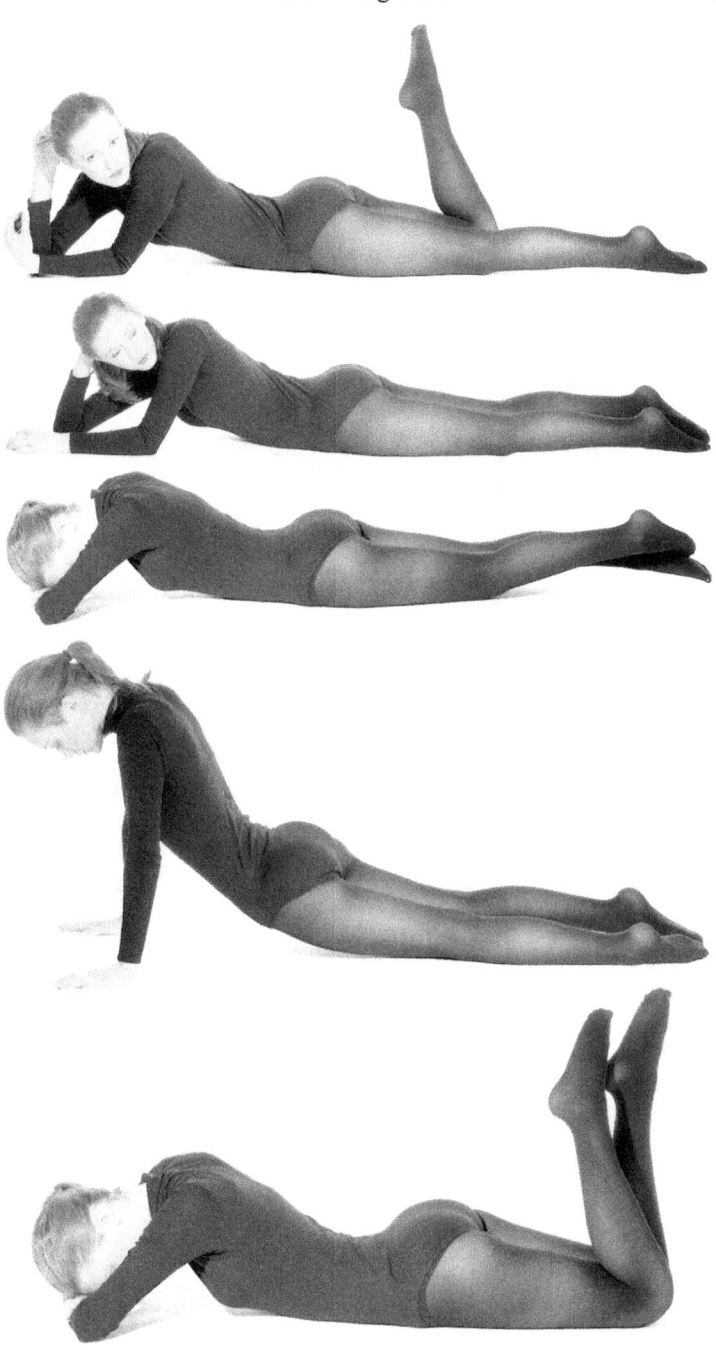

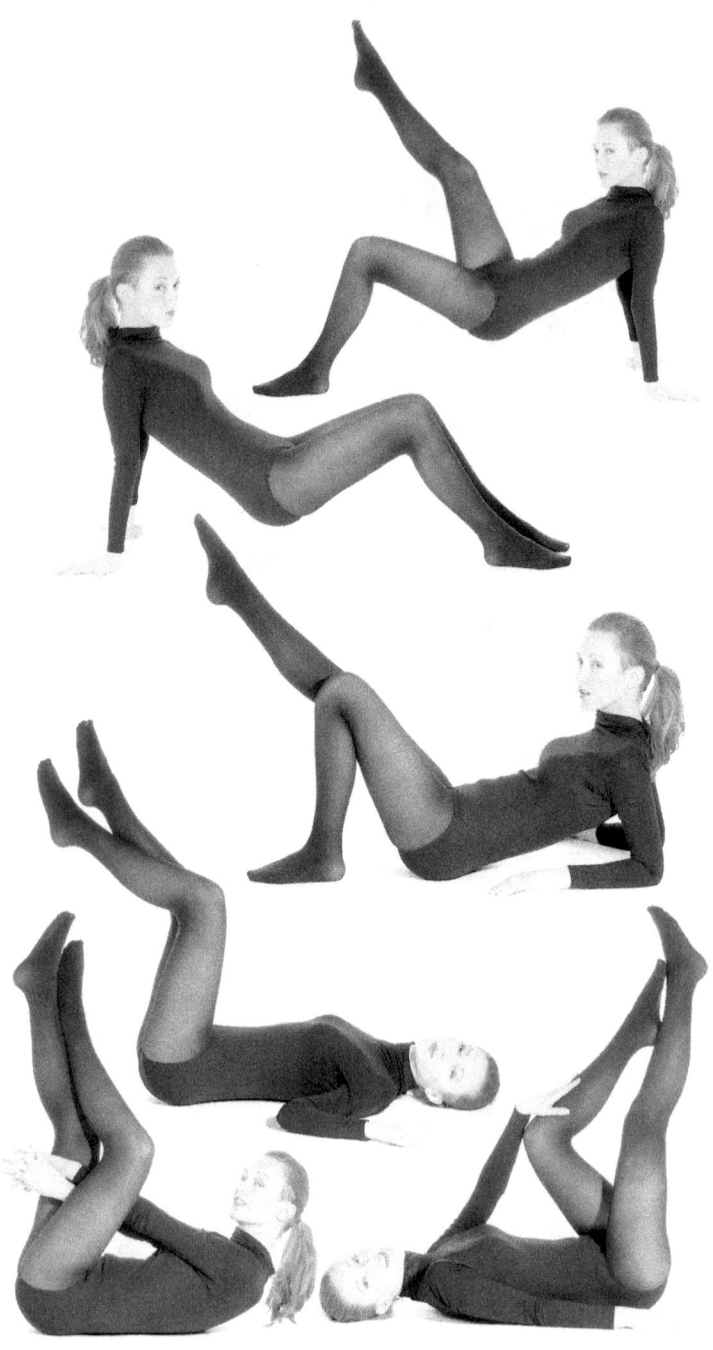

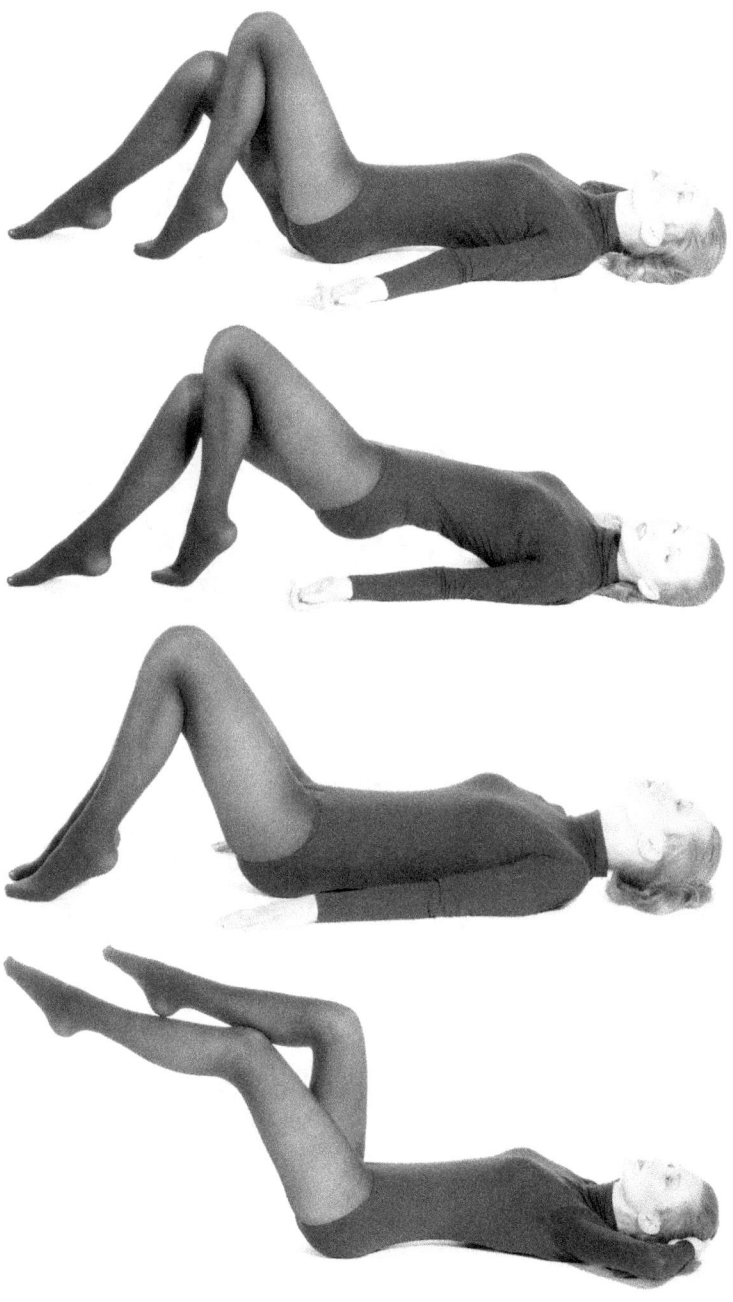

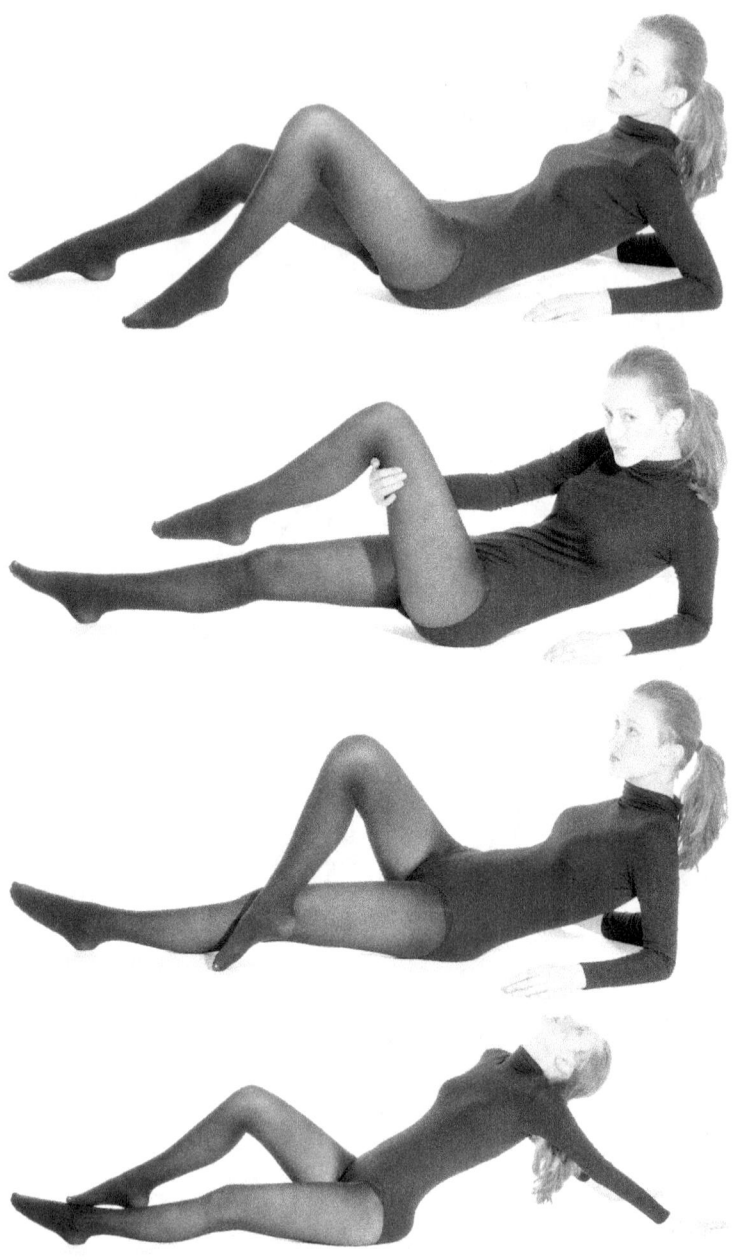

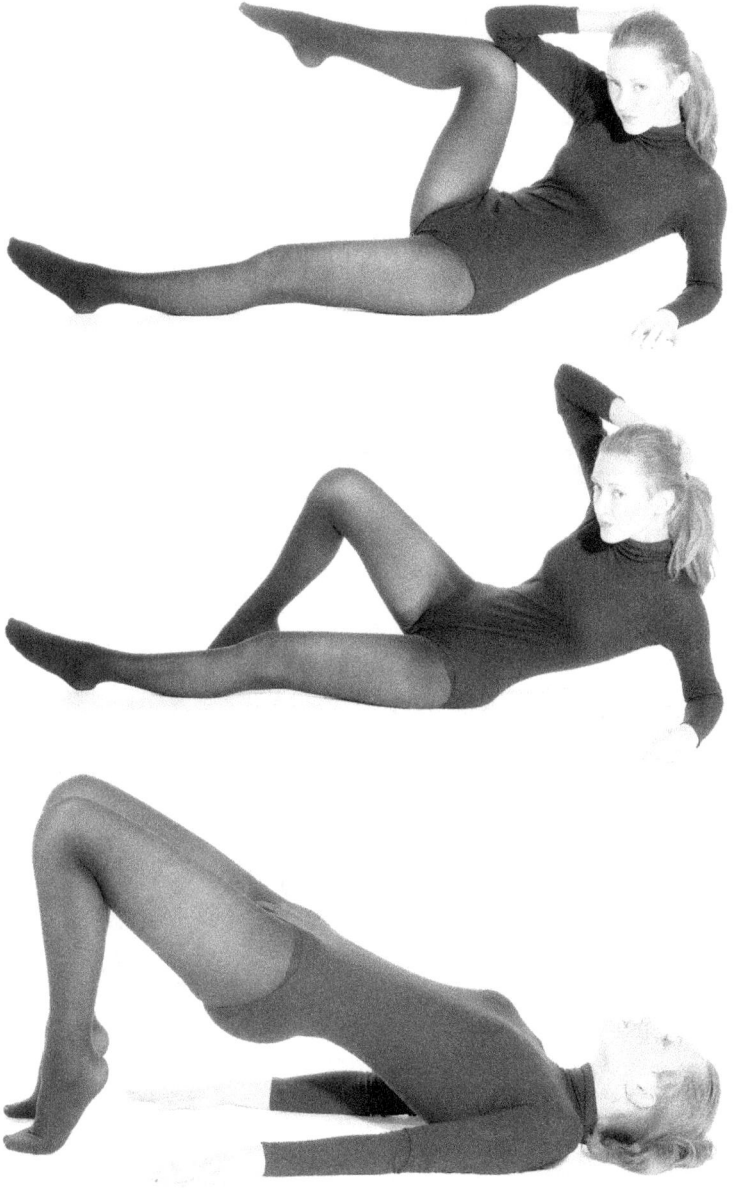

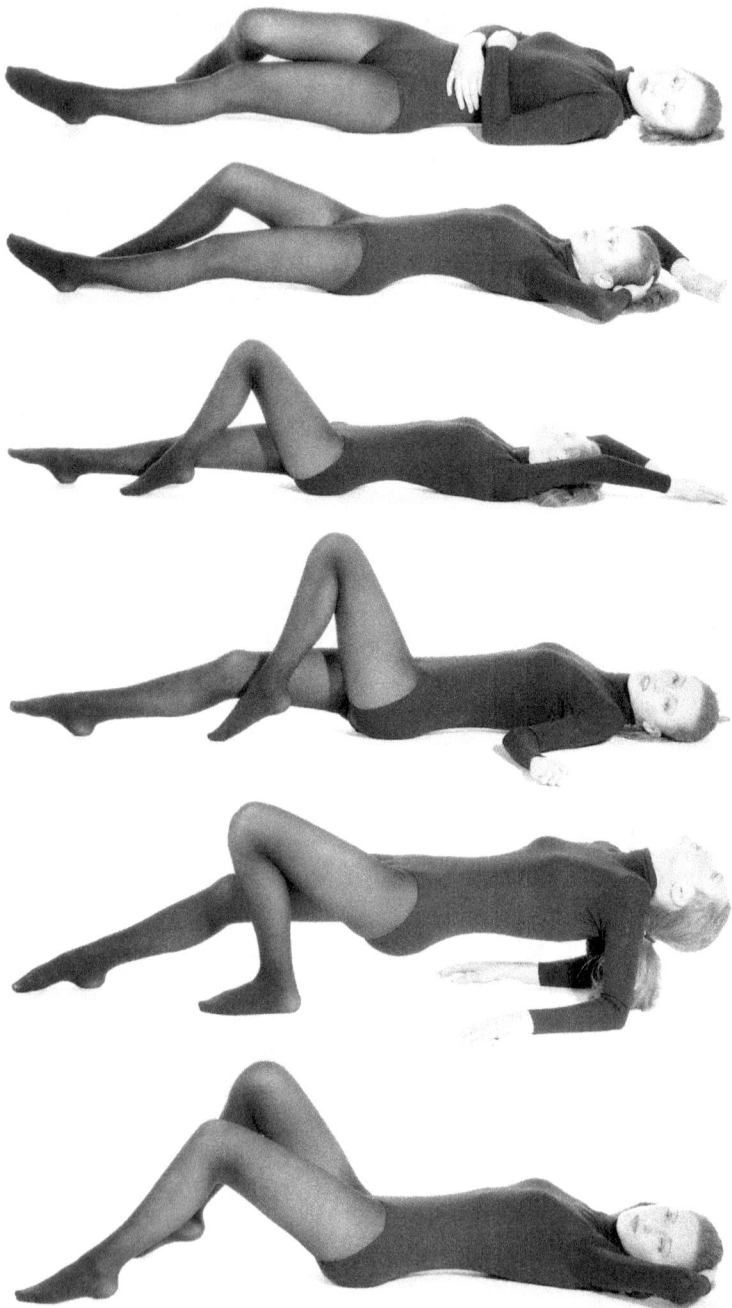

PROP AND CLOTHING SPECIFIC POSES

The key to posing with any type of prop (clothing included) is interacting with it. Use your imagination when it comes to the sections that follow. *The poses in this section tend to be defined by the apparel worn, so the sample photos here were done in the appropriate apparel. Many are Glamour Photos as Fashion Photos for these types of apparel tend to have a Glamour style to them.*

SKIRTS AND DRESSES

A skirt can be rather dull if you just let it hang, but is fantastic when you use it as a prop. Playing with the hem line and moving the fabric around adds life to your photos. And, showing a flash of what's underneath can add a touch of excitement to your glamour photos.

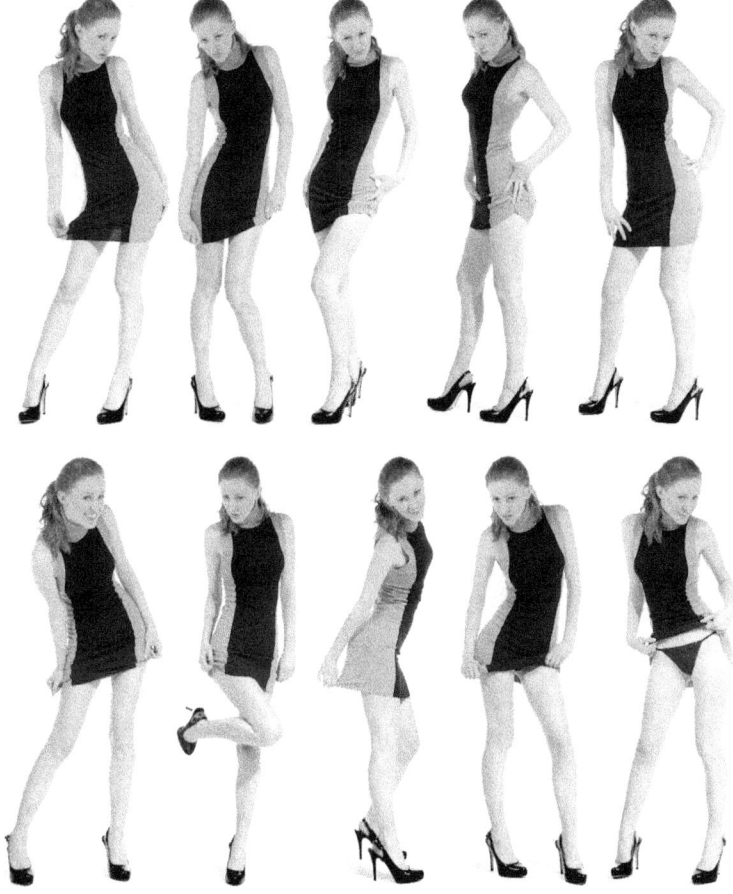

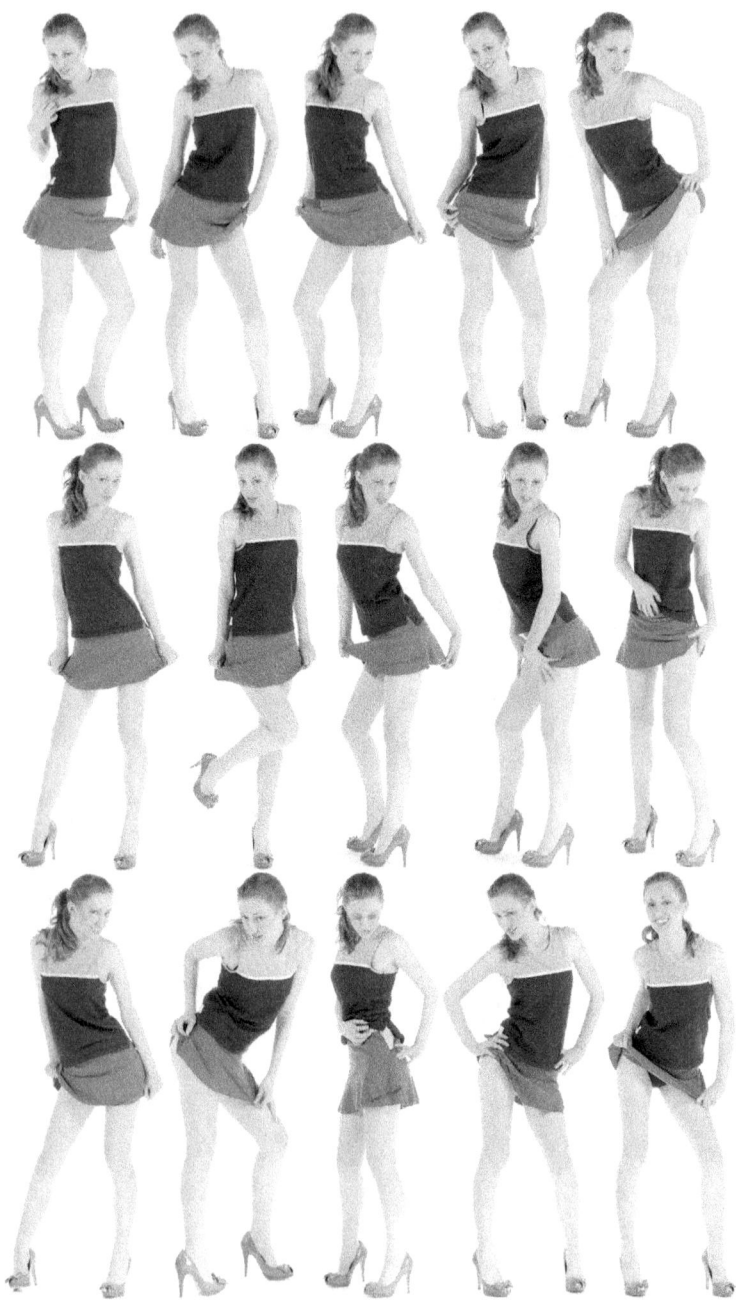

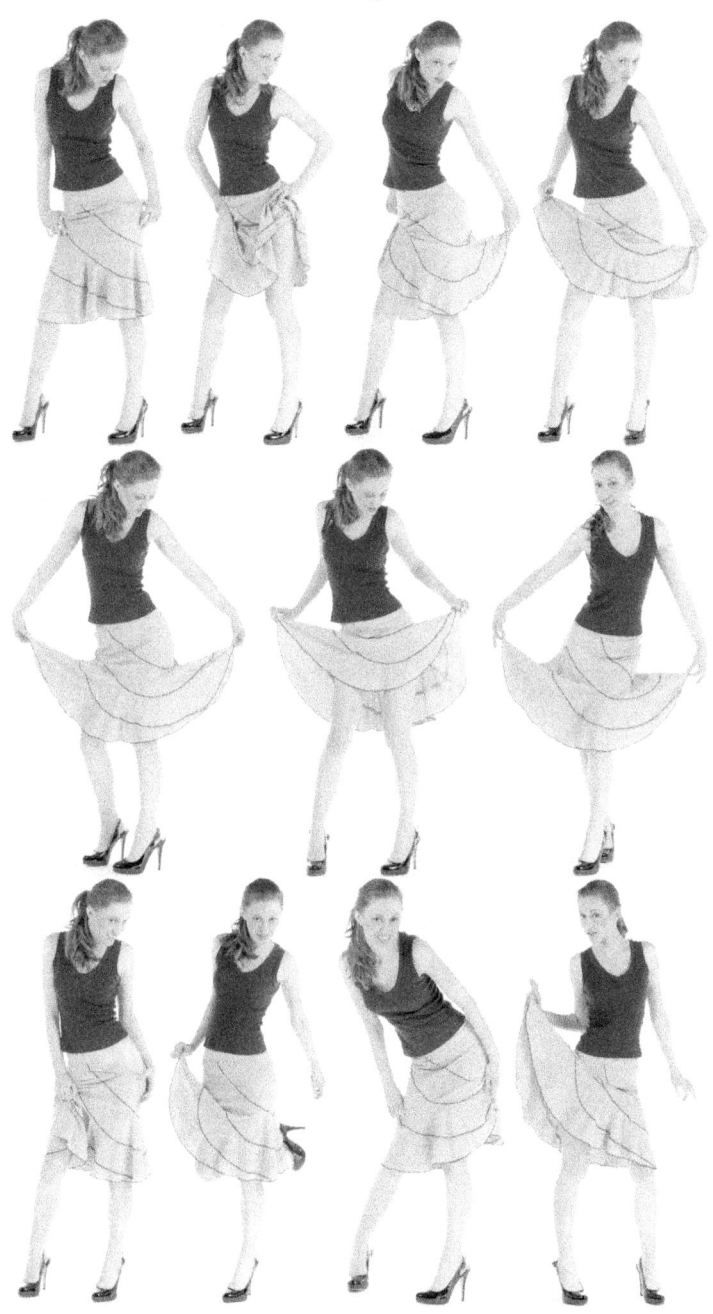

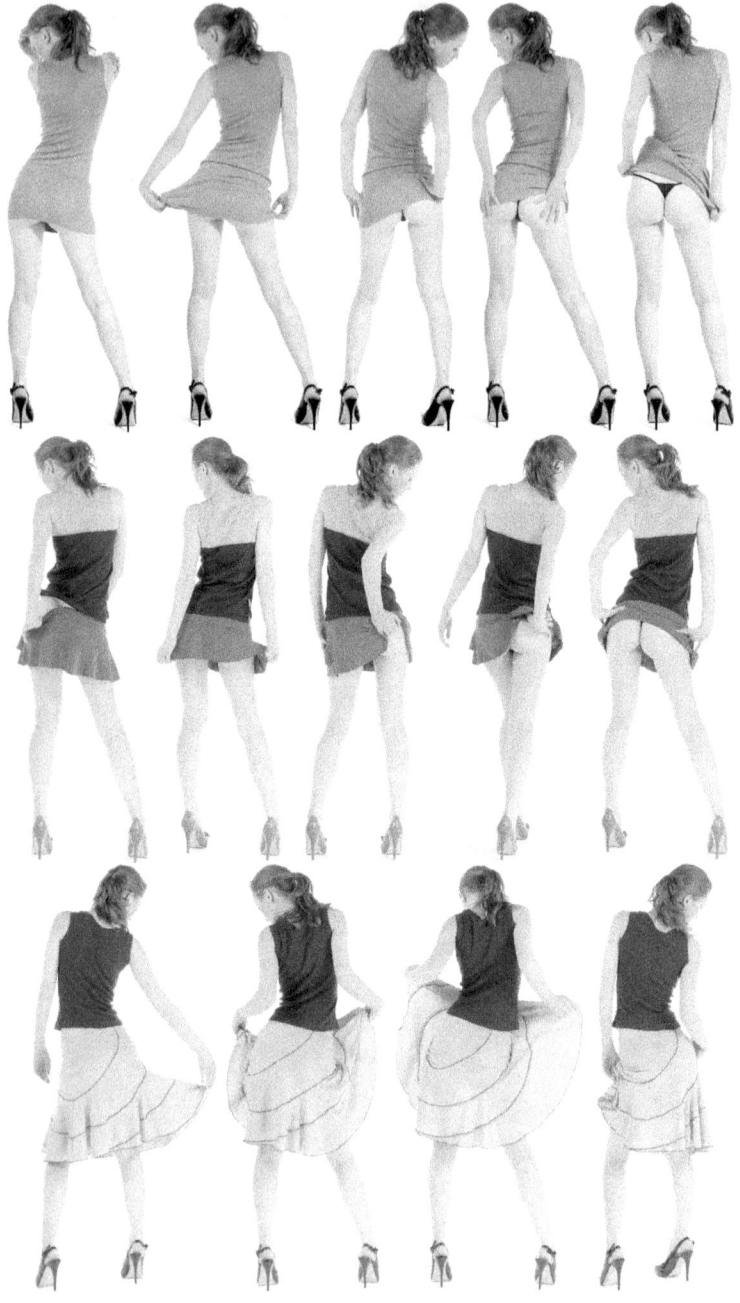

JEANS OR OTHER PANTS

Jeans or other types of pants can be used in Glamour Photography to great affect. Some apparel companies promote their product through sex appeal, so similar posing is often used. It's funny, but some of the most effective images of jeans are of the model not quite wearing the clothes.

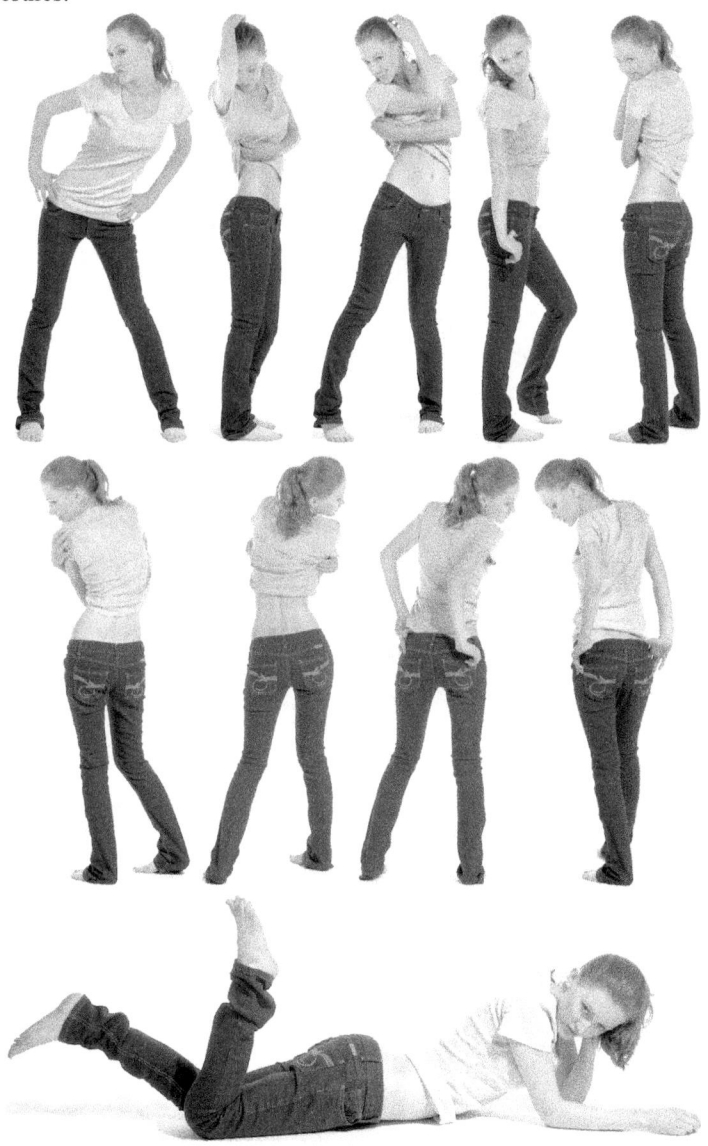

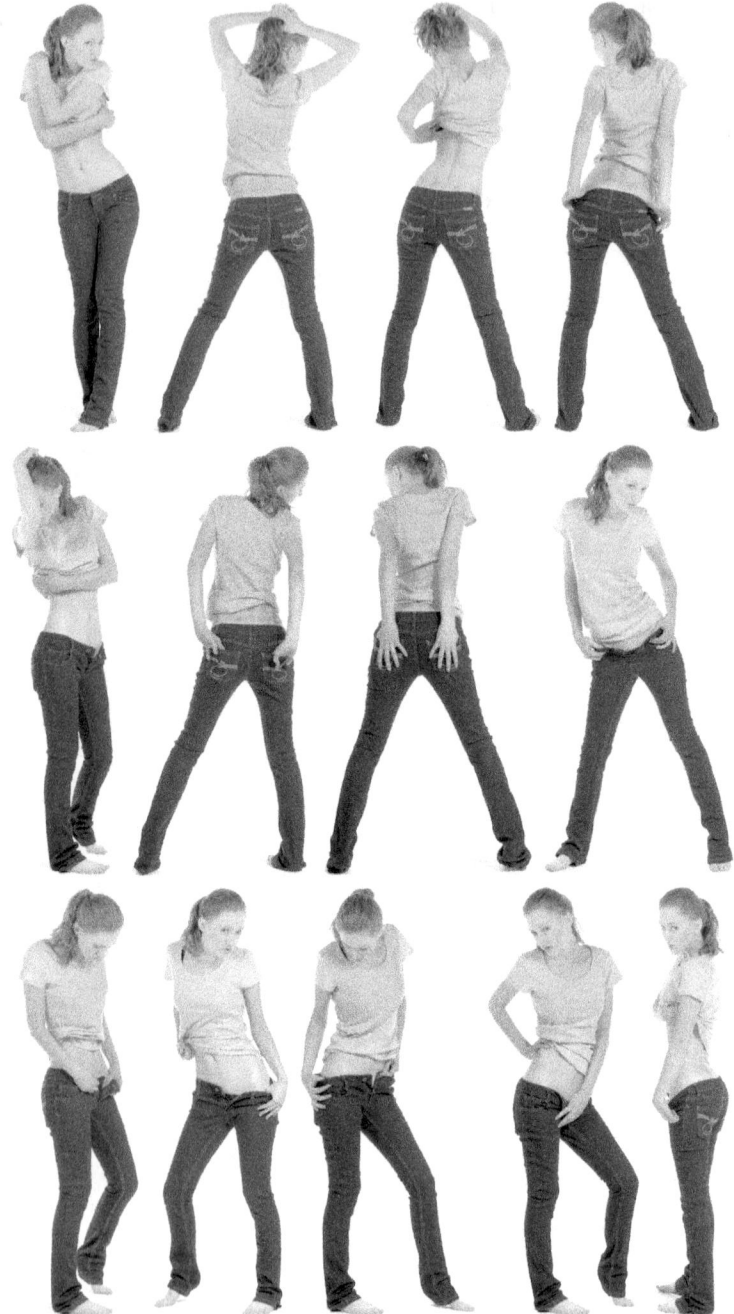

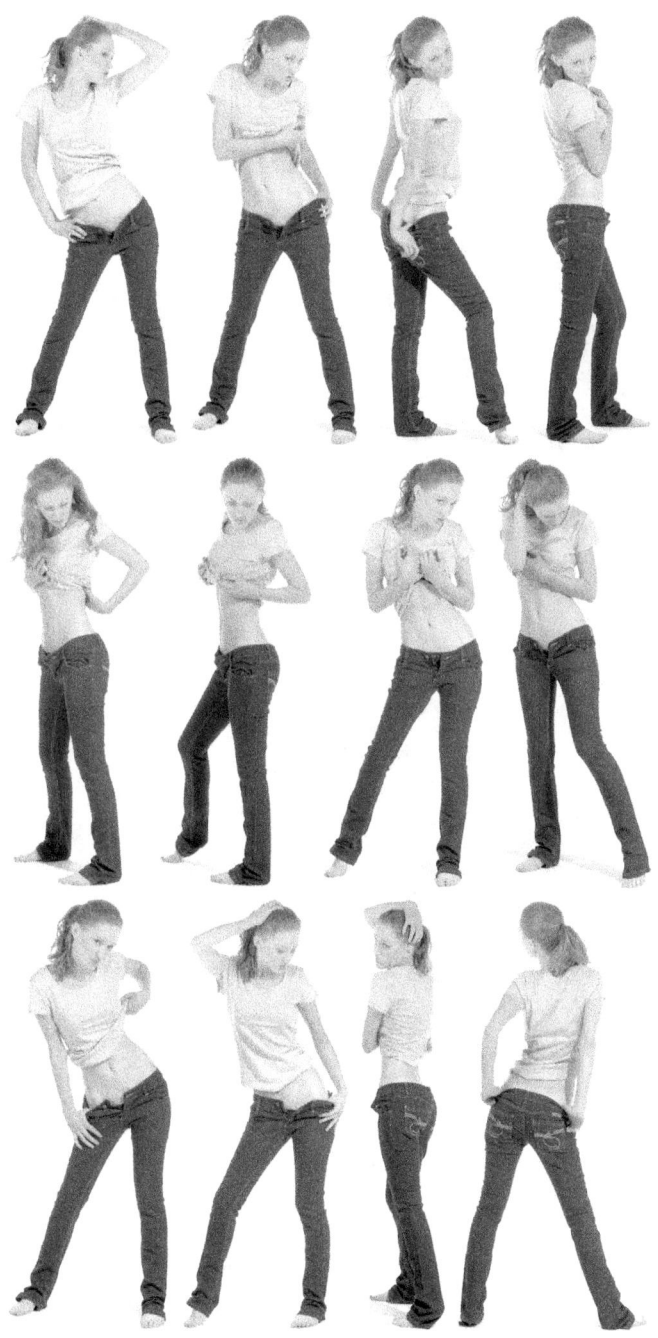

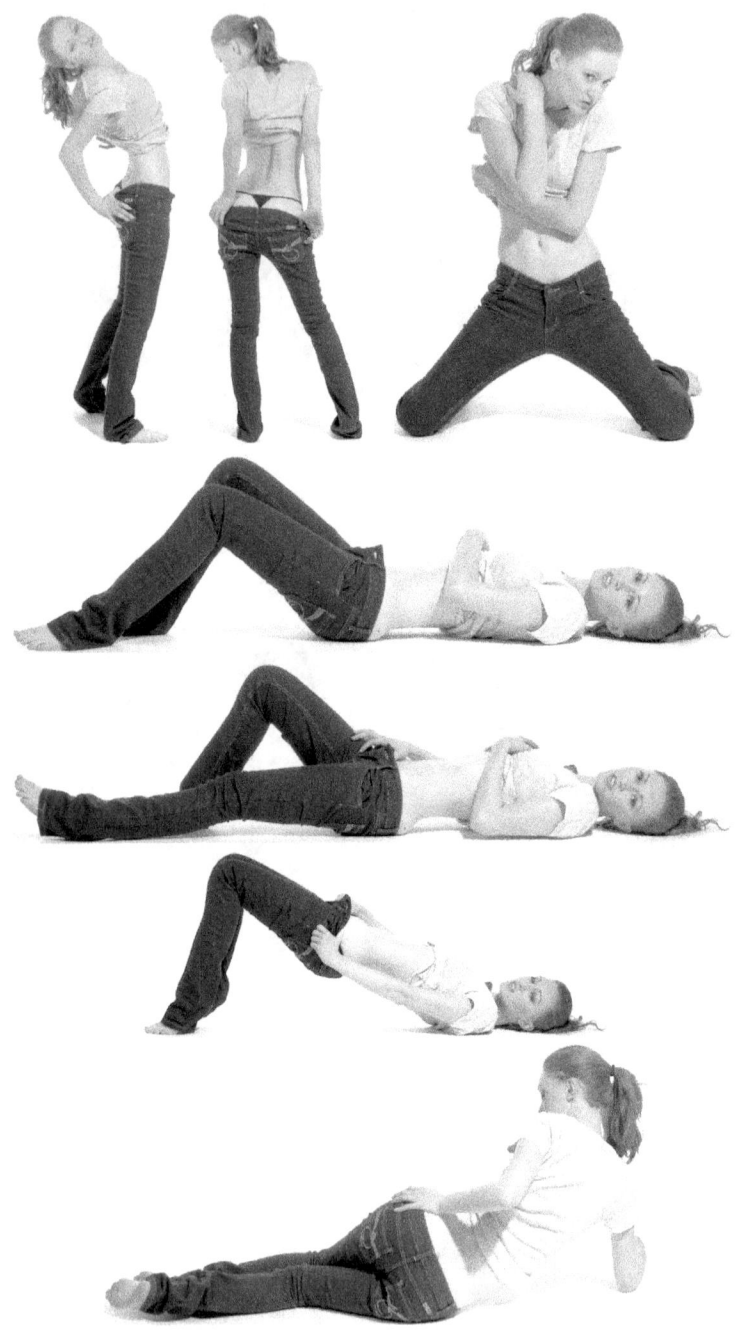

BEDS

Posing on beds is mainly limited to lingerie fashions and glamour photography. You need to make sure that the lingerie is visible for Fashion Photography. In certain cases, careful posing, strategic use of props or covering up with the hands needs to be done so that the photos will be publishable.

You need to have an idea of what you are going to look like in your head. Lay flat on your back (or stomach) and the photographer will need to climb a ladder to see you. (That's not a bad thing, unless there's no ladder around!) Ideally, you should be on one hip facing (or facing away) from the camera for a 'lying down' position.

The model is wearing lingerie in the sample photos not only because that is typical of the apparel used when posing on a bed, but also so that you can easily see the orientation of her body and get a better idea of how the poses work.

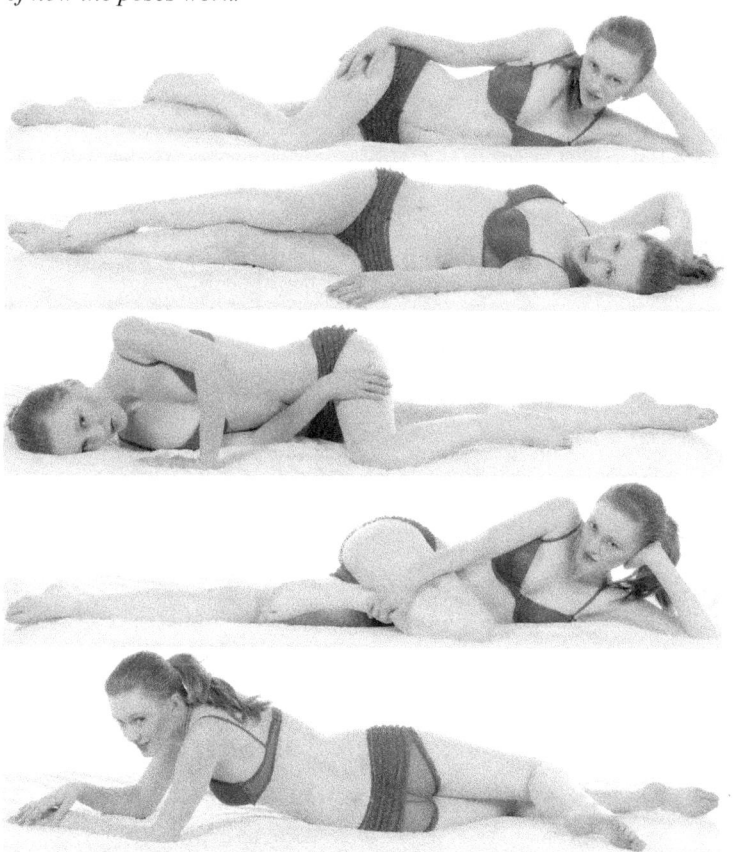

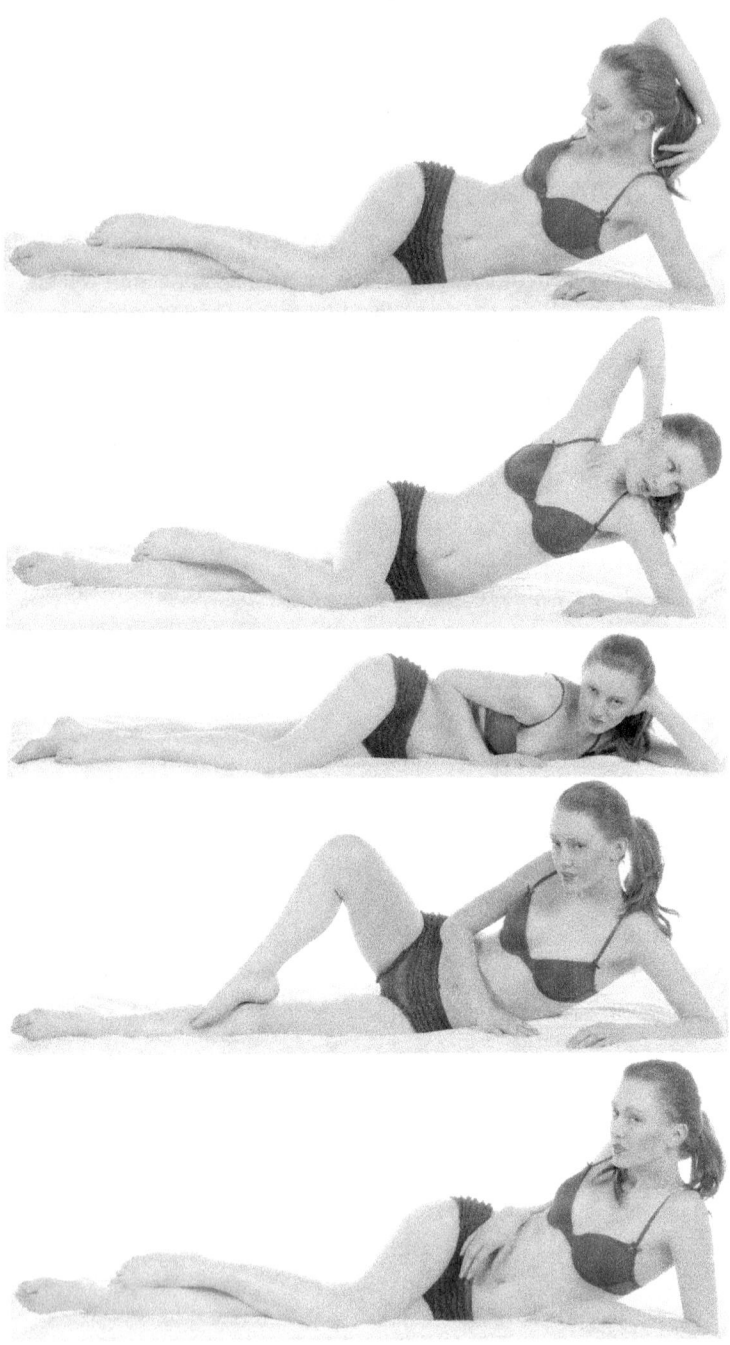

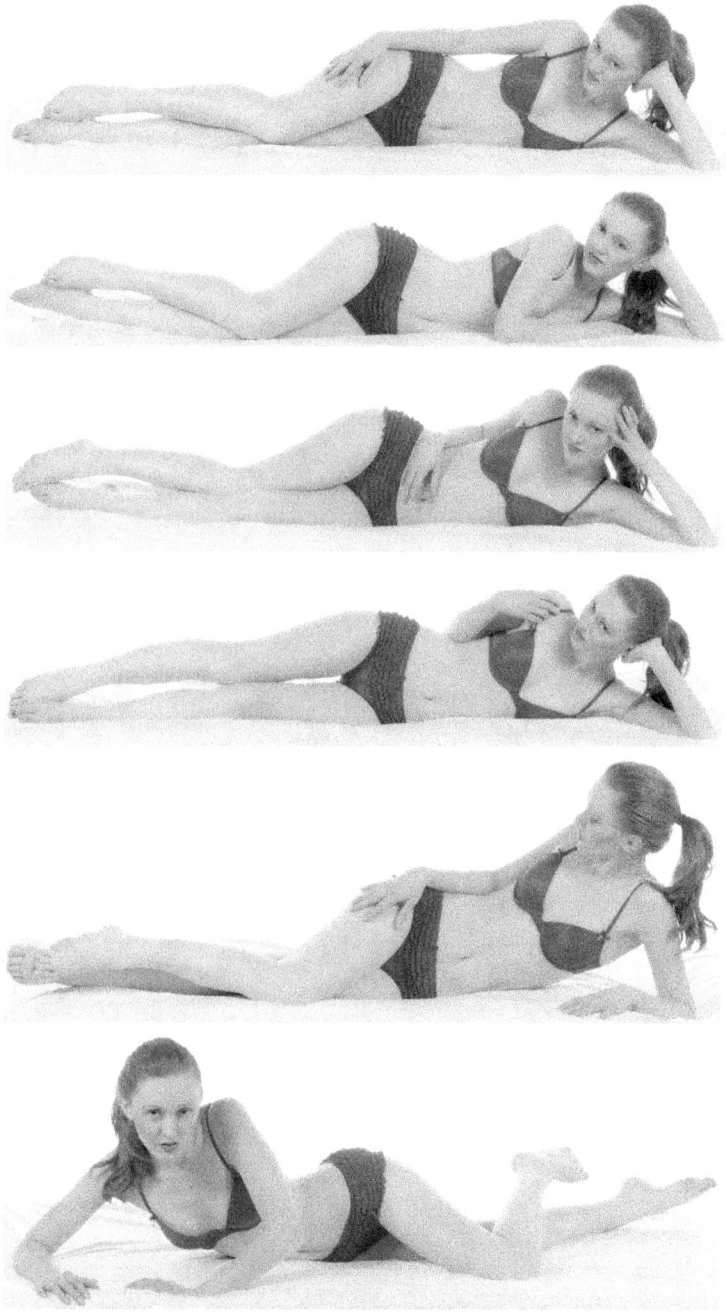

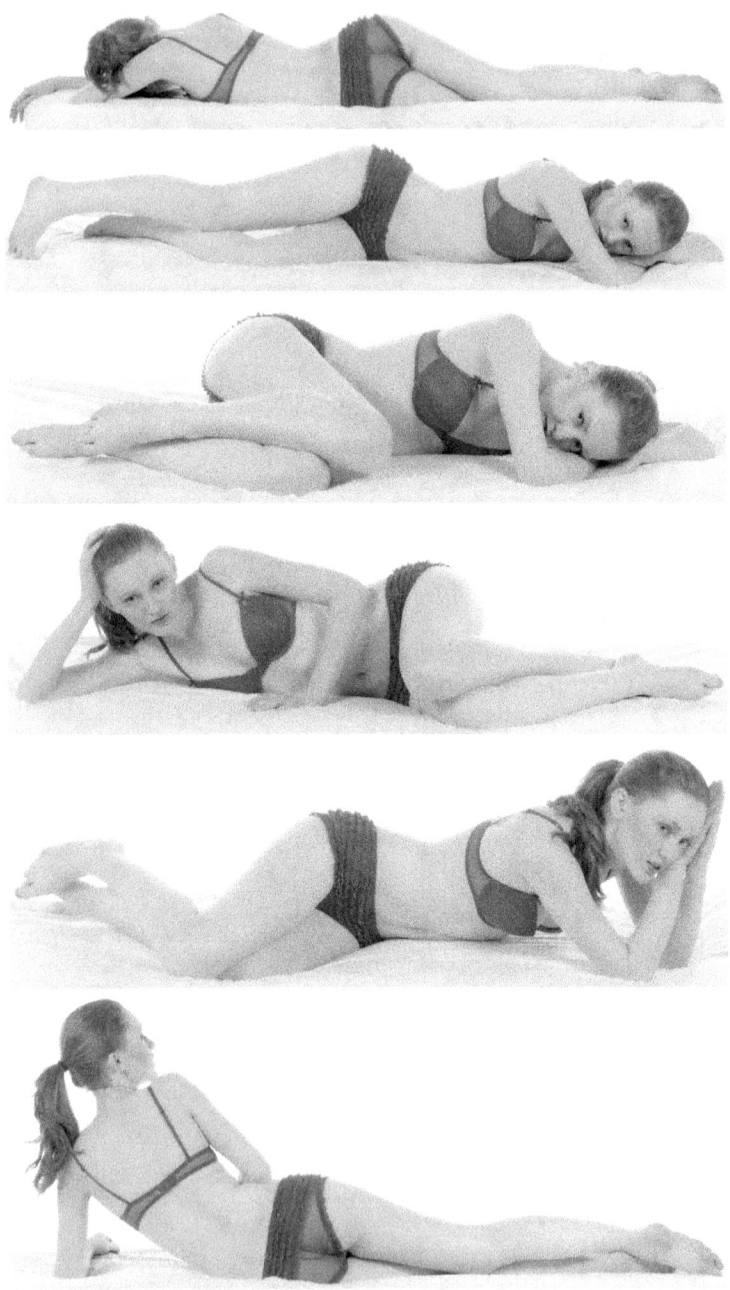

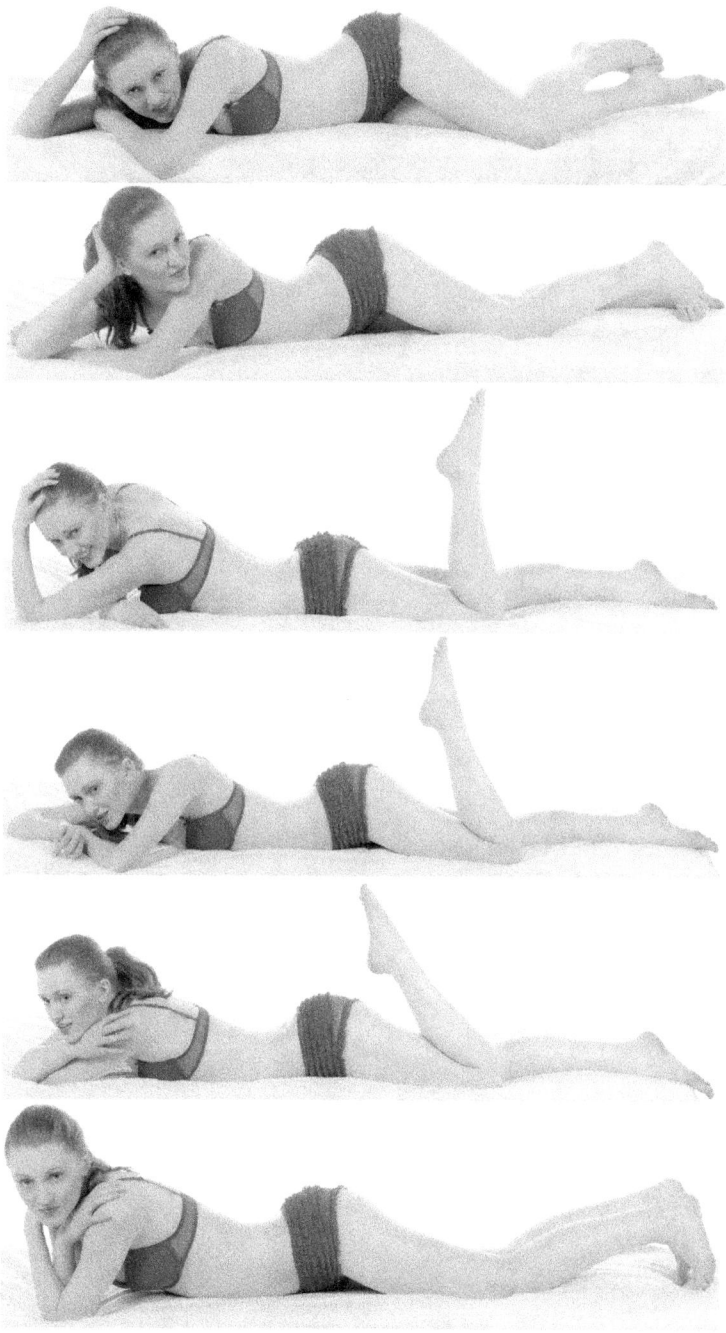

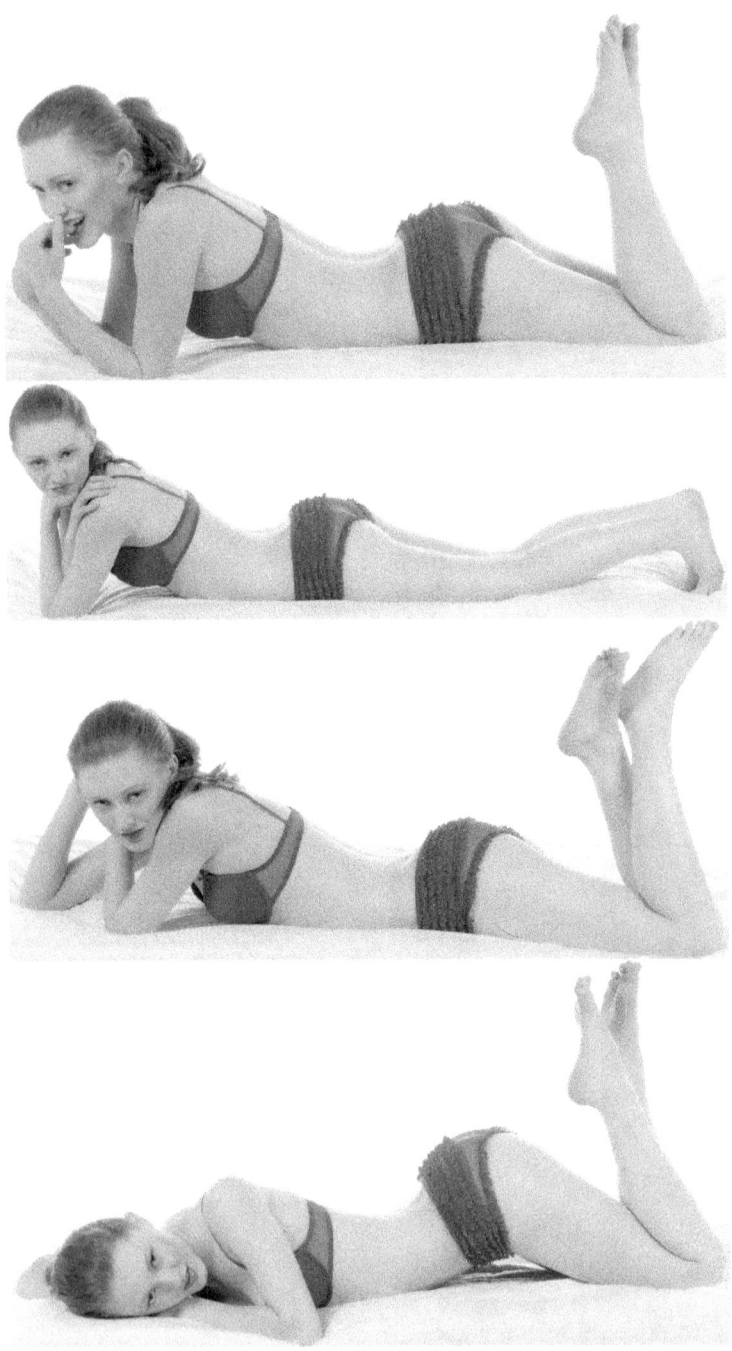

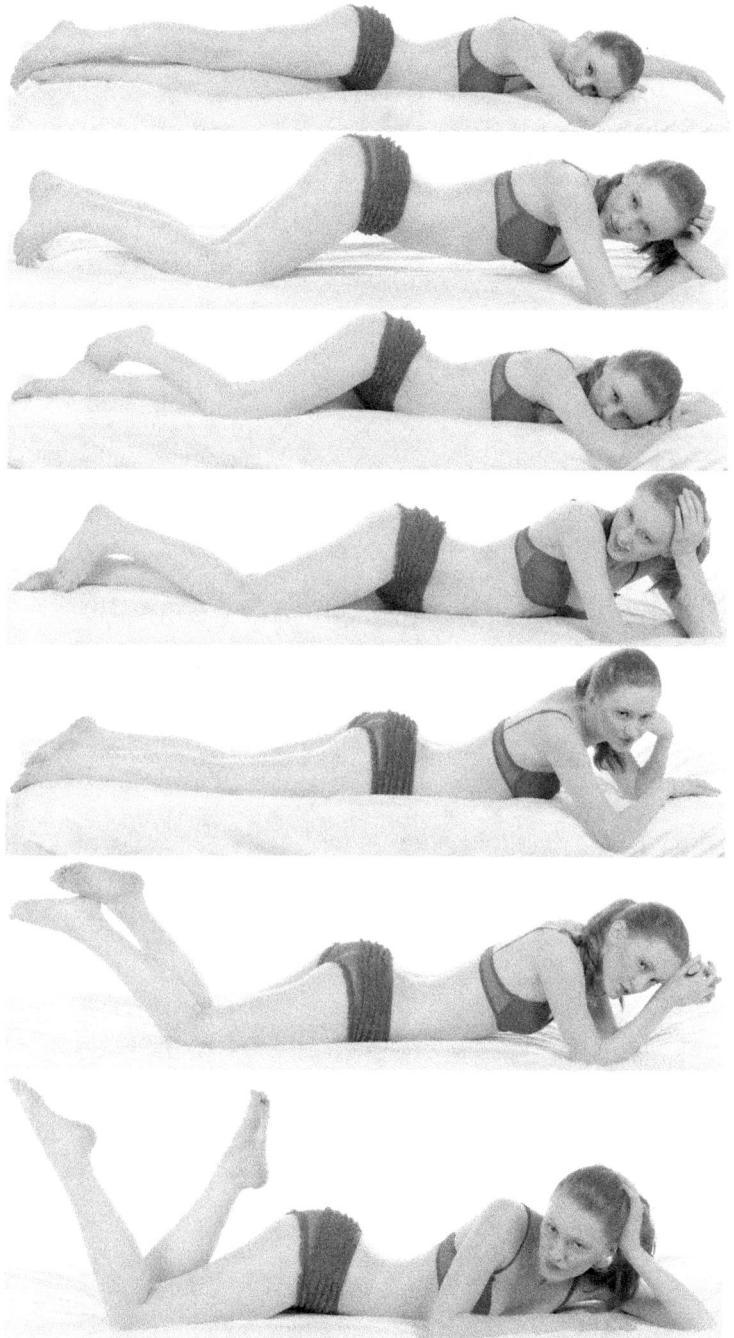

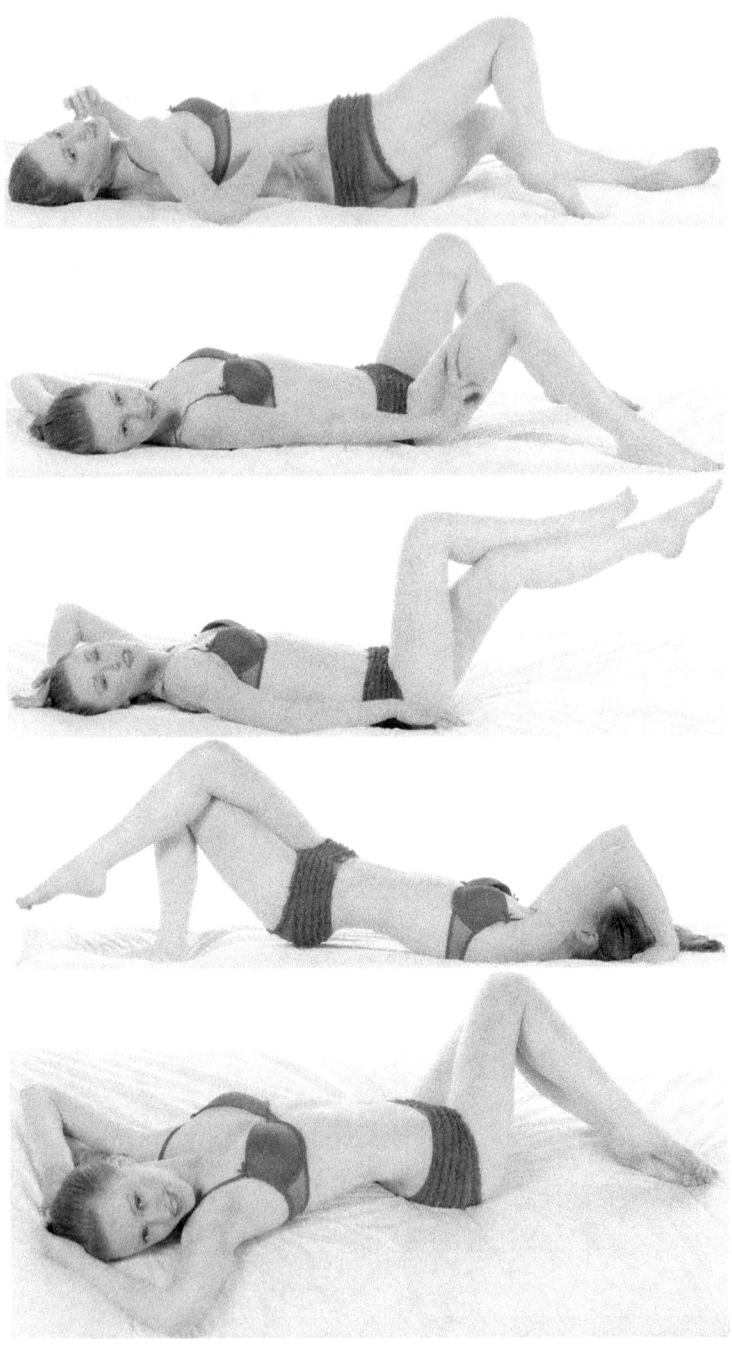

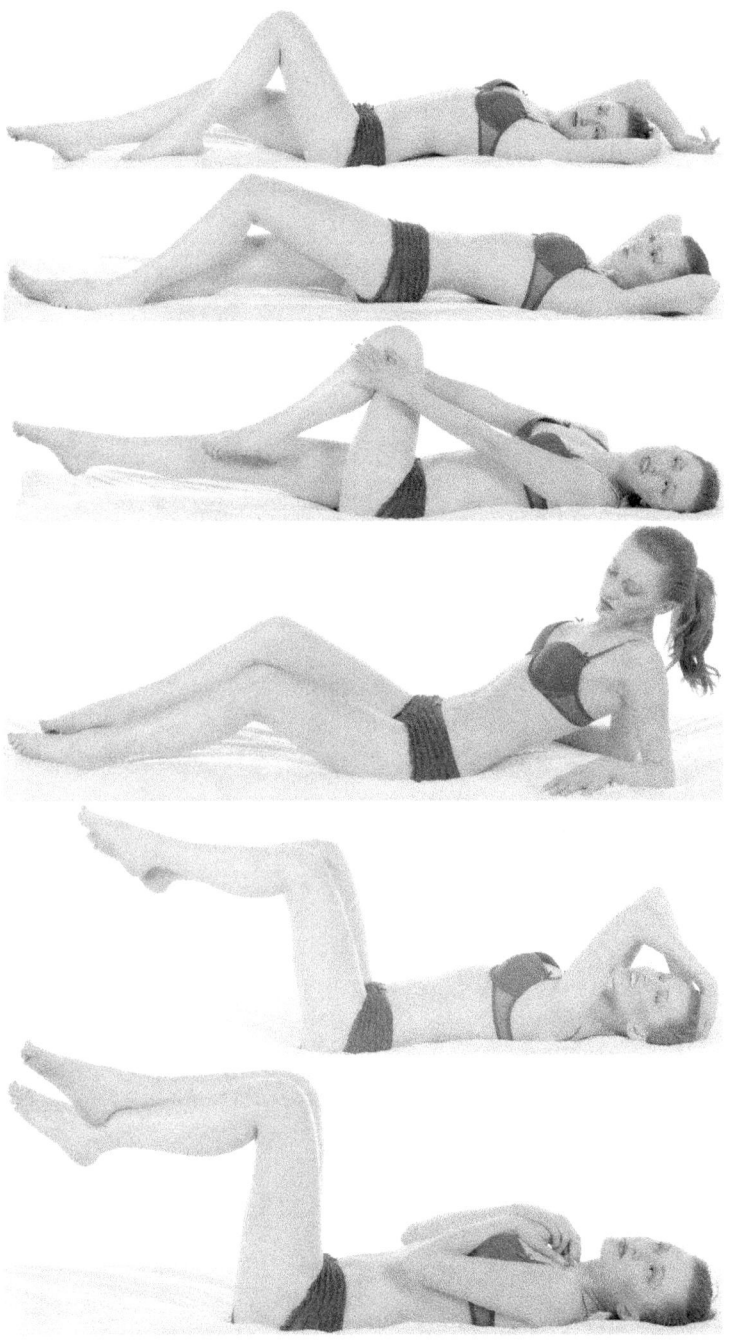

Don't forget that the sides of the bed can be used as well.

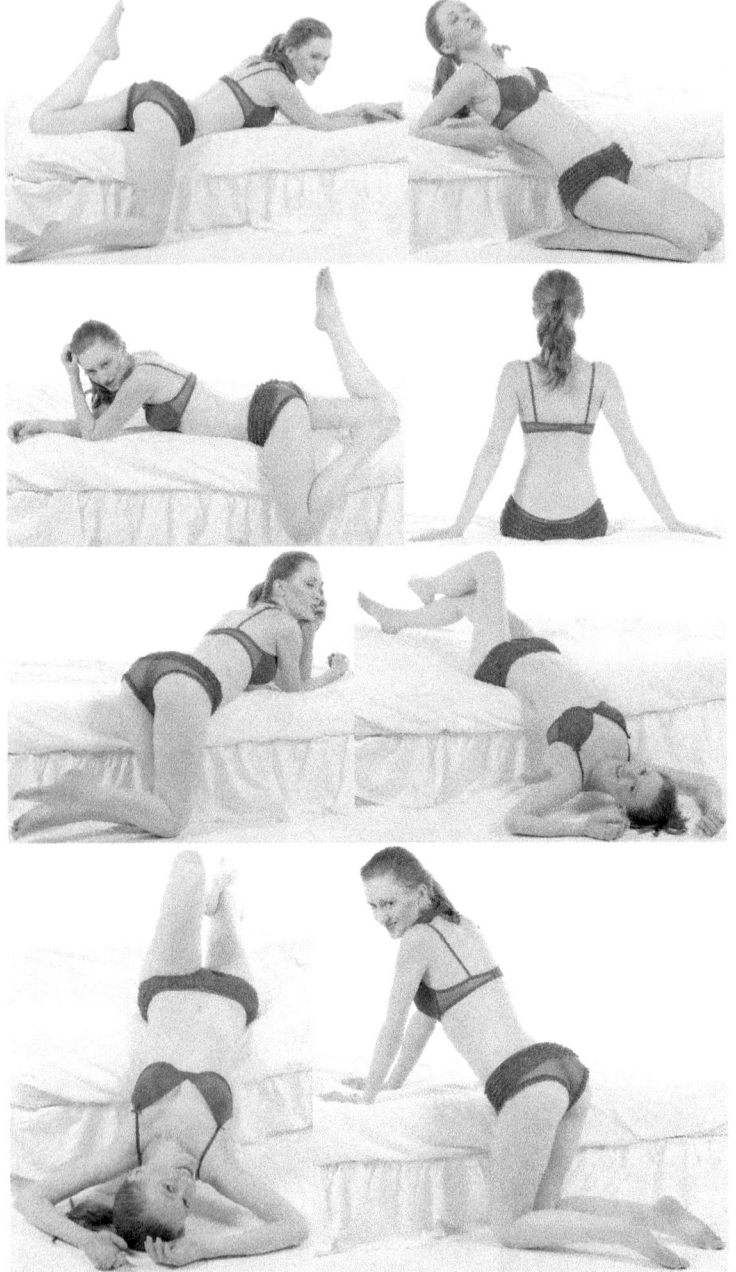

Expect the photographer to not only shift perspective, but also the position of the bed and you during the shoot.

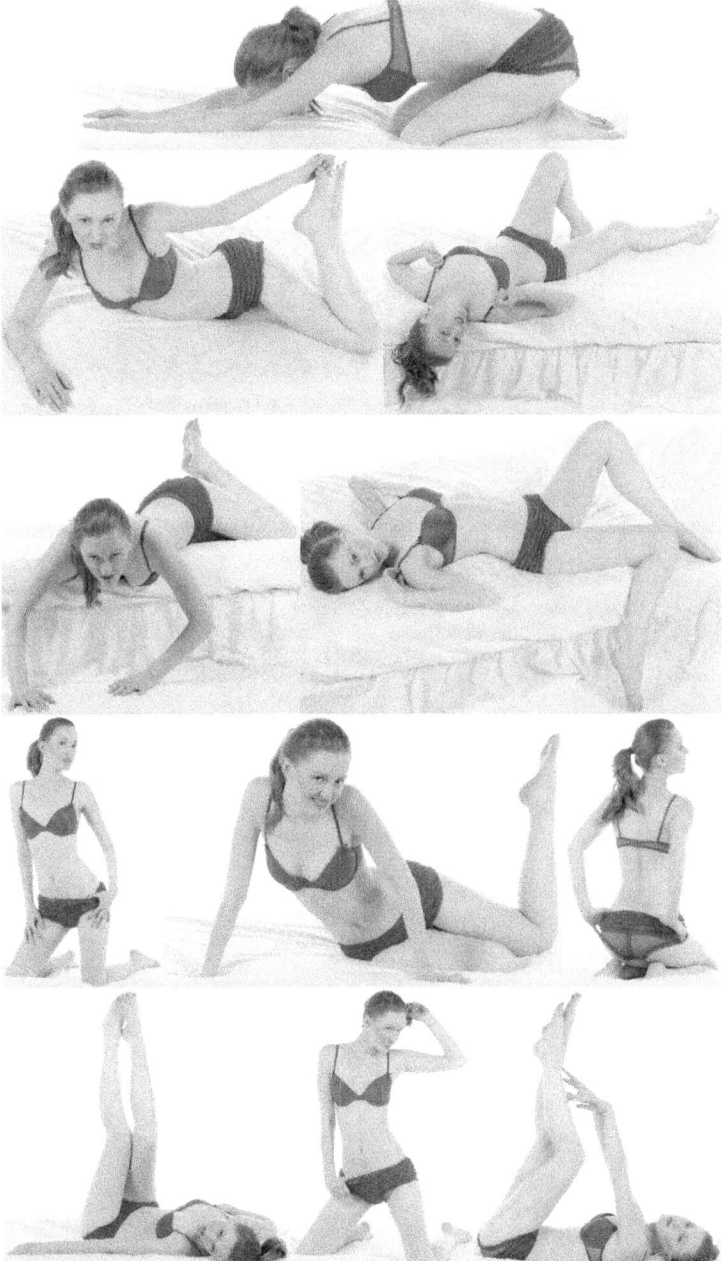

Think of other things other positions to get into too.

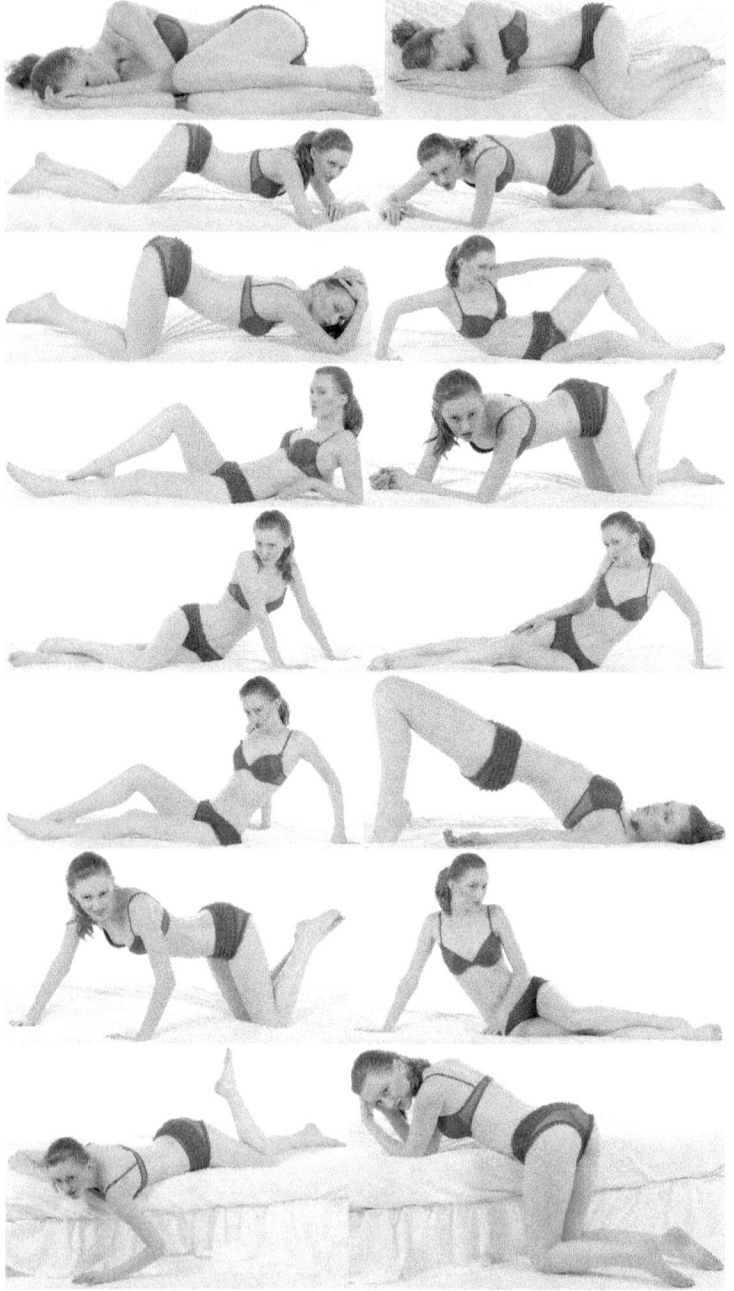

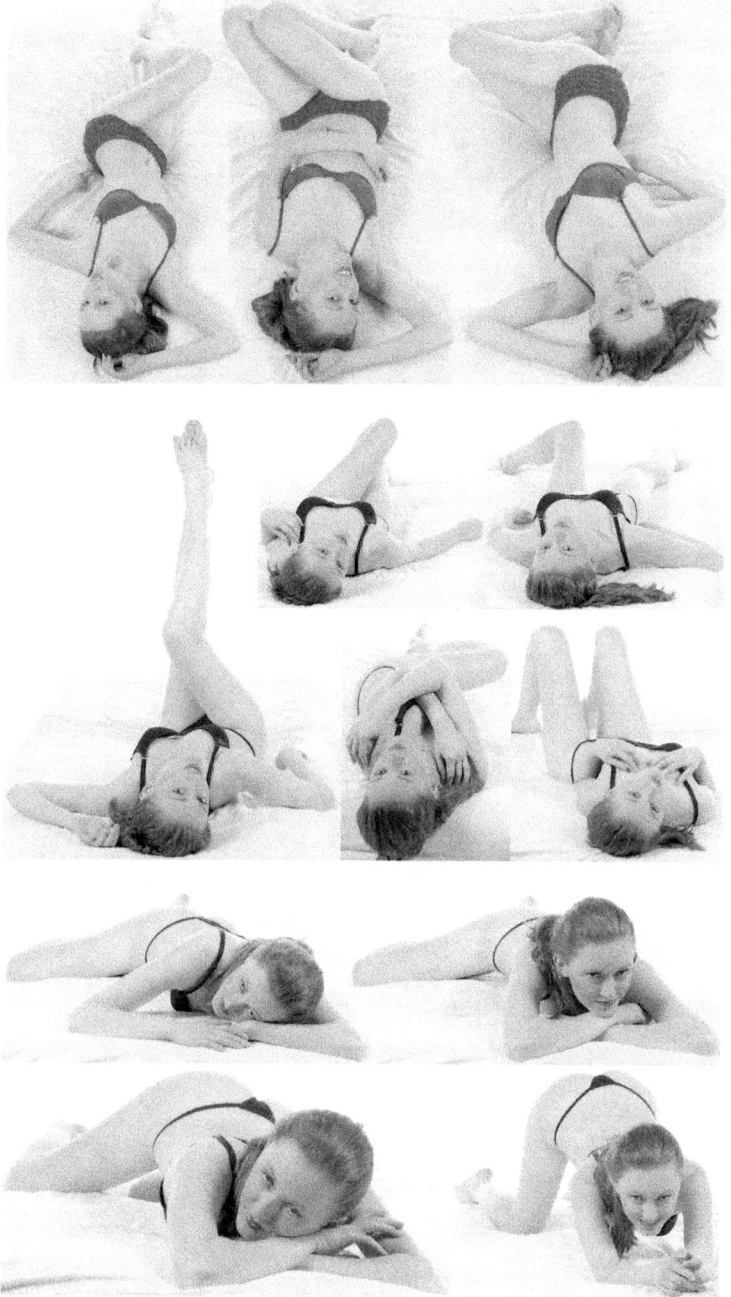

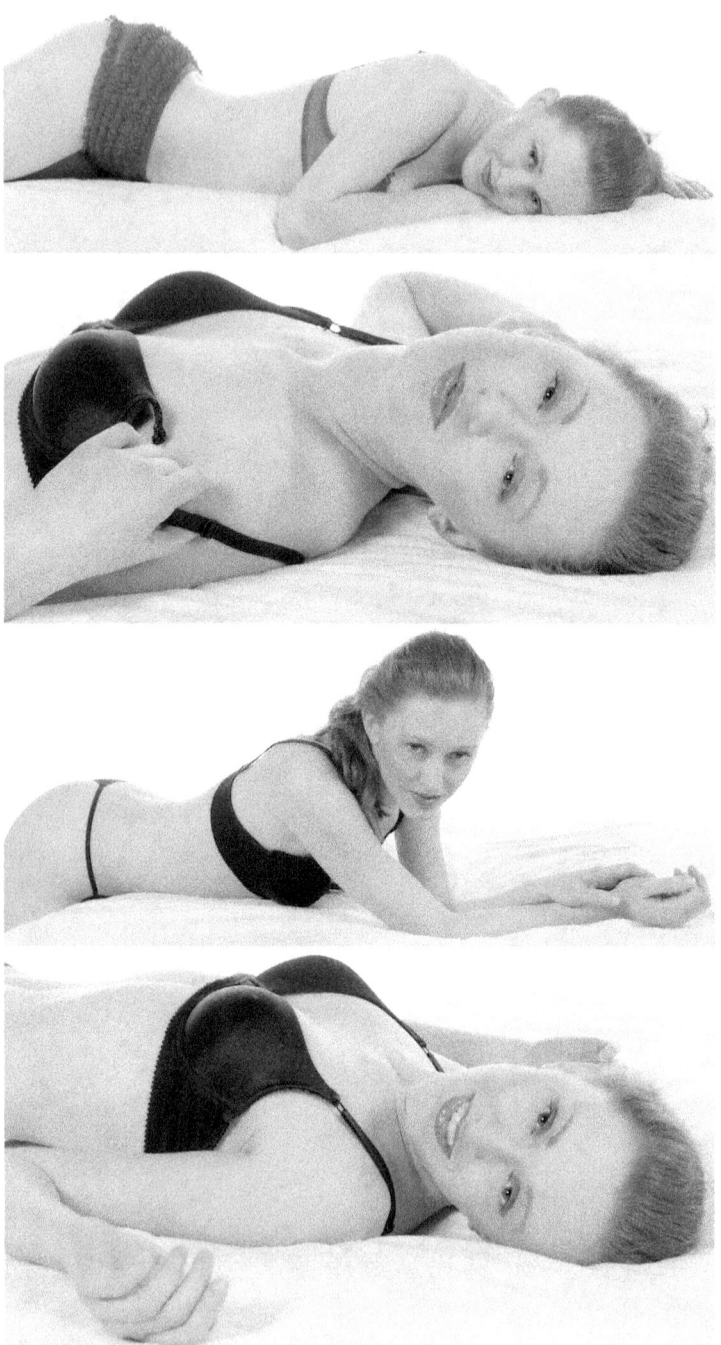

Remember that small variations to your pose can save you work while still generating a variety to choose from.

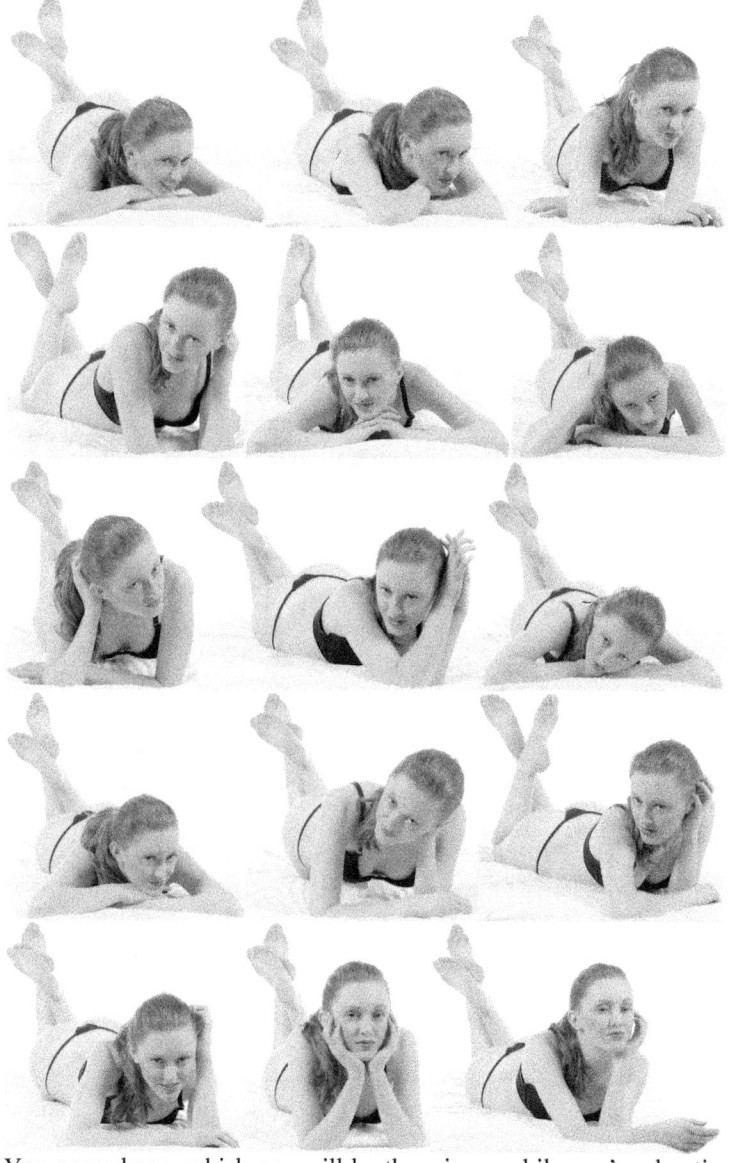

You never know which one will be the winner while you're shooting, *but the more variety; the more likely you are to have one!*

LINGERIE

Lingerie is a huge industry and the types and styles are nearly endless. If you are modeling for a fashion shoot, things should be spelled out in advance as to what's desired. For any other purpose, let your creativity flow but always try to think about what the camera is seeing and what the final destination of the photographs will be. With a little imagination, you should be able to use any of the examples from this book for lingerie. A common item to use with lingerie is a robe.

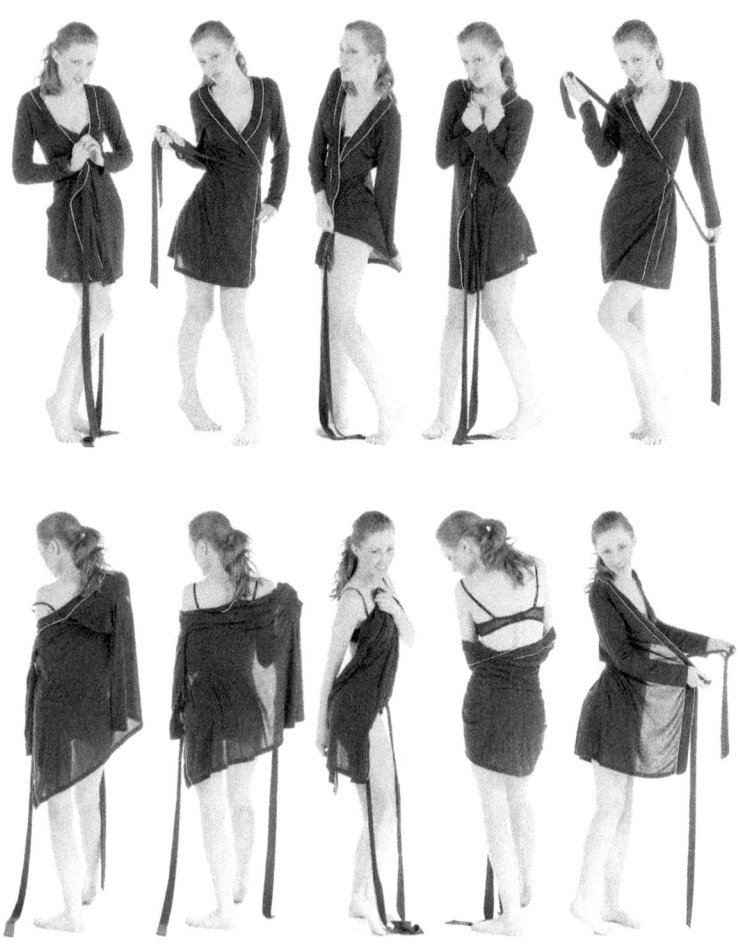

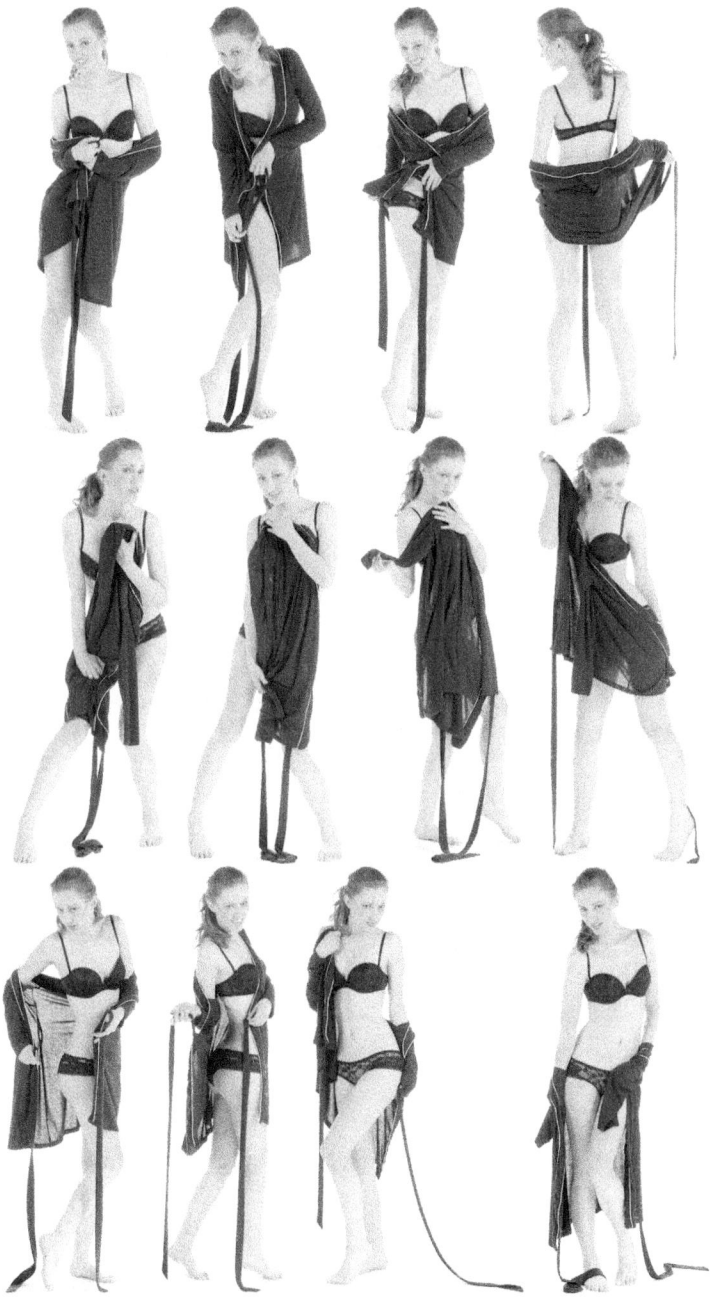

COVERED AND IMPLIED NUDES

Covered and Implied Nudes are almost the same; the obvious difference is that in a covered nude, the model is, in reality, bare. That comes in handy if you are posing and your shoulders, sides, hips or rear-end are visible, but is otherwise just a matter of comfort between the model and photographer. Both are truly a glamour style and have little use for a fashion shoot. Some common 'covers' are a sheet, scarf or blanket, a screen or wall, or any item large enough to partially conceal the model's body.

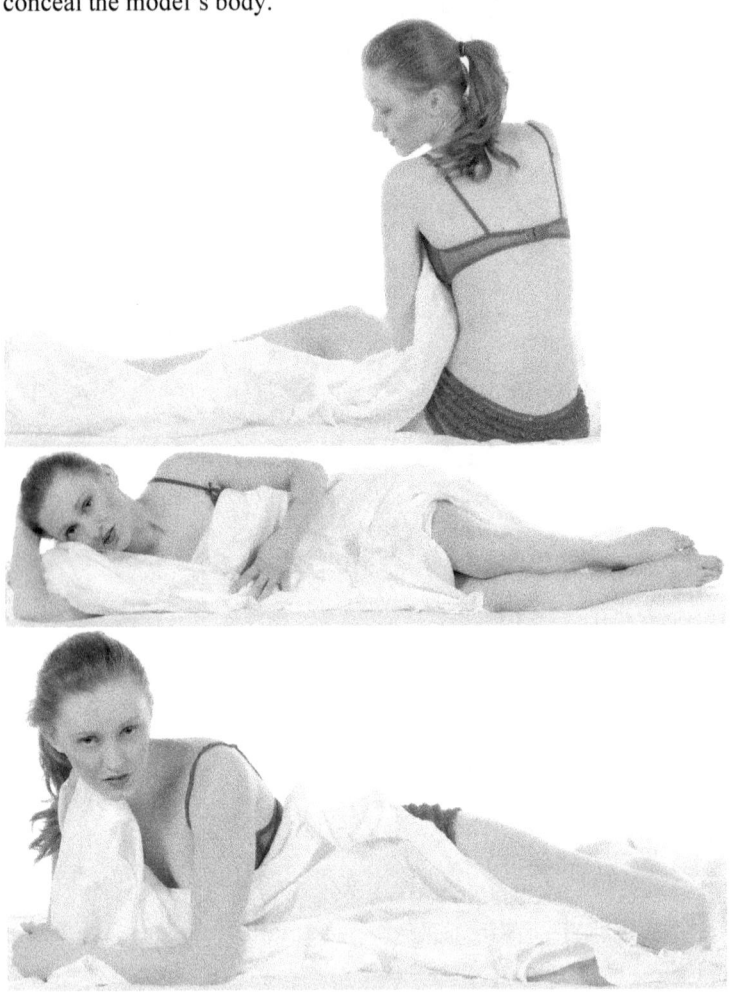

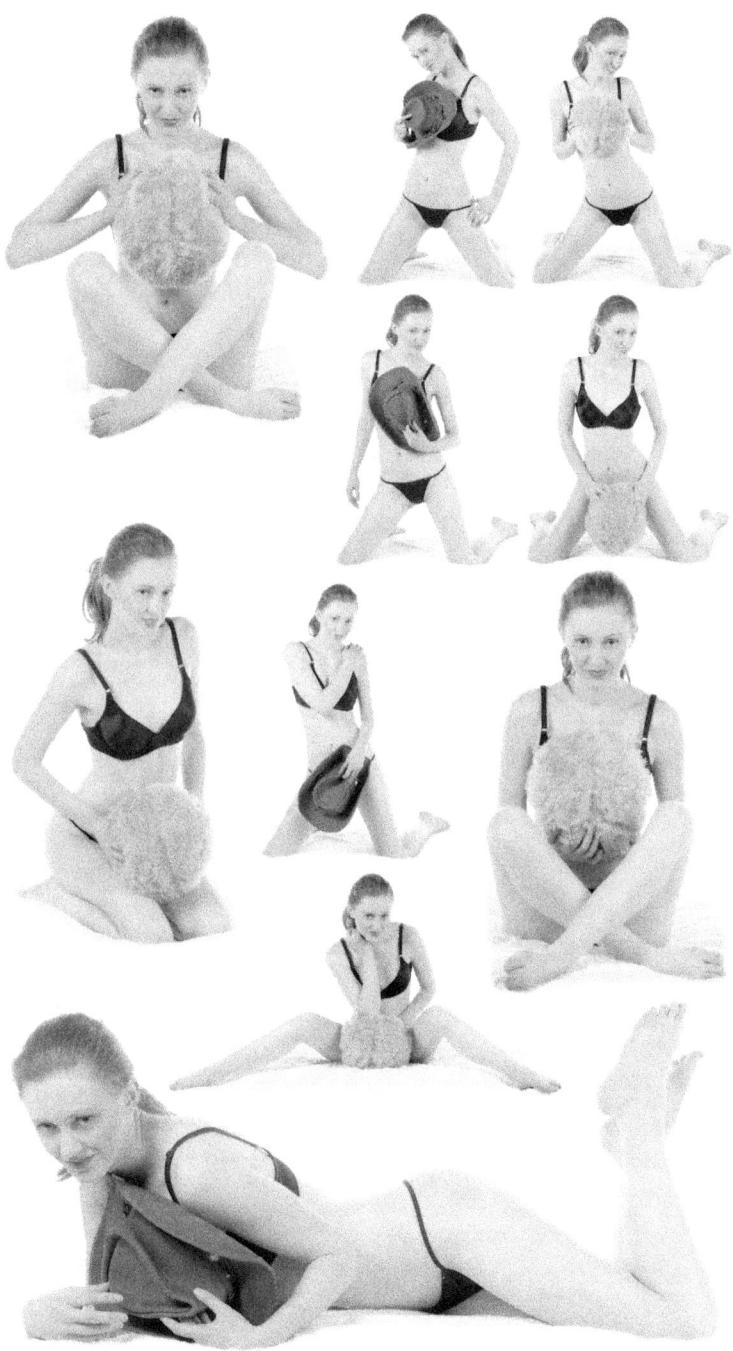

A scarf, sheet or any piece of fabric can make a versatile prop.

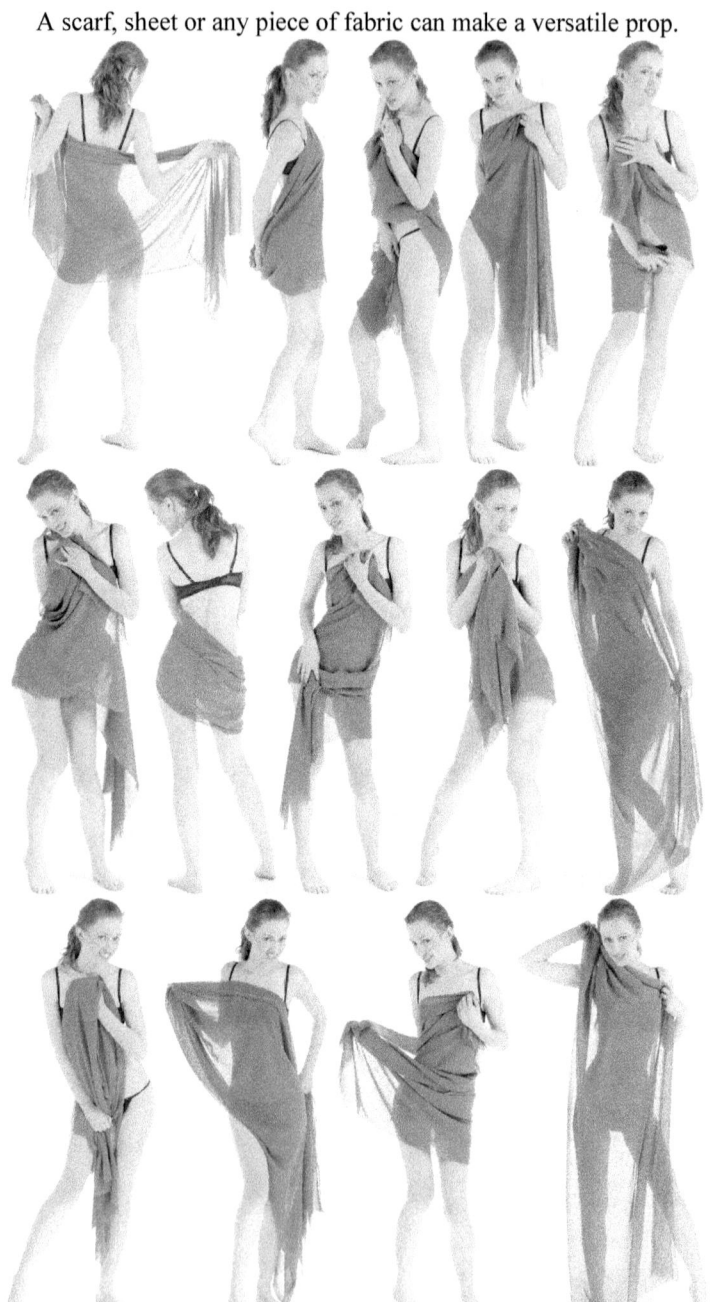

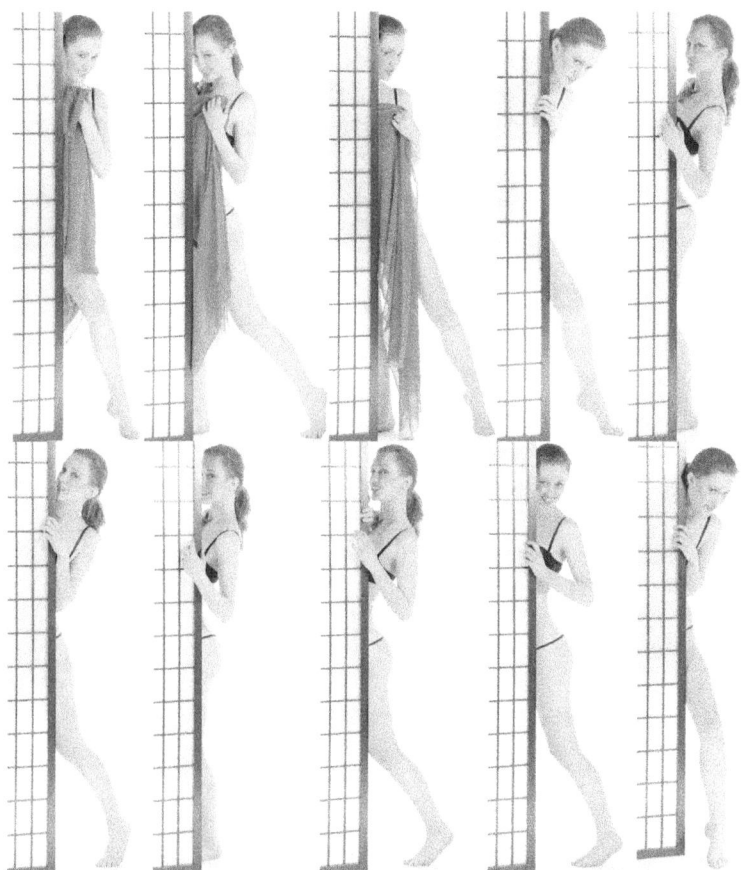

NUDES

When it comes to nudes, you can use any of the poses from the previous sections. The same rules apply with a few caveats. If you are posing topless it may be important to provide your own support (in lieu of a bra). More attention is needed to make sure that your stomach doesn't create 'folds' when you are sitting. Body hair is, of course, something that needs to be taken care of long before the shoot.

Nude shoots come in many flavors: Topless; Bare bottoms; Full frontal nudes; Provocative nudes; and Explicit nudes. You should know what you're doing before you are actually booked for the shoot. There are no actual nude photos included in this book, and truthfully you don't need them; you just need to use your imagination with the poses you've already seen.

SWIMWEAR

Swimwear, especially bikinis, can be a lot of fun, especially if you can escape to a tropical location to shoot in them! Fashion poses are typically standing to show off the suit, but sitting or laying poses are not uncommon.

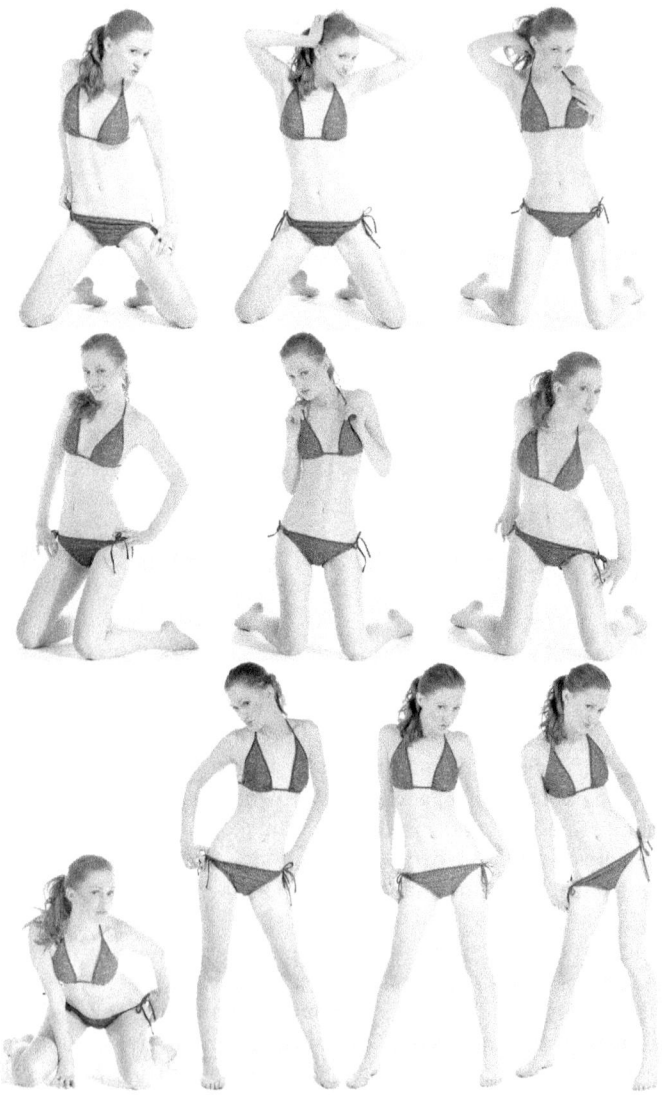

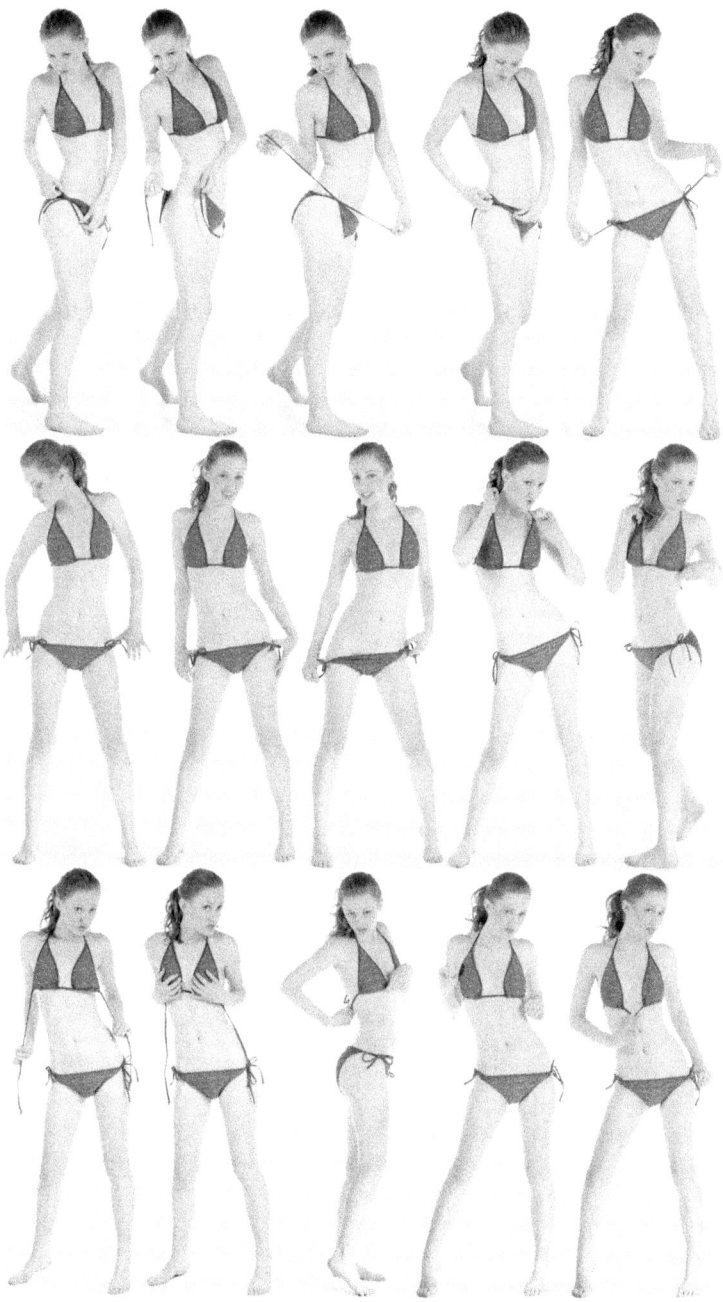

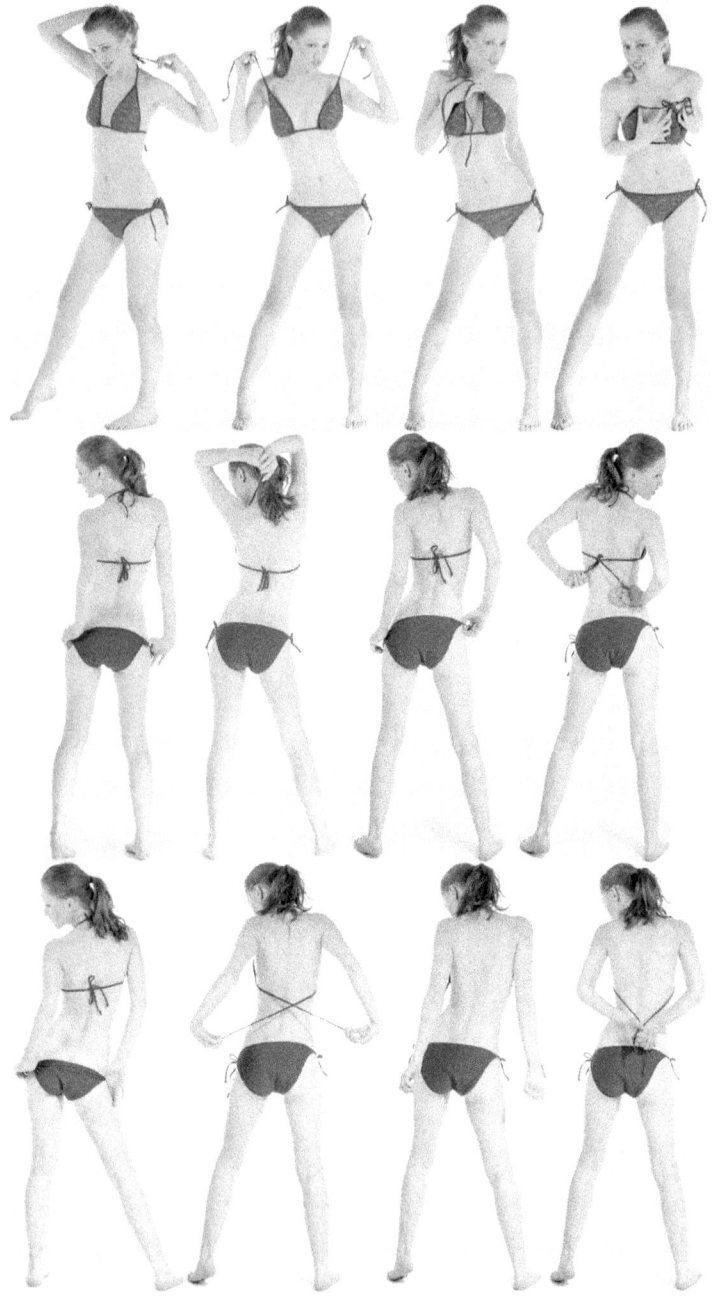

A towel combines well with a bikini.

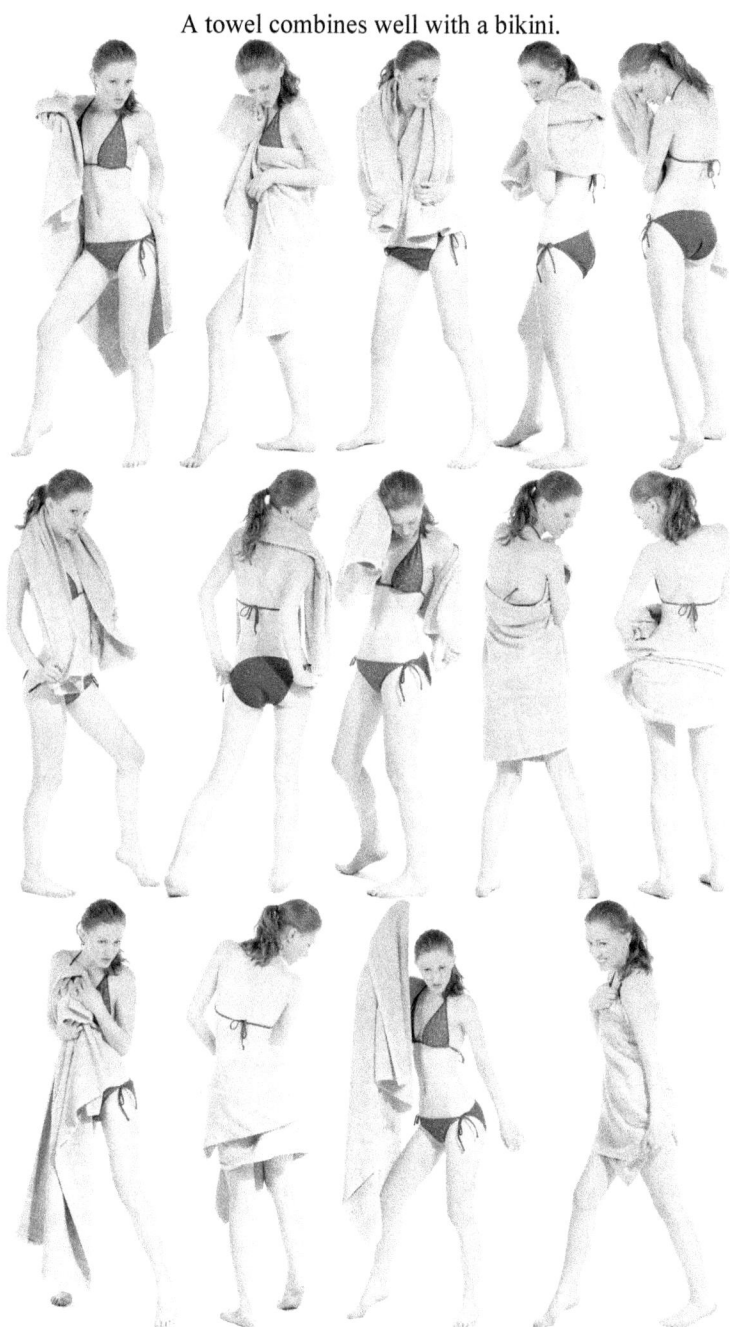

Some of these might work for lingerie or nudes as well.

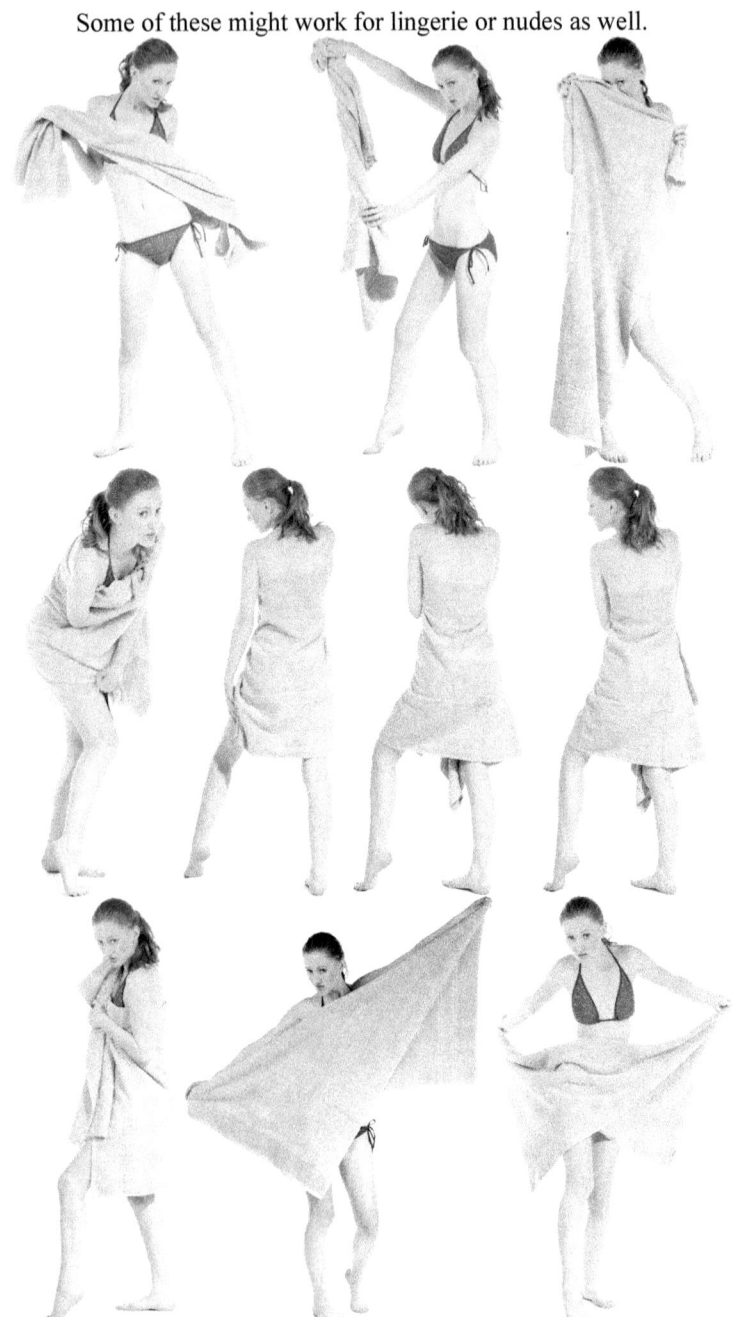

Note to Photographers

This book is written as if I'm talking to a model. This is because I expect models to read and benefit from it and YOU as a photographer will most likely be telling YOUR model the same information yourself in a similar way. This book is meant for a model, but I hope you can benefit from using it too. These two pages are meant to help you as a photographer when it comes to seeing and capturing the actual photo.

Cropping:

When shooting, remember that you have several choices of framing for each pose: head and shoulders; bust (from the chest up); half (from the waist up); three quarter length (crop anywhere from just above the knees to just below the crotch; and full length (don't cut off the feet!)

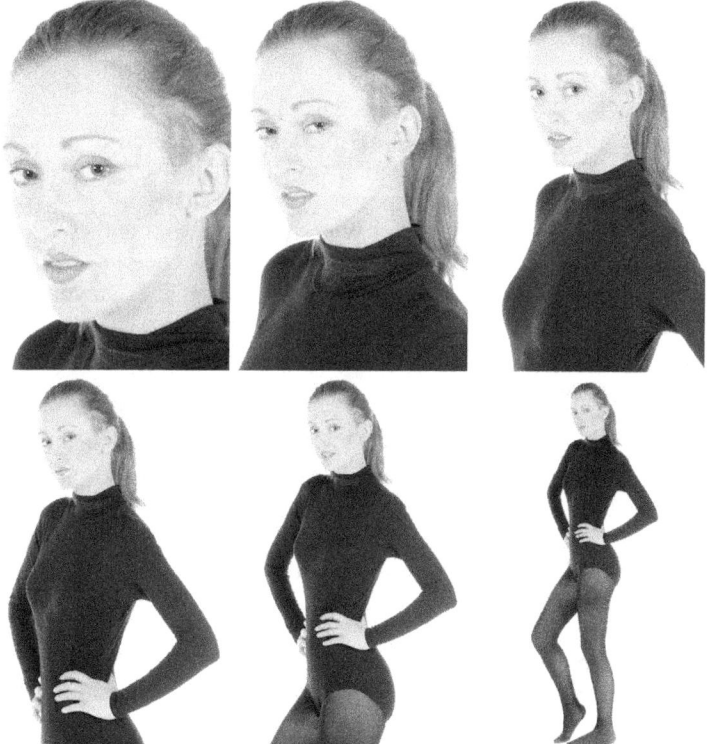

If you need to, ask your model to hold a pose so that you can take a few photos with different framing. Try different angles by using a chair or ladder to get elevated or get down on the ground. Keep in mind the intended use for the photos you're taking and remember to leave room for text if they are being published. If that's the case, then try to make sure that your 'text space' is relatively uncluttered and low-contrast so that the text will be readable. If you are doing a fashion shoot, remember to include the entire garment in the photo! If you are doing a glamour shoot, some close-in head shots and some tight crops on different body parts are a nice addition for you and your model.

Fashion Photography falls into two categories: Editorial and Advertorial. The main difference (for you) is in relation to the cropping & posing. On an advertorial shoot, time will be spent on a limited number of images for a specific ad OR time will be divided among many outfits to be placed in a catalog with most of the shots cropped in so as not to waste space. Editorial work may be more creative or storytelling in nature, including more of the set or background and time is more likely to be spent on a smaller number of outfits, possibly with a number of models in each shot.

Working with your model:
Occasionally, you will run into models that glide easily from pose to pose with no direction from you. While that makes for an easier shoot, you should still be paying attention to what she is doing and all the details before you. If she is not posing in the way that you'd prefer, you will need to speak up and tell her! Watch out for creases at the neck and waist from twisting (sometimes this can be fixed by covering them with hair, hands, arms or props.) Look for details that might ruin your shot, like clothing tags, uneven ties or even loose strings. When on location, keep an eye on the background. Watch out for people or other things going in and out of your photo.

While shooting, you should also not be static. Look for different angles to shoot from. Get down low, climb a ladder, move in and move out. You need to use your own judgment to determine where the best place to shoot from is and what to include in the frame, but if ALL of your photos are full length, taken while standing from 20 feet away; you're just hitting the button!

One last thing:
Depending on the situation, remember to take some photos for yourself and your model while shooting. It's normal that you'll both want some portfolio images from the shoot that may not follow the exact guidelines of the shoot, but you may need to request permission to do so from your client, and you'll most likely need some sort of release from the model to use the images. This is NOT a case where it's easier to beg forgiveness than ask permission, so make sure you ask!

Notes

www.ingramcontent.com/pod-product-compliance
Lightning Source LLC
Chambersburg PA
CBHW051524170526
45165CB00002B/594